How Small Firms Can Increase Their Productivity and Profits with Personal Computers

The Art of Computer Management

Jim McNitt

SIMON AND SCHUSTER
New York

Published by Simon and Schuster
A Division of Simon & Schuster, Inc.
Simon & Schuster Building
Rockefeller Center
1230 Avenue of the Americas
New York, New York 10020

Designed by Irving Perkins Associates
Manufactured in the United States of America

10 9 8 7 6 5 4 3 2 1

Library of Congress Cataloging in Publication Data

McNitt, Jim.
The art of computer management.

Includes index.
1. Small business—Data processing. 2. Microcomputers.
I. Title.
HF5548.2.M3647 1984 658'.022'02854 83-20432
ISBN 0-671-46471-X

Acknowledgments

The inspiration for *The Art of Computer Management* can be traced to one man, one place, and two sentences.

The man is Dr. Robert Jastrow, chairman of NASA's Lunar Exploration Committee. The place is his extraordinary book *The Enchanted Loom*. The sentences read: "The era of carbon-chemistry life is drawing to a close on the earth and a new era of silicon-based life—indestructible, immortal, infinitely expandable—is beginning. By the turn of the century, ultra-intelligent machines will be working in partnership with our best minds on all the serious problems of the day, in an unbeatable combination of brute reasoning power and human intuition."

Dr. Jastrow opened my eyes to the world-transforming power of the computer. But it took hundreds of interviews and conversations with computer scientists, management consultants, and business people to put that power in perspective. A few of those who gave so generously of their time to help make this work a reality are credited in the text. Some others I'd like to acknowledge here.

In particular my thanks go to David Delong, currently of Harvard University, Peter Beren of Sierra Club Books, Bruce Brown, founder of the Connecticut Computer Society, Janice Van Collie of Xerox Learning Systems, and Russ Walter, whose series *The Secret Guide to Computers* has become one of the underground classics of personal computing literature. Their help came at a time when *The Art of Computer Management* was still a fragile and uncertain thing.

Bruce Page, now of Quantum Science in New York City,

was the researcher-reporter for this book. His talents, especially his self-reliance, were invaluable assets.

Also invaluable was the forbearance of the Special Projects staff at *Newsweek International*—Carol Wilk, Jay Harris, and Hugh Roome—who not only put up with my preoccupations during the year this book was in progress but did so cheerfully.

On the subject of forbearance, perhaps the person most deserving of praise is Bob Bender, Senior Editor at Simon and Schuster. Moreover, his ability to keep this work on course, even when the helmsman was apt to wander, along with his readiness to place quality ahead of expediency won my heartfelt gratitude and admiration.

Finally, special thanks to a few special people whose encouragement, support, and friendship have extended over many years and many projects: Richard Laurence Stevens, Marty and Edith Luray and, above all, James and Helen McNitt.

J.M.

For Audrey

Contents

Preface

Jim McNitt describes the personal computer as the catalyst for the renaissance of small business. Those of us at the American Stock Exchange can testify to the awesome impact of computer power.

A decade ago, we were awash with millions of pieces of paper. Today, our computerized trading operation handles volume levels inconceivable back then far more quickly, accurately and efficiently.

We've also seen the innovative companies listed on our Exchange use their computers to discipline and spur their own dramatic growth.

So the fact that now smaller companies will have access to computers is a welcome development. The timing is particularly propitious because the good news for our nation's future is that entrepreneurship has recaptured the American imagination.

On campuses where business was once denigrated, students are now flocking to courses on how to start your own business. Each year, hundreds of thousands of new businesses start up. Add to that even greater numbers of Americans gathering their savings, weighing the risks and awaiting the opportunity to become entrepreneurs.

This phenomenon is more than statistics. It is deeply ingrained in our nation's psyche and it gives a special vitality to the way we tackle challenges in every field—the arts and sciences as well as business.

Unlike many societies, we do not frown in disapproval when a man or woman leaves a secure position with a large corporation to plunge into his or her own untried venture. Nor do we scoff when business people who have seen their enterprises collapse lick their wounds and plunge again, tougher and wiser, into a new undertaking.

We are a nation that cheers the small business person who can enter terrain dominated by giants and through agility and audacity make good. Our history is replete with products that owe their origin to this type of initiative: the vacuum tube, power steering, the self-winding wristwatch, FM radio, insulin, the helicopter and many more.

The process continues today. And as it does, the nation benefits from new products, new services and new jobs. It is estimated that many, if not most, of the new jobs needed twenty years from now will be created by companies that don't even exist or are barely known today.

To compensate for the enormous difficulties facing small businesses, fledgling entrepreneurs enjoy natural advantages —fierce commitment, hard work, long hours, knowledge of customers, stress on services, insistence on quality and other marks of personal involvement. These entrepreneurs are not afraid to break the rules and fix things *before* they break.

They also run lean. Departments considered essential in larger operations are simply omitted.

Because of the often precarious balance between success and disaster, any tool that can help control such business essentials as inventories and billing, that can improve productivity and extend the range and flexibility of an operation is enormously welcomed.

The small computer would seem to be that tool. Today, the same ingenuity that entrepreneurs bring to survival in the business world is being applied to the computer. Once mastered, I am confident we will see many new creative applications that will once again testify to the power of an unfettered economy and an unfettered imagination.

Arthur Levitt, Jr.
Chairman
American Stock Exchange

Introduction

Why the Personal Computer?

This book is for businesspeople and professionals who don't know where to begin—or even whether to begin at all—with the personal computer.

Personal computers work in most small firms. And they work well.

When one considers their potential for saving time, boosting productivity, and providing vital management data, personal computers seem preposterously inexpensive. A complete desktop computer system—including video monitor, printer, and a pile of good software programs—can cost under $3,000.

If you consider that in many offices each personal computer workstation eliminates the need for at least one full-time clerical position, then you can understand why trade unions resist—even oppose—microelectronic technology. "All jobs which are totally repetitive or with repetitive elements are at risk," complains one union official.

Yet, contrary to popular wisdom, in the well-run firm the personal computer does not eliminate jobs—it creates them. Personal computers help small companies get bigger, often with very high, sustained growth rates. The long-term impact of the personal computer is more jobs, not fewer.

Meanwhile, when managers and staff exert less effort shuffling paper, they can devote more energy to patients, clients, or customers as well as planning, thinking, learning, and selling. Personal computers, in short, free people from repetitive, nonproductive tasks to do the kind of creative work machines cannot perform. And when it comes to decision-making support and managerial control—especially financial control—the adding machine and paper-filing systems compare to the personal computer in much the same way that quill nibs and lampblack inks compare to the photocopier.

What specifically can the personal computer do for the small firm? Here are the four application areas where personal computers are helping managers in "sunset" and "sunrise" industries alike operate more productively and more profitably:

Word processing: With a personal computer, correspondence, proposals, and reports can be composed, edited, and typed in a fraction of the time it takes to do the same job with a pencil and paper or an electronic typewriter. You can expect to cut writing, proofreading, and retyping time by 50 to 300 percent. If you like, you can dress up documents with bar graphs, pie charts, and other business graphics. And you can use the computer memory to store form letters or "boilerplate" text that is used repetitively in forms, contracts, proposals, or in answering routine inquiries.

Spreadsheeting: You can use your personal computer to build precise financial models of your business or professional practice that provide a day-to-day picture of operating costs and margins. Which projects are profitable? Which aren't? Change one variable and see how it affects an entire budget or business plan—instantly. An electronic spreadsheet eliminates most managerial guesswork and increases decision-making accuracy.

Information management: With this, you can create electronic files that are automatically stored, updated, retrieved, sorted, evaluated, and even typed into standard reports. A simple computerized "data base" will maintain a customer or client list, sort it by zip code, state, city, or any other category, and type up the envelopes or address labels. A sophisticated data base will store thousands of records ranging from patient histories to invoices to personnel files. Unlike paper files, a computer **data base** can sort or search thousands of records in a few minutes' time. As a result, business managers have instant access to sales, marketing, and other information that would be prohibitively expensive to obtain from paper files. Data-base management can increase the efficiency and usefulness of a small firm's filing systems by as much as 500 percent.

Accounting: You can automate payroll, journals, general ledger, receivables, payables, order entry, and inventory. Do monthly customer statements in hours, instead of days. Reduce inventory shrinkage, pinpoint problem accounts, speed collections, and control cash flow. Look for a significant improvement in the timeliness and accuracy of your accounting figures, while reducing the time spent on bookkeeping activities by up to 200 percent.

So, why haven't you computerized already?

Too expensive? Forget it. Your personal computer will probably pay for itself within a month. Almost certainly within a year.

Afraid? Forget that excuse too. Computers don't bite, irradiate, or dehumanize. As long as you anticipate the consequences of computerization, and are prepared to deal with them (see chapter 4), there is no reason to fear the personal computer. Indeed, you'll be better served worrying about a more pressing concern—what happens if your competitors computerize before you do?

Perhaps you are under the impression that personal computers require world-class programmers to perform useful work. They don't. Most small-business problems are solved with packaged software programs that can be mastered in a few hours, or at most a few days.

Still, there are legitimate reasons for some people to resist computerizing. For all its benefits, the personal computer is no sure cure for poor business judgment. Rather, the evidence suggests that a personal computer may be the last thing an incompetent manager needs. "The personal computer accelerates the speed at which decisions are made," notes one management expert. "If you're already headed for the precipice, a personal computer may only hasten your journey."

So, personal computers are not for the incompetent. And they may also be avoided for reasons of management style. Jeff Finn, a Seattle computer consultant, sometimes tells his clients they are better off with manual systems that work than with computerized systems that could jeopardize a successful management style. But this advice applies only to very small firms that have built their success on the personal charm or style of the owners or partners.

Like children, personal computers can be demanding. The benefits of automation are far from automatic. Teaching yourself to do productive work with a personal computer requires investing "sweat equity." Moreover, there are good ways to introduce the personal computer into the small firm, and there are not-so-good ways.

When computerizing a small business, the human dynamics—not the electronics—should be the first concern. Unfortunately they seldom are. If you fail to consider people first you may increase office productivity at the cost of company morale. I discuss how to avoid this most common of tactical errors in chapter four, "Tactical Deployment."

There is also the very real danger—and this is perhaps the most compelling reason why some managers should avoid the personal computer—of being seduced by the intellectual appeal of computer technology. The personal computer is the means to an end, not an end in itself. Some users become so fascinated with the tool, they lose sight of the problem it was supposed to solve. "If you're using instant coffee," says one computer consultant, "you don't spend an hour stirring it."

While these are valid reasons to approach computerization with caution, there are many more reasons for taking the firsts steps toward computerization, be they ever so tentative, instead of clinging to manual procedures.

Do you, for instance, receive a weekly statement showing which receivables are 30, 60, or 90 days old? You ought to, if you want to avoid selling to accounts that are past due.

Do you know what your cash position is right now? What it will be next week? Next month? Next quarter? You can, if you teach yourself to use an electronic-spreadsheet program such as Visi-Calc.

What about sales? Are your daily sales reports broken out by profit centers or sales territories? Can you compare your daily and weekly sales figures to those of the same period one year ago and to those of a realistic projection for the present year?

Can you generate a balance sheet, a profit-and-loss statement, or key financial ratios at any time? What about such typical small-business headaches as inventory control? Sales taxes? Mailing lists? Order entry? Job costing? Payroll? Departmental budgeting? Customer service? Is a growing professional practice straining your ability to manage client files, patient scheduling, billing, estimates, proposals, or long-term financial planning?

Is your firm really as productive as it could be? Are your decisions based on hard facts? Or are you managing by instinct, by "gut feel" and subjective benchmarks?

If the manual systems and procedures in your firm get the job done in as timely, effective, and *profitable* a fashion as you would like, read no more. The personal computer is not for you.

But if you sense the need to improve the management of information at your business or professional office, *The Art of Computer Management* can help make your firm more productive and more profitable.

This book will not make you a computer expert. It won't teach you how to design computers or even how to write their programs. Nor will you be assailed by computer jargon.

Instead, you will be introduced to the basic concepts of personal computing as they apply to three fundamental managerial challenges: office productivity, decision making, and financial controls. You'll discover the basic strategies and tactics for deploying the personal computer in the small firm. You'll see how to evaluate computer hardware. And most important, you'll learn the real secret of the art of computer management: how to choose and use inexpensive software programs that expedite such fundamental tasks as word processing, financial forecasting and budgeting, recordkeeping, inventory control, and accounting.

Where computer jargon is unavoidable, it will be confined, as one computer manual says, "to places where it is the best correct description of what's happening." The first time an unfamiliar term is used in a chapter it will be marked in **boldface.** When you have finished this book you won't be an expert. But you should be able to converse intelligently with computer consultants, vendors, and programmers.

Ideally, the purchase of a personal computer should be the final step, taken only after you've decided which software programs your business needs. Without software programs, computers are useless. Software determines how you apply the personal computer to your management problems. Not every software program runs on every personal computer—far from it. Finding the right software should be your first priority.

But this is not an ideal world, and if the question of which personal computer to buy is a burning issue with you, here is some advice. The *historical* standard for business applications has been the Apple II. You will find the Apple II and its variants mentioned in this book more than any other machine.

The new personal-computer industry standard—without question—is the IBM Personal Computer, usually referred to as the "IBM-PC," or simply "PC." This does not mean the IBM-PC is the best personal computer around. It isn't. Nor is the IBM-PC necessarily the best value for your dollar. Again, it isn't. But if you must buy a personal computer fast, the "machine for modern times" has some compelling advantages.

One advantage to the PC is its universality. With many hundreds of thousands in service, finding advice, assistance, and even employees that already know how to use them is much easier than with less-popular brands.

But it is the library of IBM-PC program software, as much as the IBM-PC hardware, that makes the IBM-PC a winner. However, it is not necessary to buy the IBM-PC itself to gain access to this splendid software since IBM-PC–"compatible" machines built by other firms will run most (but not all) of the PC's software programs.

The abundance of both the personal computers and off-the-shelf small-business software packages makes it easy to forget that a decade ago there was no such machine as a "personal" computer. But it is not so easy to forget the difficulties small businesses have faced in these same ten years. The recessions of 1974–1975 and 1980–1982 were the most devastating since the Great Depression. Inflation has turned accurate long-term planning, and even daily price quotations, into a statistical nightmare. Regulatory edicts and government requirements continue to bog down small-business managers in paperwork. And, finally, big business increasingly trains its sights on regional markets, services, and even professions that were once the province of small firms.

During this past decade it often seemed that the small firm was destined to drift into oblivion. No more. Instead, the microprocessor seems to be inaugurating an era of transformation that will benefit small business, just as some economists predicted. "The microprocessor shares an explosive logic with certain crucial technologies of the past, those transforming inventions—the printing press, the clipper ship, the steam engine, the electric generator, the railroad, the automobile and the telephone—that transfigure an economy and extend the dimensions of the world," asserts economist George Gilder in *Wealth & Poverty*. "Like these key technologies, the microprocessor does not operate within the confines of the existing industrial structure, but makes possible a new one."

One feature of this new economic structure is already evident. It is the reversal of the trend toward dominance by ever-larger bureaucracies and bigger businesses. Small businesses are already playing a pivotal role in the new industrial structure that is emerging in the wake of America's declining smokestack industries. The revitalization of small business is recognized as a social, political, and economic necessity and thanks in part to the computer, it is already happening.

We stand at the threshold of a renaissance of small business. The personal computer is the catalyst; it is the key that unlocks new possibilities and powers that not long ago were beyond the dreams of the small-business manager or professional. The machines exist in prolific variety, as do the small-business software programs that power them. Personal computers and their software are affordable, user-friendly and effective. There are few businesspeople whose firms will not benefit—often profoundly—from mastering the art of computer management.

Jim McNitt
Greenwich, Connecticut

Chapter One

Big Savings for Small Firms

[The computer] will alter the entire nervous system of social organization.

—*French government study*

SOME DRAMATIC POSSIBILITIES

This is a book about how men and women—many without any technical inclination or training—are using powerful, low-cost personal computers to manage their small businesses and professional practices for increased productivity and profits—and how you can join them.

The smallest of the firms discussed here are unincorporated sole proprietorships. The largest are small corporations, public and private, with payrolls of approximately two hundred fifty people. They share one uncommon trait: an owner, a partner, or a manager of innovative persuasion who, a year or more ago, took a chance on a new machine—the personal computer. In retrospect, the risks were minimal: a few thousand dollars, a few dozen hours, and, as always, the possibility of failing at something new. The rewards, however, both financial and psychic, have proved abundant: growth, prosperity, and even some measure of peace of mind.

In America today there are over seventeen million small businesses, mostly proprietorships and partnerships, and over sixteen million working professionals. A few use large-scale **mini-** or **mainframe** computers. Most use no computer at all. Only a fraction have discovered the managerial benefits of *personal* computing: lower overhead, greater financial control, better decision-making support, and increased time and energy for creative action.

Faster, Better, and More Profitably

There are very few small enterprises that cannot profit from the personal computer and its software. From teaching pharmacology in the People's Republic of China to designing buildings in Ireland or wholesaling meat in New Jersey, the personal computer is helping managers and professionals get their jobs done faster, better, and more profitably.

One reason is that personal computers have grown extraordinarily powerful, both in the range of the managerial tasks they can perform and in the memory capacity they offer. "Although personal computers are physically very tiny," says Mike Mara, a data-processing specialist at Oxoco, a Houston-based oil-and-gas exploration company, "some of them actually are as powerful as the IBM 370 series mainframe computers."

By using inexpensive software programs this power can be channeled into literally thousands of time- and labor-saving business applications. From word processing to automated accounting, personal computers eliminate repetitive manual chores, such as retyping successive drafts of a memo or letter, while increasing the speed and accuracy of the task being performed. On the individual level the personal computer can double, triple, and even quadruple the productivity of those who know how to use it. And individual productivity gains can translate into significant company-wide savings. Since Oxoco began using personal computers the firm has doubled its business volume, but increased staff by only 20 percent.

But the real secret to the microcomputer explosion is that personal computers are easy to use. "A person will be comfortable with a microcomputer after eight hours," says Dr. Eugene Galanter, a full-time professor at Columbia University and a part-time personal-computer instructor. "And you will be able to run complex business software, say spreadsheeting, after another four."

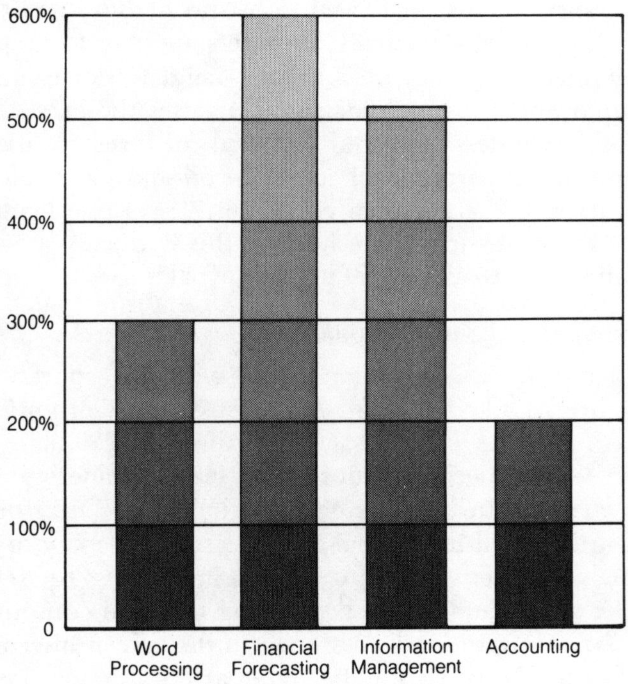

RANGE OF PRODUCTIVITY GAINS REPORTED BY INTERVIEWEES FOR BASIC SMALL-BUSINESS APPLICATIONS

Productive and Profitable

When *Inc.* magazine released their 1983 survey of America's fastest-growing small public companies, I interviewed officers of the top ten performers in two categories, productivity and profitability, to find out how they were using computers. One answer was not surprising: All twenty firms used computerized data-processing systems for their financial recordkeeping. But in addition to these central computing systems, the majority of the *Inc.* top performers also used low-cost personal computers for jobs ranging from simple word processing to complex financial forecasting.

How Hadson Attains a Net Income of 50 Percent of Sales

At Hadson Petroleum of Oklahoma City, Oklahoma (the firm topping *Inc.'s* list of the ten most profitable small corporations), six IBM Personal Computers are used to prepare quarterly financial statements and long-range forecasts. Even more important, Hadson's management uses the persuasive power of computer-generated financial analyses to attract and keep limited partners for its seven oil-and-gas exploration ventures. "The personal computer," says one Hadson official, "was instrumental in helping this company attain a net income equal to almost 50 percent of sales."

How Liz Claiborne Saves $600,000

Liz Claiborne, a Manhattan-based women's sportswear manufacturer, ranked fifth on *Inc.'s* list of most productive small corporations, with sales of almost $250,000 per employee—an especially impressive feat considering the labor-intensive nature of the garment industry. Director of Marketing Mitchell Lewis makes no secret of the key to Liz Claiborne's productivity. "We've been in business for seven years," he says, "and we've been using personal computers for five." Among the tasks assigned to the fifteen micros at Liz Claiborne's New York City headquarters are "word processing, recordkeeping, general ledger, merchandising accounts, piece goods control, sales statistics and forecasting." Says Lewis: "Each personal computer *saves us the equivalent of three $15,000-a-year employees.*" At that rate, in 1982 Liz Claiborne's fifteen personal computers added approximately $600,000 to the firm's bottom line.

Back from the Brink and a One-Man Show

Many professionals and executives computerize in an effort to fine-tune an already successful career or small business. But not everyone.

Manhattan's Haworth Press was in the throes of a desperate cash-flow crisis when its owners purchased six personal computers. Just two years later, Haworth saw its revenues double from $1 to $2 million, even as the publishing industry suffered its worst years since the Great Depression.

Why the dramatic turnaround? Co-owner Pat McLoughlin credits the computers and the financial control they allow him. By automating his office, McLoughlin claims he is now using Haworth's resources—including his own time—more effectively and more profitably. "Instead of devoting our entire earnings to administrative overhead, we've been developing new products and improving production. Without the computer," says McLoughlin, "we'd still be in trouble."

"The computer gives you a different feeling about what's happening in the company," he explains. "Because the computer provides instant information, you can see your business more clearly. At Haworth we now look at only ten pages of computer printout, rather than the hundreds of pages of records we once needed to get the same data. And we use the time we save to build the business. The computer has freed us to think more clearly. As a result we are creating new products, more sales, and new jobs. The computer has made life a lot more enjoyable."

Without his computers, life would certainly be different for Michigan petroleum broker Graham Eddleston. Last year Eddleston's Sterling Oil & Chemical Company reported annual revenues of over $16 million.

Granted, $16 million a year is small change in the oil industry. But you haven't heard the whole story: Not only is Graham Eddleston founder and chief executive officer of Sterling Oil & Chemical—he is also marketing manager, comptroller, sales director and, in fact, *sole employee*. How does one man do it? "My whole operation is computerized," he says. "That's what saves me."

The Productivity Crisis

Running a small firm has always been risky, but never more precarious than today. "America's diminishing rate of productivity is a sinister force that causes inflation, suppresses initiative, reduces living standards, increases taxes, creates unemployment, stifles innovation, and that has been largely responsible for the most all-encompassing bureaucracy that has ever existed in the history of the world," declares productivity expert John A. Patton.

Unhappily, small firms, with their limited resources, bear the brunt of America's productivity crisis. Managing the small firm can often mean contending with negative cash flows, unruly inventories, accounting systems gone berserk, and groaning piers of unfinished paperwork. The usual scapegoats are a turbulent economy, burdensome taxation, foreign competition, ill-conceived regulation, and poorly motivated workers. But the obstacles themselves are not the real culprit so much as the failure to overcome them.

"Most managers are not making the most of what's available to them," suggests management consultant Robert H. Schaffer. And internationally respected statistician W. Edward Deming agrees, saying that inefficient *managers,* not blue-collar workers, may be to blame for up to 85 percent of America's productivity problems.

For professionals, the situation is equally ominous. By one estimate some physicians now devote two-thirds of their time to such administrative chores as recordkeeping and filing health insurance claims. Less than a third of these doctors' day goes to practicing medicine. Nor is the field of medicine unique. A recent Louis Harris poll found 70 percent of professionals dissatisfied with their own productivity.

When it comes to the productivity crisis, many managers and professionals are barely keeping afloat. With their desks awash in a sea of unfinished paperwork, they are more concerned with surviving the next wave than with raising their sights to more distant horizons. But flagging productivity is not inevitable.

The Personal Computer: An Analytical Tool

If you are a professional practitioner or specialist, a business owner or a business manager, the personal computer *can* increase your productivity and ultimately the profitability of your firm or practice. It can help pare the cost of doing business, while upgrading the quality and the quantity of your goods or services. It can bring a runaway inventory, a slipshod set of books, a disheveled filing system, and even elusive cash-flow problems under steadfast control.

This is because the personal computer is an analytical tool of unprecedented power and capacity. With it, for the first time in history, the small firm can afford to quantify the business assumptions upon which fundamental decisions are premised. With the assistance of computerized accounting, spreadsheeting, and **data-base management** programs, for instance, small-business executives can now obtain the same kind of precise management information their big-business competitors have been receiving for years. Information such as weekly or even daily summaries of sales volume, inventory, receivables, cash flow, client or job status, production schedules, commissions, or labor costs. Information that is vital to guiding any firm through a turbulent economy, but which until now has been beyond the financial and administrative resources of small business.

The result of computerization can be nothing less than a revolution in the speed, quality, and accuracy of small-business decision making. By replacing assumptions and guesswork with an orderly, quantitative analysis, the personal computer can act as a lens that brings the realities of small-business management into razor-sharp focus. In addition, through its functions as a word processor and electronic filing system, the personal computer vastly reduces the volume, and hence the cost, of many routine clerical tasks.

Computer Literacy

Best of all, the prerequisites for personal computing are minimal. The ability to add, subtract, divide, and multiply is helpful. So are a lively intellectual curiosity, a logical mind, and the willingness to master a few fundamentals of what has come to be known as *computer literacy*. But as you are about to see, computer literacy involves far less technical knowledge than is commonly presumed. Anyone who can run a small business or professional office in today's competitive economy can learn to run a personal computer. Just ask

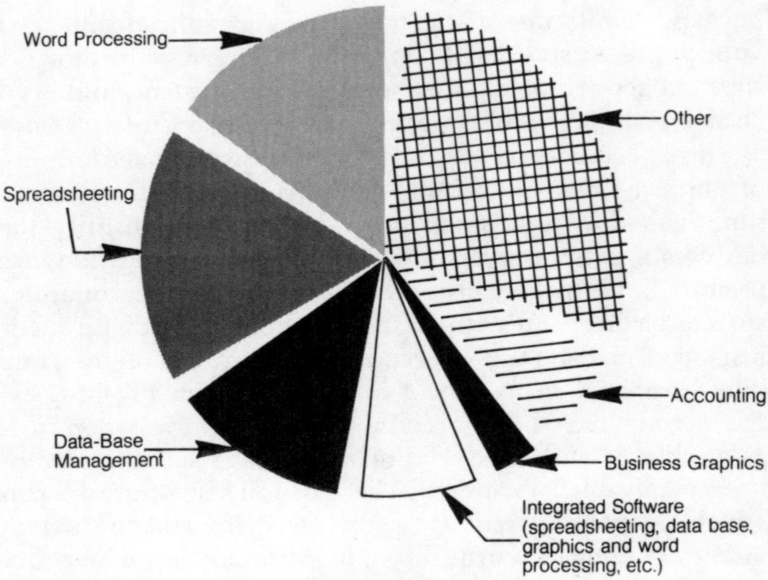

PROJECTED PC BUSINESS APPLICATIONS—1988

Maurice Maio. When Maio acquired his first personal computer his plumbing and heating business was little more than a one-man operation grossing under $150,000 a year. Thirty-six months later Maio could boast twenty-five employees and projected revenues of nearly $2 million. "There are a lot of little reasons for our success," says Maio, "but there's just one big reason—the personal computer. Without the computer we'd be a fraction of our size, and we'd have a lot of troubles."

Computer Power in Perspective

Not everyone, however, is enthusiastic about personal computers. "Personal computers in no way solve data processing's major problems," says a data-processing consultant who advises *Fortune* 500 corporations. "They are nothing more than powerful calculators. They affect only small problems. They have limited power, a basic incompatibility problem, and limited ability to handle data—especially when the integration of data from various sources is needed."

True, compared to the giant computers at General Motors, AT&T, or Eastman Kodak personal computers *do* have limited power and they affect only small problems. And not every personal computer is "compatible" with the large firm's corporate **mainframe** or divisional minicomputers. *But today's desktop micro is still more powerful than yesterday's room-sized mainframe.* And the kind of problems personal computers are good at solving may seem small to the data-processing professional, but they don't to the millions of business managers worldwide for whom controlling cash flow, inventory, or accounts receivable can mean the difference between survival and oblivion.

The Personal Computer Is the Only Computer for Most Small-Business or Professional Settings

In many small-business and professional settings, the personal computer is the *only computer* that makes economic sense. At China's Tientsin Medical College, Professor Cia-Li Vhang uses an Apple II computer to help teach pharmacology. Were it not for the personal computer, Dr. Cia-Li Vhang would use no computer at all. And what goes for Professor Vhang also holds for the Dave White Company in Newark, New Jersey, Gaston's White River Resort in the Ozark Mountains, Manhattan's Haworth Press, and millions of other enterprises. Very few small businesses or professional offices can justify an expenditure of $40,000 or $50,000 for a large-scale computer. On the other hand, small firms today really can't afford *not to* invest $4,000 or $5,000 in a device offering a potential savings equivalent to two or three full-time clerical employees.

How small is too small for a personal computer? Some management consultants place the cutoff for small businesses at $100,000 in annual revenues. But the fact is that almost no well-run business is too small to benefit from a personal computer. When the small-business manager learns to use a $5,000 personal computer, instead of adding $15,000 or $30,000 in staff overhead, there is more cash available to help the business grow through increased merchandising, advertising, marketing, product development, or capital investment. And professionals—including lawyers, doctors, engineers, accountants, consultants, sales representatives, pharmacists, and many others—can exploit the personal computer in their daily work as well as in the business management of their firms.

Better Service, Lower Overhead

In Tuakau, New Zealand, Bruce Barnard is writing a database program to help pharmacists in that country "handle all the dispensory functions of a pharmacy, including the recording of patients, their medications, the name of their doctors, and their medication profile." Barnard's program will save New Zealand pharmacists thousands of dollars a year in administrative overhead. It may even save lives. Similar personal-computer programs are under development, or already in use, for scores of professions and industries—from group medical practices to family farms and independent insurance agencies.

In Dublin, Ireland, Fred Quinn is a partner in a twelve-employee architectural firm. He has been using a Radio Shack computer and its software programs for two years to prepare proposals, manage his payroll, and maintain a company data base. "We key in all fundamental job statistics," he says, "such as the date the project was first briefed, names of the initial contractors and the subcontractors, cost increases, unusual problems, materials specifications, and the performance of each element of the operation. This becomes our reference base for costing future projects and determining whether certain types of construction proved difficult or easy and how well they hold up under stress."

How difficult has it been to use the personal computer? "You have to be disciplined to make it successful," says Quinn. "But having a computer tends to discipline *you* as well." And how important has the personal computer become to managing his office? "It's indispensable," says Quinn. "I can't imagine how we got along without it."

Neither can Ruben Wolcovinsky, a general management consultant in El Dorado, Panama. He uses the personal computer for developing "inventory sheets, special annuity schedules, and accounts receivable programs" for his clients.

"Latin America is about two years behind the United States in computer awareness," he says, "but microcomputers are starting to get down here now, mainly because prices are coming down."

Productivity Success Story

Brian Taylor, the administrative manager at Nippon Vicks in Osaka, Japan, has been using personal computers for five years. "We brought in a few TRS-80s and used them initially for games," he says. "Anyone could use the computers for anything they wanted during work hours." Today Taylor has five microcomputers in the office, "and that still isn't enough. They're all running full blast from nine in the morning until five at night."

What about office productivity? "We've increased our productivity five times over since we began using the micros," says Taylor. "The computers have enabled people to work smarter, faster, and better than they ever have before. In today's economic conditions you're forced to evaluate a number of rapidly shifting conditions. The microcomputer makes it possible."

Are personal computers a major business tool in Japan? "From what I read about the United States," says Taylor, "Japan seems to be behind. But I wonder for how long."

Saving $100,000, Analyzing Trends, and Cutting Bookkeeping Time

In Tokyo, Masanori "Woody" Hayashi helps manage a thirty-employee office for Smith, Kline and French Overseas. "We have three Apple II computers and we use them for preparing budgets, spreadsheeting, forecasting, and what-if simulation." How have his employees responded to the computers? "The more they get involved with the personal computer," he says, "the more I see them adapting it to their own application or work areas. The advantages of the computer have spread by word of mouth. Over half our employees are now using the computers, a very high number, considering that both the keyboard and the software are in English."

At Lillian Vernon Corp., a New York mail-order house, Fred Hochberg uses his computer to analyze sales trends. Hochberg estimates that by helping him determine the best weeks for catalog mailings, the computer has saved his firm at least $100,000.

In Lengerich, West Germany, Nadam Munk uses a personal computer to manage the finances at his primal therapy center. "In the last year there have been many more clients coming to the center, so we needed the Apple II. It cuts the time I spend on bookkeeping in half. And it's fun." Does he see the personal computer catching on among other professionals and businesspeople in West Germany? "It's not like the United States," he says, "but the growth is coming. I can feel it in the air, see it in the ads, read about it in the newspapers. The growth is definitely coming."

And why not? For $2,500 to $5,000 you can buy a personal computer in Bahrain, Bangkok, or Bangor that is more powerful—and far more useful—than the mainframe computers that guided Neil Armstrong to a lunar landing.

The Personal Computer as a Decision-Making Tool

For those like California attorney Steven Guralnick who has been using a microcomputer in his law practice since the late 1970s, the personal computer long ago became an indispensable management tool. "The personal computer," says Guralnick, "has made it possible for this office to expand, to build a client base, to produce high-quality serivce, and to make a decent living."

The impact of the personal computer is not limited to office productivity and financial control. Personal computers can also be used as decision-support tools. They can enhance the quantity, quality, and accuracy of management data available for small business and professional decision making. "I've learned more about my business in the last two years," says Massachusetts publisher Dennis Curtin, "than in the first fifteen." Others report seeing their businesses and their careers "more clearly" and "more logically." And when decisions are based on facts, not guesswork and intuition, managers gain better control over their companies and their careers.

"All sorts of enormous improvements in human affairs can come about if we are able to enhance human thinking with large amounts of computer thinking power," says computer pioneer Herbert A. Simon, winner of a Nobel prize for his research into the decision-making process. "Using computers, we'll make a lot of decisions more sensibly."

Personal computers change not only how people work, but how they think. Computers encourage logical, organized analysis, especially in complex problem solving and decision making. They accelerate learning, improve concentration, and stimulate creativity. "The computer changed my outlook on retailing," says a California store owner. "I hadn't realized how the pressure of routine paperwork was leaving me physically exhausted and mentally paralyzed. With the personal computer operational, I felt as if a great weight had been lifted. The business became fun. I felt more alert, more energetic and, for the first time in my life, willing to take risks."

In at least three vitally important areas—spreadsheeting, data-base management, and accounting—personal computers and their software programs provide executives with information that is more detailed, timely, and precise than anything that can be obtained by manual systems. Managers and professionals who master these tools will acquire a powerful competitive advantage. Moreover, learning to use today's decision-support tools will put you on the inside track when, as expected within the next five years, personal computers assume the role of "intelligent expert advisors." Says one leading industry observer: "Artificial intelligence will be a key ingredient in the makeup of personal computers of the late 1980s. 'Expert systems' functions will be available, allowing interaction with an expert program capable of being a 'helper' to the user."

EVOLUTION OF THE PERSONAL COMPUTER AND THE IMPORTANCE OF SOFTWARE EXPLAINED

The biggest problem most executives face with personal computers is getting started. They don't know where to begin.

Don Ethan Miller is a student of American subcultures. "With reference to computers, there are basically two groups of people," he points out. On one side are the computer "jocks"—programmers, designers, systems analysts, double E (electrical engineer) wizards, and data-processing managers. "In the other camp fall the rest of us who couldn't tell a 'loop' from a 'floppy,' and wouldn't know an **'algorithm'** if we fell into one."

For most of us, this state of grace—the blissful ignorance of "computerese"—might have continued into the twenty-first century, were it not for a discipline known as "solid-state physics." It is the solid-state physicist, and his tinkering with the crystal lattice of doped silicon, that is responsible for pocket calculators, digital watches, video games, cruise missiles, and now the personal computer.

Miracle of the Microprocessor Chip

At the heart of the personal computer is the famous **microprocessor chip**—a triumph of electronic miniaturization developed at the Intel Corporation in the late 1960s. It is difficult to overestimate the importance of the microprocessor. Imagine the consequences of reducing a nuclear reactor to the approximate size and cost of a digital watch battery; the equivalent in the information world has already occurred.

Ironically, at the time of its invention, the significance of the microprocessor was largely overlooked by the mainstream computer industry. Few computer engineers or executives in the late 1960s took seriously the idea of a desktop

microcomputer built around a powerful microprocessor chip.

One reason for this oversight is understandable. Before the microprocessor could be "instructed" to perform much useful work, hundreds, perhaps thousands, of man-years of effort would be needed to develop software programs to communicate with and control this freshly minted silicon sliver.

The First Microcomputer

The first commercial microcomputer, known as the MITS Altair 8800, was built in early 1975 by a group of engineers who operated a small electronics firm in New Mexico. At the same time, the microcomputer went almost unnoticed, except by scientists and hobbyists with the expertise to communicate with it in **machine code,** the most rudimentary, and hence difficult, of all computer languages.

Within half a decade, however, the microcomputer was blazing a trail of glory across the financial firmament as one of Wall Street's fastest-rising stars. By 1980 microcomputer manufacturing had become a billion-dollar industry, heading for $21.5 billion by the end of the decade according to one 1980 study from the University of California. Recent projections are even more optimistic, with one estimating annual worldwide microcomputer sales at over 17 million units worth approximately $52 billion by 1990.

Home Computer, Personal Computer

Since the hobbyist was the principal user of the first microcomputers, it was natural for the first microcomputer manufacturers—notably Apple, Tandy Radio Shack, and Commodore—to position their products as "home" computers. However, it turned out that the American household was not the microcomputer's most fertile market. "Owners of small businesses, like their larger counterparts, were turning to computers for recordkeeping, payroll, budgeting, and inventory control. Lawyers and accountants used them for

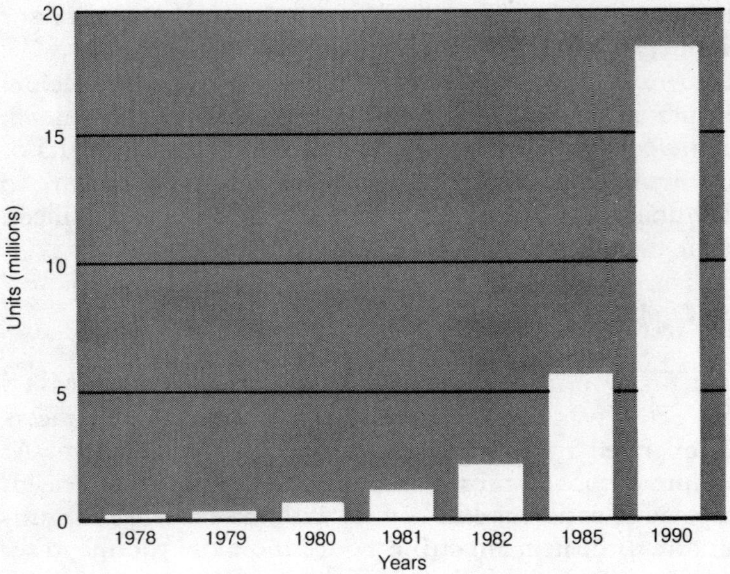

PERSONAL-COMPUTER SALES BY UNITS

billing. Scientists and technicians used them to do math and to program experiments. Writers and editors used them as word-processing machines for editing text on the display terminal," reports Dirk Hanson in *The New Alchemists*. The average home didn't, and still doesn't, have computer-sized problems.

So during the early 1980s the *home* computer became the *personal* computer, i.e., any programmable desktop microcomputer, be it a cream-puff home entertainment and game model, or a high-powered small-business computer with enough operating speed and memory capacity to handle the accounting and financial planning for a 250-employee corporation.

Two major features distinguish the personal computer from its large-scale predecessors: price and size. What strikes most people first, at least those old enough to recall the Paleolithic era of data processing, the late 1950s, is the price. "Personal computers cost as little as thirty dollars and they can sit on the top of a desk," says the marketing manager of Commodore Business Machines.

If the cost of fuel had fallen the way computer prices have plummeted, America's bill for imported oil would now be $65,000 a year instead of $65 billion. "Today I can buy a machine for five dollars that's better than one costing five million dollars twenty years ago," says MIT scientist Edward Fredkin. In fact, what contributes the most expense to today's personal computer is not the computing device itself, but the **peripherals**—the keyboard, video monitor, printer, and disk drives—that are needed to get information in and out of the microprocessor quickly and efficiently.

The Price of Muscle

Thanks to a combination of technical innovations and mass production, anyone who manages a small business or professional practice can afford a personal computer. In general, home-type personal computers in the $30 to $500 range are excellent learning aids, but they lack the memory, speed, and flexibility to perform anything but the most rudimentary business applications.

This does not mean that personal computers with enough muscle for small-business and professional computing need be expensive. For about $3,000 the typical retail computer store offers a variety of packages that include a microcomputer, its peripheral devices, and a number of powerful business-**applications software** programs.

Indeed, the real question today is whether you can afford *not* to computerize. You may be able to get along without the personal computer, but many of your colleagues and competitors are not. And closing ranks from behind is a generation of micro-kids weaned on video games and computer keyboards. "By the late 1980s," notes a 1982 study of the personal-computer market, "most young people entering the work force will be computer literate, especially college graduates."

Today, literacy in the ways of the personal computer is a competitive advantage. Tomorrow it may be essential to economic survival. For several million small-business managers and professionals worldwide, the personal computer is already an essential management tool. In 1985 the installed base of personal computers used for business applications will exceed seven million units. And by 1986 it is estimated that about 20 percent of all American workers will use computers daily.

With personal computers, most of these people will truly be accomplishing more for less. The bottom line is that personal computers will help the small business get bigger and help professional reputations grow.

The Secret Is Software

Fortunately, computer literacy does not demand an intimate knowledge of semiconductors and microcircuits any more than driving a Volkswagen requires an understanding of torque conversion.

Although the design and manufacturing of personal-computer hardware is impressively complex, using it is not difficult. Mastering the use of personal-computer hardware often takes less than an hour. Selecting the best hardware for a specific application is another matter, requiring the ability to evaluate such factors as **disk operating systems** and **random access memory.** (See chapter five.) But infinitely more important is the stuff that makes the hardware go, the computer software.

How can something as insubstantial as a few lines of program code be more important than a palpable, real-life machine with buttons and keys and a screen that glows in the dark? The answer is that in the micro-world, software is power.

Computer software is the alchemist's incantation, the *abracadabra schazaam* that brings the electronic brain to life. Without software programs the personal computer—like a cassette deck without tapes, or a phonograph without records—is useless. When you buy a personal computer you get a "black box" that runs programs. By itself, the computer is of little value, unless you happen to be a skilled programmer.

A Thing of Joy

When purchasing software you are acquiring "business solutions": complex instructions that can keep your books, figure your taxes, analyze your cash flow, project your monthly expenses, and perform any of a thousand and one other routine chores. With substandard programming even the world's sexiest computer hardware is merely an expensive paperweight. But a good program is a thing of joy—and utility—no matter how primitive the machine that runs it.

Software programs are instructions written in a language that the computer hardware understands. The good programs are precious. Personal computers can be mass-produced on an assembly line at the rate of one or two a minute, but **writing** and testing a complex program for, say, accounts receivable or word processing may consume man-years of effort. The biggest challenge facing the beginner—aside from making sense out of the mumbo jumbo of computer jargon—is finding *good* computer programs.

The most common mistake made by the novice is to buy a personal computer—regardless of how famous the manufacturer might be—and assume that the software needed for your business is available. It may well be. But if it's not, be prepared for no end of grief.

Software First—The Cardinal Rule

The cardinal rule of computer management is to find good software first: software that suits your tasks and, if possible, your personality. This is no simple matter. One small-business consultant tested over three hundred software packages. He found less than thirty that he could recommend. Once you find good software, and only then, should you buy a computer that will run it.

Choosing and using the right software is the secret of personal-computer management. Understanding software, how it works and how to make it work, is the prime objective, the real key to computer literacy. The later chapters of this book will explore how managers and professionals are using well-proven off-the-shelf programs, as opposed to expensive custom-written software, to increase their administrative productivity and control.

"The computer is the Proteus of machines," says MIT professor Seymour Papert. "Its essence is its universality, its power to simulate. Because it can take on a thousand forms and serve a thousand functions, it can appeal to a thousand tastes." The problem is not so much in dreaming up new ways to apply micro-power; after a few hours with a personal computer anyone whose desk is awash in unfinished paperwork can name at least a dozen. The real problem is simply illiteracy—computer illiteracy, not knowing how to ask the basic questions so you can get started: Can the personal computer do the job you need done? Where do you begin? What are the risks? How long does it take? Until you reach that elusive middle ground that lies between ignorance and expertise, the personal computer will remain dimly menacing. But it need not remain so for long.

TRANSFORMED SMALL BUSINESSES: ANCHORING THE ECONOMY

The personal computer strengthens the small firm's ability to compete in a troubled economy by increasing the efficiency of its managers and staff. A healthy small-business community, in turn, is an essential ingredient of regional and national prosperity.

Small firms anchor the economy. They are the industrial world's most important source of new jobs, technological innovation, and economic expansion. A return to robust economic growth in an inflation-free environment will not occur until small businesses regain their position as a significant economic force.

Even big business's most ardent enthusiasts recognize the virtues of small-scale organization. During their study of America's top-performing corporations, management consultants Thomas J. Peters and Robert H. Waterman, Jr., discovered that smallness and efficiency can go hand in hand. "For us, the story on plant size was nothing short of astonishing. Repeatedly, we found that the better performers had determined that their small plants, not their big ones, were most efficient," Peters and Waterman note in *In Search of Excellence*. "The point of smallness is that it induces manageability and, above all, commitment. A manager really can understand something that is small and in which one central discipline prevails."

A Revolution in Small-Scale Technology

How can we reverse the social, economic, and technological momentum of a century-old trend that results in bigger machines, greater concentrations of wealth, and increasingly violent consequences for the international economy and the environment? British economist E. F. Schumacher advised looking "for a revolution in technology to give us inventions and machines that reverse the destructive trends now threatening us all."

Specifically, he suggested, "We need methods and equipment which are: cheap enough so they are accessible to virtually everyone; suitable for small-scale applications; and compatible with man's need for creativity."

Schumacher believed that a man's basic tools should cost no more than a year's pay. Even a decade ago this seemed a wishful academic fantasy. Today, Schumacher's idealistic call for inexpensive, "accessible" tools, "suitable for small scale applications" and "compatible with man's need for creativity" are an everyday reality—in the shape of the personal computer and its software programs.

Fortunately, this "revolution in technology" is concurrent with two fundamental economic trends. One is a rebirth of the entrepreneurial spirit in America. The other is the decline and restructuring of America's smokestack industries in the face of strengthening international competition from Western Europe, Japan, and the developing nations.

Entrepreneurial Explosion and Restructuring of Industry

"In 1950 we were creating new businesses at the rate of 93,000 per year. Today, we are creating new companies in this country at the rate of about 600,000 a year," John Naisbitt points out in *Megatrends*. This entrepreneurial explosion is more than an event of passing academic interest. It is one of America's best hopes for breaking the grip of economic stagnation brought on by decades of compounded big government and big business expansion. It is the small firms, many with under twenty employees, not *Fortune* 500 companies or government agencies, that create the vast majority of technical innovations and new jobs, while also providing the major gains in productivity and sales growth. Small firms and cottage industries are the cornerstone of international economic stability.

The Birch study at MIT discovered that 66 percent of new jobs created during the late 1960s and early 1970s were *in firms with less than twenty employees*. By contrast, the 1,000 top *Fortune* companies provided almost no job growth during the same period.

Small businesses contribute more to economic prosperity and stable growth, however, than just new jobs. Small firms are also more innovative and productive than most big businesses. A recent National Science Foundation study concluded that small firms produce four times more innovations per research dollar than medium-sized business, and twenty-four times more innovations than big business. Says Arthur Levitt, Jr., chairman of the American Stock Exchange, "Small businesses literally can't afford to be unproductive. They have no margin for slack: Productivity is essential to their survival."

In addition, the vast majority of small-business growth occurs in the industries of service- and information-based technologies. And compared to old-line smokestack industries, these emerging technologies have little potential for environmental harm.

While the well-financed, politically organized special interests of big business, big labor, and big government dominate American society, it is actually the small firm that generates new jobs, growth, innovation, productivity, and the industries of tomorrow. "Entrepreneurs are fighting America's only serious war against poverty," concludes George Gilder. "The potentialities of invention and enterprise are now greater than ever before in human history."

Winning Proposition

It is through the renaissance of America's 17 million small firms, not its 200,000 big businesses, that we can achieve relatively high and sustained rates of economic growth and job creation throughout the 1980s and beyond. "The real choice," says Harvard economist Robert B. Reich, "is between protecting an old industrial base—historic preservation, I call it—which is a losing proposition, or trying to accelerate the transition to a more competitive industrial base."

The new technologies revolutionizing agriculture, oil refining, pharmaceutical production, health care delivery, telecommunications, energy exploration, and virtually all the informational professions—law, education, engineering, systems analysis, medicine, architecture, nursing, journalism, advertising, social work, accounting, library science, and even religion—are already pointing the way toward an emerging new knowledge-based American industrial system. The leaders in this new economy will be men and women with the flexibility to adapt their management style to the technologies and requirements of the information age. The personal computer is the key.

The low-cost personal computer—immensely powerful, yet available to all who care to learn how to use it—is the ideal managerial weapon for increasing productivity while resisting the pressures of bureaucratization. Personal computing is the winning proposition for small firms and, by extension, the American economy. It is in precisely the very areas of our recent vulnerability—insufficient job growth, failing productivity, overly centralized organizational structures, faltering innovation, and widespread environmental damage—that the personal computer offers new promise and new power. Together the entrepreneurial explosion and the personal computer will give rise to a new era of economic stability and prosperity.

Chapter Two

Strategic Deployment—How to Use the Personal Computer to Keep the Cash Flowing

Which of you, intending to build a tower, sitteth not down first and counteth the cost, whether he have sufficient to finish it?

—Luke 14:28

WHEN TO BUY?

The first problem confronting the professional or small-business executive is when to computerize. The question is often asked, Won't computerizing now mean installing a machine that may soon be obsolete?

The answer is that it's better to install a machine that might become obsolete than never to computerize at all. Any differences between the present generation of personal-computer hardware and the next pale compared to the differences between using a personal computer and not using one.

Barry Wolkon says it would take five full-time employees to accomplish what his one secretary does in twenty hours with an Apple II. Yet the Apple II is now an obsolete computer—and it has been for years. It doesn't matter. The difference between using a personal computer and not using a computer at all is so vast that distinctions between one generation of computers and the next are virtually irrelevant. "You probably would prefer a Mercedes to a Volkswagen," says one computer expert. "But compared to walking, there really isn't much difference between them."

The Default Option

Sitting on the sidelines while competitors computerize is really no strategy at all. It's like a computer program's **default option,** the choice requiring no action on the user's part. Computer literacy takes time. Learning to use most computer programs is akin to taking up a new sport or musical instrument. The requirements are practice, patience, and concentration. The ability to prepare budgets and financial forecasting models with a spreadsheet program such as VisiCalc or SuperCalc, for instance, is an enormous competitive advantage for executives; some compare it to the invention of the wheel or the plow. But spreadsheeting is a skill that is not acquired overnight. It takes anywhere from five to fifty hours to become proficient with the program itself. Next comes the problem of building a model that accurately represents your business. Microcomputer consultant Jeff Finn suggests that this phase often results in a "ripple effect." By attempting to quantify what appears to be an isolated relationship, say, the impact of your promotional spending on gross sales, you are actually forced to unravel the dynamics of your firm one thread at a time.

"For most executives," says a Boston general management consultant, "the financial model unleashes a chain reaction of unanswered questions. What are the various relationships between period costs, product costs, gross factory margins, and net income? What about rental mix, cost of revenue, field engineering, and marketing research? To be effective a financial model must capture the interaction of every revenue or cost flow area that impacts the profits and losses."

Modeling your business in all its detail, most spreadsheet users find, is an open-ended process. "After two years," says Massachusetts publisher Dennis Curtin, "I'm still refining my models." But Curtin, like many managers who have tried spreadsheeting, is not about to stop. One reason is the financial control that spreadsheeting gives him over his business. Control that comes through knowledge. "The net benefit of having to do it all yourself is tremendous," he says. "The one aspect of the personal computer nobody has addressed is the power of it as a learning tool for the person using it."

Get Started *Now* with Inputting

Another reason to computerize now: "Inputting" sufficient data to give your calculations validity is an arduous and time-consuming process. This is especially true in data-base management and accounting, where entering historical records can require months of intensive clerical work. Unfortunately, the only practical method for computerizing hard-copy records is to type—or *enter*—them through the computer's keyboard. At Seven Associates, a small California manufacturer with $1 million in annual sales, thirty-five employees, and approximately 300 customers, typing the past year's manual accounting records into the automated accounting program was a twelve-week ordeal. But not until data is entered into the system can the small firm realize the benefits of automation. (Incidentally, when you are computerizing accounting and other vital recordkeeping systems, most consultants recommend that you run your manual system *and* your automated system in tandem for a period of three to six months . . . just in case.)

Perhaps one of the most important positive side effects of computerizing is that business procedures and systems that have often grown up catch-as-catch-can must be reviewed and revised. In planning for a computer many managers are forced, often for the first time in their careers, to make a systematic analysis of their business procedures. Effective personal-computer management entails significant groundwork. Employee morale, lines of power, and professional esteem must all be considered.

Expand Creativity—and Your Competitive Edge

There are also intangible benefits from computerization. Computers change people. As Professor Stanford B. Weinberg of St. Joseph's University in Philadelphia figures it, about one person in twenty who try using computers suffer from vertigo, nausea, hysteria, cold sweats, or stomachaches. But for every cyberphobe, half a dozen people find using personal computers an intellectually challenging, even consciousness-expanding experience. Says a Beverly Hills screenwriter who uses her Radio Shack TRS-80 for word processing: "It energizes consciousness in a way no typewriter or legal pad ever could. It forces you to respond quickly, to think logically, and to focus your attention on content, not form. The personal computer increases efficiency. But as far as I am concerned, it also expands awareness." But to find out, you have to use one. "Even if you are on the right track," said Will Rogers, "you'll get run over if you just sit there."

Peter Drucker, who has been called "the man who invented corporate society," notes that "the computer, for those who understand anything about it, is emancipation for the individual. The purpose of the computer is to enable us not to spend time on 'controls,' but to use the time for tasks that require perception, imagination, human relations, and creativity." This is the essence of computer management.

Today the ability to manage the small firm with the personal computer is a dramatic competitive advantage. But for how long? Presently less than 15 percent of America's small-business and professional offices have personal computers. Those who own them, and know how to use them, hold a significant competitive edge. But the situation is changing rapidly. In 1985 professionals and people with small businesses will enjoy an installed base of at least five million computers. By 1987 at the latest, the personal computer will no longer be seen as a competitive advantage in most fields. It will be a fundamental prerequisite.

AN ARTICULATED BUT FLEXIBLE STRATEGY

Effective computerization requires using the personal computer not just as a tactical device—say, as a machine for automating the payroll or accounting system—but as a strategic weapon capable of helping attain long-range objectives. By thinking of the personal computer only in tactical terms, you box yourself into information systems that may be adequate for today, but will not serve your needs tomorrow.

And the fact is that no firm is too small to benefit from the personal computer—not the twenty-employee firm, not the five-man shop, not even the one-man band—if the personal computer helps achieve long-range strategic objectives.

This presupposes that you have an articulated strategy. Many, indeed most, firms do not. A generous estimate might put the number of small businesses and professional offices working towards well-defined strategic goals at fewer than one in ten. But what is a strategic plan? How is it developed? And why must you have one to use the personal computer effectively?

You may already have a strategy for dealing with a competitor's price cut or finding a new job. You may have strategies for winning a new account, client, or project. And perhaps your firm has annual sales objectives and perhaps even a five-year marketing plan. But these are not strategic plans any more than a sacrifice bunt, a lob return, or an economic embargo are strategies. They are tactics—functional, small-scale maneuvers designed to further a larger purpose.

Business strategy is a long-term, large-scale plan, integrating the thousand individual battles and tactical maneuvers into one purposeful whole. Strategic plans are realistic, action-oriented, and, above all, comprehensive. They are *not* wishful projections of current revenues or ratios. They *are* rational appraisals of where your business or professional career should stand five or ten years hence. Strategic objectives must consider products, competition, materials, clients, customers, labor, machinery, inventory, business systems, key management, markets, financing, economic conditions, and, above all, your best perceptions of fundamental economic trends. "An essential feature of all strategic planning is a forecast of the world ahead," say Columbia Business School professors Boris Yavitz and William H. Newman. "This scenario of the future should cover social, political, and technological changes as well as economic shifts."

The first aim of strategic deployment is to develop business systems that are as open-ended and flexible as possible. This means finding software packages that can be **integrated** so that numerous computerized tasks can operate from a single set of computer files, or **data base.** Note that the emphasis is on finding the right *software,* not hardware.

Personal-computer hardware is cheap, and getting cheaper. Choosing good software, however, remains an undertaking with great implied expenses. Not because the software itself is necessarily expensive—although many off-the-shelf packages may actually cost more than the actual computer—but because software demands a precious commodity from you—time.

Software takes time to master, and it takes time to enter enough data to make it useful. Accounts, clients, customers, inventory, sales, markets, demographics, dates, dealers, distributors, employees, tax tables, addresses, phone numbers, zip codes, and the other details that are grist to the mills of commerce have to be typed into the system and verified.

Building computer data files may take a few afternoons for high-margin, low-volume professionals such as real estate agents, consultants, authors, yacht brokers, graphic designers, advertising photographers, or architects. But for businesses or professions with large inventories or many customers, clients, or suppliers—medical, legal, and dental practices, retailers, wholesalers, mail-order firms, or small manufacturers—constructing an adequate data base may demand hundreds, even thousands, of hours. Having to build a new data base every time an additional program is implemented is a waste of valuable time and resources. Yet this is exactly what happens to many who take a piecemeal approach to micro-power. "Successful implementations don't just happen," says Donald Shaw, former vice-president of Automatic Data Processing, Inc. (ADP). "They're planned in meticulous detail, and progress is checked each step of the way."

PERSONAL COMPUTERS AND THE STRATEGIC PLAN

Two Methods

Imagine for a moment two fictional retail videocassette outlets called "VideOne" and "VideoTwo." Both have good geographic locations, ample working capital, and the identical problem: With over two thousand titles in stock, their manual inventory-control systems are breaking down. Slow-moving films such as *Hiroshima Mon Amour* clog the shelves, while recent hits are not being reordered until after a sale is lost. Additional sales are missed because the owners must spend several hours a day in the back office monitoring the "paper trail" of 250 weekly videocassette rentals. Both owners recognize the need for a computerized inventory system.

VideOne's owner is a competent, task-oriented small-businessperson who takes charge and gets things done. He visits several computer stores and finds the best buy on a popular microcomputer and an inexpensive software package that will run a real "perpetual"—or continuously updated—count of stock items. He hires his part-time bookkeeper to keyboard the basic data, spends about twenty hours learning the system, and within two months he can push a few buttons every Monday morning and summon up a sales profile of the previous week, complete with volume leaders, inventory levels, and a complete history of rental transactions. There is only one catch. VideOne's inventory package is just that—inventory. It does its assigned task famously, but that is all it does. It cannot be integrated into an accounting system that includes cash journal, accounts receivable, general ledger, and the other good things that help monitor cash flow and build financial records. It doesn't keep track of the names of cash customers to build automated mailing lists for promotional mailings or sales to other area merchants. In addition, the data-base files that VideOne is building will probably have to be reentered through the keyboard should he ever decide to upgrade to more flexible software.

VideoTwo is also owned by a take-charge entrepreneur. Like her competitor at VideOne she has recognized the enormous growth potential of the industry and is convinced of its high profit potential. In addition, she has a strategic plan. Selling videocassettes at $49.95 apiece is nice, but selling franchise leases for $20,000 plus 4 percent of gross is even better. Her objective is to establish VideoTwo as a model retail outlet, and then, relying upon her financial statements and expertise, form a Sub S corporation and go shopping for $250,000 in venture capital to open two additional outlets.

With three stores and a growing reputation within her industry, she hopes to arrange volume discounts and launch a high-visibility advertising and public relations campaign. If this stage is successful and the VideoTwo name becomes established in her geographical market, the next phase will include a fresh infusion of venture capital in order to undertake a sales and training campaign for a statewide VideoTwo franchise operation.

This strategic overview adds a new dimension to her shopping assignment. Her immediate requirement is the same as VideOne's: to have an effective inventory-control program "on-line" (i.e., in operation) as soon as possible. But she also can foresee many other eventual needs, including an integrated accounting system (for payroll, receivables, order entry, general ledger, and for producing financial statements and a business plan), mailing lists (for potential customers, investors, franchise operators, vendors, etc.), financial modeling (for preparing various "what if" scenarios as a part of her *pro forma* monthly profit and loss forecasts, cash-flow analyses, balance sheets, and break-even charts), and word processing (letters, reports, mailings, promotional literature, updated title lists, etc.).

She may, indeed, purchase the identical computer hardware as VideOne. But she will buy an inventory package with one significant advantage that VideOne never considered (and that few, if any, computer salespeople are able or willing to point out): hers is capable of painless integration into a full-scale microcomputer system. She will add many new programs as her business prospers, as well as many new and exotic hardware devices such as high-speed "line printers" and **Winchester hard-disk** drives, and perhaps even replace her first computer with a newer, more powerful model. But she is planning her initial purchases so that these changes will evolve gracefully, not with abrupt fits and starts. If she does her homework carefully, new programs and equipment will be "upwardly compatible." She will no more need to junk a data base, entering for the second time thousands of items through the keyboard, than her early customers would have to abandon their costly videotapes, though the scope of their collections grows and the quality and power of their playback machines increase.

Synergy

Personal computers and strategic plans are synergistic; that is, the two create a whole that is greater than the sum of their parts.

A knowledge of strategic objectives makes computerization more effective, since you can select systems—both hardware and software, but especially software—that will fulfill long-term priorities and objectives. A few hundred dollars spent on more flexible software today saves thousands of dollars in clerical expense and disruption tomorrow.

Micro-power provides you and your workers with the productivity tools—word processing, electronic spreadsheeting, inventory and accounting systems—to meet strategic objectives faster, cheaper, and more efficiently. And it allows you to monitor progress and evaluate changes in the marketplace, or within the firm, that may affect the strategic mission or its objectives.

Finally, micro-power provides the raw, number-crunching muscle necessary to revise the minutiae of *pro forma* budgets, financial statements, and strategic targets at frequent intervals, thus keeping objectives practical and realistic, given the reality of ever-changing conditions.

"The principle of strategy is having one thing, to know ten thousand things," Musashi wrote in *A Book of Five Rings*. As you read the discussion of personal-computer applications in the later chapters of this book, keep the long-term objectives of your professional career and your firm in mind. One well-defined strategy can give meaning, direction, and purpose to ten thousand tactical details.

Avoiding the Cash-Flow Crisis

The strategic plan is a vital step toward a basic goal of business—as well as life: the ability to alter and ultimately control your destiny. The specifics of control depend on your business activity or profession. Manufacturers, for instance, must track orders, perform job-cost accounting, analyze product performance, and control inventories of raw materials and finished goods. Retailers have inventory problems of their own, and sales and promotion analyses are also crucial concerns. For professional offices and agencies, administrative overhead for clerical, secretarial, and special client services is a major drain on profits. In warehousing and distribution firms, margins may be fixed, but expenses vary widely, making efficient inventory and delivery scheduling essential.

This diversity of specific problems, however, masks a universal theme that transcends all others. Small businesses and professional practices of every persuasion demand one absolutely essential nutrient: cash flow. When the flow of cash, either from receipts or financing, ceases, so does the business. "The modern professional manager knows as a matter of routine that cash-flow management is basic to business," says Robert Heller, author of *The Business of Business*. "Unless his finance people are half-witted, cash coming in will be efficiently budgeted, controlled, and monitored, so enough will always be available when needed." But as an attorney, real estate agent, dentist, or small-business executive you probably aren't a "professional manager," not in the corporate sense anyway. And your "finance people" may consist of a part-time bookkeeper and a CPA who visits every three months to reckon your Employer's Quarterly Federal Tax Return and perhaps the dozen other federal, state, and city tax forms required to do business in most regions. For small firms, even high-tech ventures with impressive products and a brilliant future, having cash available when it's needed isn't easy.

Even a bulging order book is no sure antidote to the liquidity crisis. Too much business can be as bad as too little. Small firms are as apt to lose control of their cash in good times as in bad. However, according to Dun & Bradstreet, about half of all business failures are precipitated by inadequate sales, while one quarter fail because of competitive weakness, and the remaining quarter go down because of heavy operating expenses, receivables difficulties, or inventory problems.

Few small firms and professional practices have weathered the economic gales of the early 1980s without at least one near-brush with a liquidity crisis. Those that survived with their rigging intact are now in a position to enjoy a period of sustained and rapid growth.

Growth for these small businesses should be a cause for joy and celebration. Unfortunately, for some it may be the harbinger of ruin. Unfair as it seems, businesspeople who have safely crossed the troubled seas of double-digit interest and inflation and the severe recession can still find their dreams shattered on uncharted shoals, even as their landfall is in view. "For far too many small- and medium-sized businesses," says Peter Drucker, "growth turns into nightmare. Just as the company seems poised for rapid and profitable growth, it gets out of control and into severe trouble." Some firms survive—many do not.

Cash Flow and the Growing Firm

Consider Evolution Technologies. Their product is a line of minicomputers of acknowledged quality—six machines ranging in price from $34,000 to $250,000—capable of competing in the high-tech marketplace. Evolution's forecasts call for winning a one-half percent share of the exploding minicomputer market by 1986, which would give the company an estimated $100 million in annual sales.

But if Evolution reaches its goal, it will not be without deep financial scars. These include the trauma of defaulting on a $345,000 loan from California's Wells Fargo Bank as well as seeing their stock removed from the NASDAQ listings for failing to meet working capital requirements.

How did a firm with a solid product line—"probably the finest data-base management system in the world," says one Laguna Beach, California, minicomputer dealer—find itself in such dire financial straits? Rapid growth combined with inexperience were major contributing factors. "None of the four founders had manufacturing or financial experience when they started," notes Robert A. Mamis in *Inc.* magazine. Despite half a dozen financial strategems—including a $500,000 secured line of bank credit, discounting advance payments, venture capital funding in the form of a $1.1 million subordinated note, and a "reverse merger" that made Evolution a public company without the expense of issuing stock through an underwriter—Evolution simply couldn't keep any cash in the company till.

"Growth requires investment," points out Drucker. "It always strains the financial resources of a business. And unless the business is managed for cash flow, growth is likely to create liquidity pressures that might force the growing business into insolvency." In the case of Evolution Technologies the founders had stretched their financing to the limit in an attempt to simultaneously build inventory, production capacity, a dealer network, and R&D facilities. Yet just as big interest payments were coming due, sales softened, creating the sad, but similar plight—the cash-flow crisis.

Rapid expansion almost inevitably siphons off badly needed working capital. "It's quite easy to expand yourself right out of business," points out small-business consultant Kenneth J. Albert. "You may have thousands of dollars in accounts receivable, but if you don't have money to meet the payroll or to pay suppliers, you're in big trouble." Paradoxically, one of the signals of an impending cash-flow crisis is an *increase* in accounts receivable. Customers or clients that are suddenly slow in paying may be having cash-flow problems of their own. The likely results are slower sales, collection difficulties, and bad debts.

Managing the Essential Paperwork for Financial Control

To avoid the liquidity crisis, management consultants point to some basic guidelines. These include consideration of capital investment requirements, long-range financial planning, information management, and the efficient use of human resources.

They are simple, even commonsense rules. But putting them into operation has often been impractical for the harried professional or entrepreneur. For one thing, few small-business managers or professionals know "Sub S corporations," "trial balances," or "subordinated notes" from "nested loops" and "line gremlins." And you don't have to —until you strike out on your own. Responding to the immediate demands of clients and customers is time-consuming enough without being sidetracked or diverted by the essential paperwork of accounting, recordkeeping, and financial planning.

Yet, it is in accounting, recordkeeping, and financial forecasting that micro-power management has so much to offer the small firm. At the Kish Glass Company, Ltd., in Dublin, Ireland, Eamonn Marnell uses a data-base management program to keep his business records in electronic form on an Apple II computer. "One of the big money savers is the computer's ability to store information," he points out. "Records and reports can be printed out without the cost or delay of having them typed by a secretary. Annually this adds up to a very, very big benefit." Recently, Kish Glass moved its offices. "After the move I had to make a lot of changes in our files," says Marnell. "It would have taken me months to do it by hand. With the computer I just pulled out the disks and updated the information. We were back on track within a few days."

Marnell also uses his personal computer to manage cash flow. "You can put in your formulas on the spreadsheet," he says, "and all you have to do is change one number, for instance annual sales, and it will give you corresponding figures for your other variable expenses."

Frederick G. Frost III is president of the A. T. Wall Company in Warwick, Rhode Island. "I used to get reports every Monday morning that allowed me as boss and owner to make judgments and decisions. Then we started growing. Those Monday morning reports became Monday afternoon reports, became Tuesday afternoon reports as there were more and more customers, more and more transactions, more and more checks to deposit and invoices to post."

In 1982, with the assistance of general management consultant Peter Lawson, the A. T. Wall Company installed a network of IBM Personal Computers. "The personal computer has brought back to Monday morning my ability to get the kind of information that allows us to map out our week ahead," says Frost, "and to find out if our budgets and plans are on track or not.

"We haven't laid anybody off," he points out, "but it's allowed us to spend more time chasing accounts receivable and getting invoices posted for payment to our suppliers. Now we can plan our payments better and watch our cash to find out where it is and whether it's invested properly."

Marnell and Frost are typical of millions of small-business owners and professionals worldwide who are exploiting personal computers to get their files and finances under control. If you don't know where your receivables, payables, and cash reserves are, a few hours spent with your accountant, and perhaps a microcomputer consultant, developing an automated bookkeeping and data-base management system, may be among the most important of your professional or business career. Knowing where the cash is coming from, and where it's going, is essential to small-business financial planning; the personal computer is the key to that knowledge.

The Personal Computer and Requirements for Growth

What else can the personal computer do for your small firm? Here are the four strategic management challenges faced by the growing business for which micro-power can help play a decisive role.

1. Growth requires investment

Except in fields with low capital requirements such as consulting, retained earnings are seldom sufficient to finance new or rapidly growing firms.

Investment funds for start-ups come from personal savings, rich uncles, friends, and, occasionally, heavily secured, short-term commercial bank loans. Also, about 25 percent of the nation's most active venture-capital firms will provide long-term funds for promising new firms, usually in exchange for between 50 and 90 percent ownership (and perhaps the right to change management).

But access to such funds requires accurate financial statements, and usually a thoughtful and thorough business plan. The *Harvard Business Review* estimates a proper business plan "can easily take 200 to 300 hours" to prepare.

Where does this leave the entrepreneur or professional running a small private practice? Enter the personal computer. With automated bookkeeping not only can you monitor your financial position daily, but you can also accumulate historical financial records—a data base—that can assist in the development of long-range business plans or commercial loan proposals.

Computerizing the general ledger—the basic record of all business transactions drawn from the individual receivables, payables, payroll, and inventory journals—even for the one-man business, is a double-threat play.

First, once the intricacies of the system are mastered, micro-power cuts routine recordkeeping from hours to minutes. With an integrated system that links the "big four" individual software packages (accounts receivable, payable, payroll, and inventory) to the general ledger, information such as client addresses, orders, and billing or payment data is entered into the keyboard only once. The computer then automatically "posts" the data to the general ledger. The chance of error is greatly reduced. And errors, when they do occur, are easier to correct because they are consistent throughout the system. Federal, state, and city tax data is automatically recorded. And financial statements and critical cash-flow information such as "aged account status" can be summarized at any time.

After the routine recordkeeping has been computerized, the second area where micro-power helps is in monitoring cash flow. Such critical liquidity indicators as sales volume, inventory, receivables, and payables can be observed on a day-to-day basis if necessary. Many small businesses have only a foggy notion of where the money is coming from, and virtually no idea where it is going. "Even for the one-man band with a substantial cash flow I'd recommend a personal computer," says a New Orleans CPA. "Sure, an accountant can give you the same information. Probably more and better information. But it takes him about a month to do it. Down here that's all the time it takes to get up to your ass in alligators."

With a clearer picture of the day-to-day operations of the growing firm, the micro-power executive can anticipate and provide for future financial needs.

2. Growth requires long-range financial planning

Once again, computerization is vital. Long-range financial planning means sensible two- or three-year forecasts based on reliable information. Forecasts should always be predicated on anticipated market conditions *not* on production or staff capabilities. Even more important, forecasts should examine "worst possible," as well as "best possible" scenarios. Looking only at optimistic projections, particularly during the heady days of a growth spurt, is an error common to big business as well as small.

When it comes to financial planning, the micro-power manager holds the advantage. With VisiCalc, SuperCalc, and similar spreadsheet programs, he can project what-if scenarios, taking into account hundreds of variables. What if the price of oil doubles, Local 210 calls a six-day wildcat strike, inflation averages 7 percent, the prime is at 12 percent, production capability is increased by 36 percent, and sales fall by a quarter? Spreadsheeting allows financial plans to be laid *well in advance* of major changes in the business climate. Once new trends are detected, they can be quickly extrapolated and their consequences evaluated.

Not all parts of a firm will grow at the same rate. Perhaps, as often happens, it is necessary to extend longer terms of credit on receivables while simultaneously expanding staff or production facilities to accommodate increasing sales or work load. This may require a combination of short-term commercial loans to cover receivables and a long-term equity financing to acquire additional office space or production facilities. If changing financial structures are anticipated well in advance, well-run firms will find funds available. But if financial dealings are on a crisis-reaction basis, at best the financing terms will be onerous. At worst, poor financial planning can mean the loss of ownership, control, or even solvency.

3. Growth requires planning for future information needs

The administrative details of running the growing firm often isolate professionals and executives from the marketplace. The accounting system, even the computerized accounting system, does not recognize trends until they are history. In the information age, new technologies revolutionize major industries at a rapid clip. Businesses can be doomed long before sales turn sluggish. Witness the 8mm movie camera. In 1977, the year the portable videocassette recorder was introduced, 8mm camera sales set a new all-time record of $161 million. Within thirty-six months movie camera sales had collapsed. Today, chemical-based 8mm photography verges on extinction, the victim of a new technology.

In the information society, knowledge is power. The life cycles of products and data are contracting. Without a sensitive and discerning information system today's high-tech superstar can be tomorrow's buggy whip maker. According to the *Cox Report,* American businesses have a long way to go in improving their basic information systems. Less than 30 percent of the managers surveyed felt their companies "frequently achieve good information flow." Recognizing the need for certain basic information and developing systems for acquiring it are essential ingredients in long-term business and professional growth.

Information should come from multiple sources: newsletters, trade and professional journals, books, magazines, tabloids, space reps, service technicians, politicians, commissioned reports, conferences, academic courses, and, above all, customers and clients. But if it is not merely to increase the volume of background noise, information must be both pertinent and timely.

This is where the personal computer comes in. The personal computer is not just an isolated island of silicon logic. Like people, computers are capable of symbolic communication. Micros can converse directly with one another (though this may only work with similar models). They can also be equipped for "up-loading" and "down-loading" (i.e., sending and receiving) with powerful mainframe computers located anywhere on the international telecommunications grid. Mainframe computers act as central libraries—called "on-line data bases"—storing vast amounts of continuously updated information. Mainframes also operate as electronic relay stations, storing messages and even automatically calling your computer at fixed intervals.

Electronic mail and the master terminal. Since computer data can be transmitted over standard telephone lines at the rate of about one typewritten page per minute, the cost of sending documents across the country, or even internationally, is usually less than any overnight courier service. And delivery is virtually instantaneous. The result is a major information-gathering and communications breakthrough for small-business and professional firms.

How do you turn a personal computer into a master communications terminal? The device that makes such communications possible is known as a **modem**—short for *mo*dulator/*dem*odular. The modem is a hardware peripheral —an add-on option—that converts digital computer code into **analog** signals that can be transmitted over the telephone system. With a modem, proposals, contracts, reports, and other documents can be transmitted between personal computers. What if the addressee doesn't have a personal computer? MCI, Western Union and the Freedom Network (operated by Graphnet, Inc., in Teaneck, New Jersey) offer competing services that allow personal computers to act as terminals for electronic mail, Telex, TWX, International Telex, and Fax Gram services.

Western Union's "Access System" for personal computers allows you to send electronic mail in the form of Telex, Telegram, Mailgram, Computer Letter, International Cablegram, or International Priority Letter "to one person or tens of thousands," as their advertising says. Messages can be addressed to other "store-and-forward" Telex or personal-computer terminals. Or they can be delivered as hard copy by messenger or mail. The Access System costs $35 a month, plus usage fees of approximately four cents per word for domestic messages. Freedom Network has a lower monthly fee, but fewer delivery options.

The beauty of the Access System and Freedom Network is that you can use your personal computer as a combination of a word processor, mailing list manager, and electronic communications terminal. You can, for instance, write a personalized form letter, merge it with a mailing list of 250 potential customers or clients, and then electronically post your letters over the telephone for delivery as Mailgrams, Telegrams, or Overseas Cablegrams. When used as a Telex terminal, the store-and-forward feature offered by both Western Union and Graphnet will capture messages when you are away from your desk and hold them for your return.

Information utilities. Personal computers also provide instant access to "information utility services." The Source and CompuServe are among the most widely used information utility operations. Like your local electric company, their product, in a very real sense, is energy; or more precisely, the energy that information unleashes. CompuServe, for instance, maintains data on 9,000 securities that are updated through each trading day, as well as historical records of 40,000 stocks, bonds, and options. The Source accesses information libraries that abstract major business, financial, scientific, public affairs, and education publications. Individual information services from The Source include a commodity news service (bullion to pork bellies), business services (airlines schedules, corporate employment, listings of new business ventures), current business trends (information in about forty categories such as business commentary, company profiles, consumer behavior, economic planning, industrial production index, stock performance), and financial markets (report indexes on earnings, dividends, futures, options, treasury bills, New York Stock Exchange stock prices, and treasury Over the Counter).

To use the information utilities, you need a personal computer and a modem. You'll also have to open an account by phoning in a credit card number. In return you are given a telephone number and a password. Typically, the telephone number links you to one of two computer communication networks—either TYMNET or TELENET—that can be reached with a local call in over 300 metropolitan areas.

These networks, in turn, connect to on-line data bases such as The Source and CompuServe without incurring the expense of a long-distance toll. Instead, you are billed only for the time you "log" on your information service. Rates vary, from as low as $6 or $7 an hour for an after-midnight session on The Source to over $100 an hour for certain specialized legal, medical, and business research services.

An intriguing feature offered by many information utilities is the "electronic bulletin board." In researching this book I posted a message on The Source bulletin board asking how subscribers were using their computers in small businesses and the professions. Within a few hours I found the first reply in my "electronic mailbox," signed by a Hollywood filmmaker:

> Dear James:
>
> I operate a film production company that produces information films (sales, PR, training, etc.) for corporations and increasingly have been using the IBM-PC for most of the applications you listed.
>
> I write scripts with it, do budgets with a spreadsheet program, and am about finished writing a program that will do most of my bookkeeping, including job costs to date.
>
> I don't know how helpful I can be, since this is my first exposure to computers (I bought the PC last April). I'm constantly amazed at how helpful such a moderately priced investment can be if you're willing to spend the time to make it do things YOUR way.
>
> If I can help you, I'll be happy to.

Within a week there were over fifty similar responses from lawyers, accountants, insurance agents, salesmen, teachers, and even fellow writers. A well-known name in the microcomputer industry replied: "I use my PC about twelve hours per day. In addition to writing for *PC World, PC* and other U.S. computer magazines, I run a media service which provides computer information to European magazines. I use the PC as a word processor and The Source to get my material to Europe as fast as telex and a lot cheaper. The system has made a little guy like me able to compete with news services with millions of dollars."

One further advantage of using the on-line data base for information research—whether it's interviews, market studies, economic forecasts, or whatever—is that once the material has been saved on a **floppy disk** it can be integrated into memos, manuscripts, reports, and even spreadsheets without ever being *retyped*. The messages from personal-computer users quoted above, for instance, were typed only once—on their computers. I simply merged them into this chapter with a few keystrokes of my word-processing program.

CompuServe and The Source are among the most visible information utilities. But there are already over one thousand other data bases in the United States, 90 percent of them accessible by personal computer. Some, such as Lockheed's Dialog, act as feeders into as many as one hundred fifty specialized data bases, such as National Agriculture Library, the Social Science Citation Index, The Foundation Grants Index, and World Aluminum Abstracts. LEXIS and WESTLAW can save lawyers hundreds of hours in researching legal precedents. CANCERPROJ lets researchers study the findings of current and recently completed cancer studies. MEDLINE summarizes international biomedical literature, including health care, clinical practice, and administration, with articles culled from over three thousand medical journals.

Dow Jones. Another on-line data base, this one of particular interest to investors, is the Dow Jones News/Retrieval Service. The Dow's "Blue Chip" service costs seventy-five dollars a year plus usage fees of thirty-six to seventy-two dollars an hour. With it you can search and retrieve over 175,000 Dow Jones articles from *Barron's* and the *Wall Street Journal,* obtain current quotes on stocks, bonds, mutual funds, treasury notes, and options, as well as 10-K's, 10-Q's, and proxy statements on over six thousand publicly held corporations.

A big plus for investors: Data from the Dow's historical quotes and economic forecasts can be transferred directly into the "cells" of a spreadsheet program, eliminating the need to manually research or even keyboard basic data for many economic modeling and forecasting projects.

Distributed networks. Finally, personal computers can be joined into "distributed data processing networks"—computerese for the addition of personal computers as a company grows; all of them sharing the same central data base. Or, in the case of the small-business unit (typically a division of a larger corporation), personal computers can be linked to the parent firm's central mainframe. Sales reports, inventory levels, market analysis, comparative demographics, sales orders, and accounting data can all be entered and then retrieved at far-flung locations such as branch offices or even the portable personal computer that's carried in the salesperson's briefcase. At the A. T. Wall Company, President Fred Frost, in addition to his office computer, has an IBM-PC in his home and a briefcase-sized IBM-PC–compatible model, called the Compaq. Frost can receive and review his Monday morning reports whether he is in the office or out of town.

4. Growth requires efficient use of human resources

Even for the one-man business, growth ultimately entails adding new staff, delegating responsibilities, and recruiting a management team. But experienced executive talent from outside the business is too dear for most small firms.

The alternative is to build from within. The first step is strategic planning: to define the functions that promise to be integral to future success—sales, production, finance, research, staff administration. Whatever the functions, the small-business manager should assign his best people to these tasks now—without fanfare, titles, or promotions. Again, the low-cost personal computer plays a key role. For if these potential managers become computer literate now, their increased productivity will more than offset the burden of their additional responsibilities. In future years, as the firm grows, top management will be in place. And it will be a top management that is all the more valuable for its intimate conversance with the techniques and systems of computer management.

Right now, while you are grappling with the basics of micro-power management yourself, training others may be the last thing on your mind. But remember, in the long run, the productivity of the personal computer will gravitate toward those with computer literacy. Unless *you* conscientiously strive to delegate authority in the small firm, decision-making responsibility will inevitably be concentrated in the hands of the computer-literate manager. And that's a trend that ultimately stunts the growth and profitability of many small firms.

Where does it begin, this road to computer literacy? In the following chapter, we will introduce some of the basic considerations you will face in deciding what to buy, the common obstacles to computer deployment, and several approaches to learning some of the basics of computer functions.

Chapter Three

Basic Training—What to Learn and Where to Find It

I am a firm believer that it is far easier to teach the creative businessperson something about computers than it is to teach the programmer something about business.

—Pete Lawson,
management consultant

IMPROVED PRODUCTIVITY

With micro-power to improve productivity, small-business executives and professionals can manage information for themselves far more quickly, efficiently, and accurately than is possible even with a sizable, and costly, staff. "Businesspeople are discovering that with the microcomputer they can do things for themselves more effectively than they can delegate them," says Columbia University professor Dr. Eugene Galanter.

Once a computerized accounting system is on-line, for instance, balance sheets, P&Ls, financial statements, and projections can be produced by the small-businessperson without the need for laborious research and staff work. "As a CEO of a company," says Dr. Galanter, "if you want to pull together a report to discuss at your board meeting, a microcomputer with appropriate data base will let you do that more efficiently, and more reliably, than it could be done for you by a staff of people."

Nor are spectacular productivity gains limited to managerial tasks. Sharon Divincent uses a personal computer to keep the books for a small New Jersey food manufacturer. "I have to laugh sometimes," she says, "because my friends work in offices where there are three or four women and no computer. One will be doing the accounts receivable, someone else will be doing accounts payable, and another person will be typing up invoices. I do all that myself. And in one day too."

How much do you really have to know about personal computers to do useful work with them? Dr. Louis Robinson, director of university relations at IBM, defines computer literacy as "the ability to use computer technology in a particular discipline. It does not imply the person is a world-class programmer. It is a skill like driving an automobile and knowing how to get to Cape Cod. That is very different from knowing how to take the car's transmission apart."

FIRST: A FEW CAUTIONARY NOTES

Still, there are reefs and shoals aplenty on the course to computer literacy. "Keyboard shock," the traditional managerial disdain for anything related to typing, is one. Failure to recognize that personal computers are not simply plug-in office solutions is another danger. So is the failure to anticipate the emotional impact of the personal computer. "There are serious dangers to computerizing the small firm without looking at the human side," suggests Virginia Tech psychologist Dr. Lee Frederiksen. "Unless you plan for the personal computer and recognize that it is going to change who holds the power and how it is used, you may end up facing unforeseen consequences."

FUNDAMENTAL DEFINITIONS

How does a busy manager or professional acquire computer literacy? It's wise to begin with some fundamental definitions, such as the distinctions between the different types of computers and their software programs.

Mainframes and Minis

"Ten years ago if someone had told me that before the decade was over I could walk into Bloomingdale's and buy a 128K computer on my wife's charge card," says a senior IBM marketing executive, "I would have thought them quite mad." Until the mid-1970s there existed just two kinds of business computers—**mainframes** and **minis.**

Mainframes, typified by IBM's 360 line, cost between $150,000 and $4 million, needed hundreds of square feet of environmentally controlled space, and were run by a priesthood of white-frocked technicians. Without mainframe computers Neil Armstrong would not have taken his "giant leap for mankind," nor would modern corporations and central governments have achieved their preeminence.

But while a legion of IBM sales representatives tended the mainframe marketplace (mostly big government and big business) a new computer customer was emerging. From Wall Street brokers to college administrators and research scientists, people who had witnessed the power of big computers began searching for machines that could perform more modest tasks at modest prices. Into the breach came Digital Equipment Corporation (DEC), Data General, and about fifty others. These were the firms that would seize the latest in electronics technology—notably the down-sized *integrated circuit* that condensed a mountain of individually wired transistors onto modular boards the size of a slice of Wonderbread—to create reasonably small, reasonably inexpensive computers. In the spirit of the go-go era they were called minis.

Minis did very well. By the late 1970s, minicomputer companies founded a decade earlier were boasting annual sales in the billion-dollar range. Their customers included medium-sized institutions and operating divisions of large corporations. But while the minicomputer represented a vast departure in size and cost from the mainframe, minis were by no means cheap—either to buy or use. Even bottom-of-the-line models cost over thirty thousand dollars in 1968 dollars. Then there were programs to be written, and usually a full-time operator—the "DP" (data processing) specialist—to be hired. The minicomputer, despite its beguiling name, was at heart still a large-scale technology, inaccessible to the individual and to the great majority of America's small firms.

The Personal Computer—A Quantum Leap

The personal computer represented a quantum leap in the economics of computing power. Almost overnight the same basic capabilities that had cost between $30,000 and $300,000 in mainframe and minicomputer systems were available in a $3,000 package that covers a twenty-by-twenty-inch desktop "footprint." But the computer itself was only part of the story.

For all its power, any computer—mainframe, mini, or micro—is useless without programs. Computer hardware can be mass-produced by the truckload. Not programs. "Writing programs," says Dirk Hanson in *The New Alchemists,* "unlike producing hardware, is a labor-intensive task, more a matter of individual creativity than mass production."

There are just two fundamental kinds of computer program. One is known as **systems software.** The other is called **applications software.**

Systems Software: A Traffic Cop

Systems software directs traffic within the computer. You might imagine an organized, city-wide traffic control network composed of stoplights, left-turn arrows, and one-way streets, all intended to help vehicles get where they are going in the most orderly way possible. Systems software coordinates the exchange of data between various parts of the computer, including the printer, video monitor, and disk drives.

In microcomputers the most important systems software

is the **disk operating system,** or DOS. The technical purpose of the DOS is to enable the interchange of information between your disk drives, where data is electronically stored, and the central processor, where it is computed. The disk operating system organizes the information on your floppy disk and even displays a directory—a kind of table of contents—on your monitor when you first load a disk.

Proprietary DOS

Unfortunately, there is also a marketing aspect to disk operating systems. In an effort to carve a market niche, many computer manufacturers equip their machines with a proprietary DOS. The result has been a proliferation of incompatible disk operating systems. This in itself may not sound so bad, until you realize that the DOS determines which applications software can be run on your computer. A personal computer with Apple DOS, for instance, cannot run any applications software written for the TRS DOS (Radio Shack's disk operating system) or the Microsoft DOS used on the IBM Personal Computer.

Control Program for Microcomputers (CP/M)

The one notable exception to the proliferation of incompatible disk operating systems is called **CP/M** (Control Program for Microcomputers). Over one hundred personal computers use CP/M as their DOS, and thousands of applications programs are compatible with it. In addition, over two hundred other models of personal computers—including models from Radio Shack, IBM, and Apple—can be modified to use CP/M.

Applications Software

Applications software—usually referred to as "programs" —is designed to perform specific tasks, such as word processing, project scheduling, or file management. Returning to the traffic system analogy, we can imagine the applications program functioning like vehicles bound for one address or another within the highway network. Actually, within the computer's central processor, applications software instructions are, in fact, stored at specific "memory addresses." Systems software controls how this information gets routed to these locations. In personal computers, WordStar, SuperCalc, and VisiCalc are among the most popular and widely used application software packages. But it is the systems software, specifically the DOS, that determines which application programs run on what computers.

Precious

How important are these two kinds of software? "Users become attached to their programs and systems software," explains Tracy Kidder in the Pulitzer prize–winning *The Soul of a New Machine*. "Software is expensive. Getting it to function often takes time. Software that works is precious. Users don't idly discard it."

Behind the highly visible hardware revolution in personal computing, there has been an equally important software revolution. Because of the mass market created by the personal computer, more new software programs are being written this year than in the first thirty years of computing combined.

These new programs (programs intended for managers, professionals, and their employees—not data processing personnel) are the true source of micro-power. Not until hardware is matched with flexible, easy-to-use applications software can the power of the microcomputer be unleashed in the small-business or professional setting.

But remember: Applications programs run only on certain computers. So important is the question of software selection in personal computing that software, not hardware, should be the controlling factor in purchasing a microcomputer. "Evaluate your needs. Evaluate the software. Then find the computer it runs on," says Stephanie Burns, president of a Los Angeles computer training firm. "Don't buy a computer and then pray to God it has the software you need."

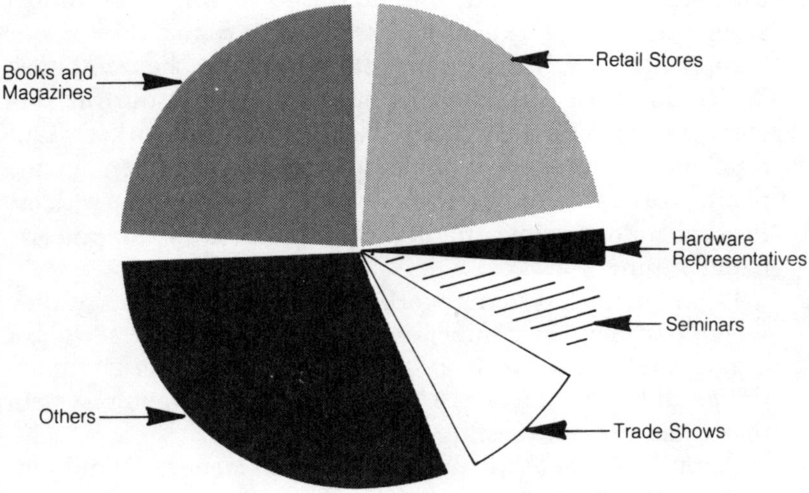

WHO HELPS USERS EVALUATE SOFTWARE

STARTING SMALL, AND STAYING FLEXIBLE

"In our small business environment," says Fred Frost, president of the A. T. Wall Company, "I'm trying to overcome the basic fear of computers and the dominance they tend to have in a business."

Why fear computers? "We have a fear of all forms of computers," explains Frost. "Because we've tried all kinds of computers, and they never helped us. There was always too much machinery. And it was always too expensive, too distant, too unfriendly."

Frost's first experience was with the mainframe. "Ten years ago we bought a fairly large NCR punch-card operation," he says. The problem? "Everything seemed to disappear into the punch cards all the time." Frost got rid of the punch-card computer, and returned to manual systems. "I had the fear that with the computer, any computer, we would lose sight of our information."

Two years ago Frost tried again. "We acquired a company that had time-sharing," he says. But after working with it for a while, Frost found computer time-sharing to be almost as inefficient and expensive as the mainframe. His major complaint: "We had to tailor our system to the computer. We couldn't use our forms or our formats. Yet our file systems worked. Our methods of doing things worked. Our reporting systems all worked. Our job cost system in the plant worked." Rather than abandon his proven systems, Frost abandoned time-sharing. Still, the need to computerize haunted him.

"Our manual systems worked, but that's not to say they weren't somewhat cumbersome," he explains. "As we got bigger and went from 100 customers to 700 customers, things didn't come as fast. We needed a computer system that could use our existing formats."

About the time A. T. Wall's revenues reached $10 million, Frost went shopping once again. The most promising proposal came from IBM. But the mainframe that IBM recommended would have cost almost $200,000. Says Frost: "I kept having memories of ten years ago."

A Microcomputer Consultant's Suggestions Lead to the PC

Frost was struggling with the decision to computerize the night he met Peter Lawson at a cocktail party. In ocean racing circles Lawson is known as a top-flight navigator—the man Ted Hood selected to plot courses aboard the America's Cup contender *Independence*. Lawson also runs Brenton Management Corp., a Providence, Rhode Island, consultancy specializing in microcomputer projects. "Peter convinced me to try the personal computer instead," says Frost. "He sat down and explained what the mainframe could do that the personal computer couldn't. Then he showed me what the personal computer could do that is just as good, if not better, and more adjustable and adaptable."

On Peter Lawson's advice, Frost scrapped the IBM recommendations. Instead he purchased eight IBM Personal Computers. Total cost? Under $40,000, including consulting fees and software.

"I thought it would take a year or two," said Frost three months after installing the machines. "But step by step we've networked our computers together into a common hard-disk memory storage so that we have all the 'mental' capacity we need. Each person in the office, instead of being handed paper, works on their own machine and is able to use the kind of programs they like and feel comfortable with. I can monitor it all and watch what each workstation or department is doing as it happens."

A System Tailored to His Business

Even more important, says Frost, is that fact that "we have changed nothing. Our operating statements, our balance sheets, our job cost cards, our order entry forms are exactly as they were when they were manually done. The information I get is of better quality and accuracy . . . and I can get it sooner."

Computerization at the A. T. Wall Company has already proven an unqualified success. "I feel I know what's going on," says Frost. "And that as time goes by I will know more and more. I'll be in a better position to shrink the company, if I have to shrink it, or to grow the business, if growth looks promising. Either way, the decisions will be based on information that is accurate and readily available. The personal computer has given us much greater flexibility to weather whatever happens in the years ahead."

Beware the Bill of Goods

Consultant Lawson helped Fred Frost make the right decision. Not every executive is so fortunate. Take Pat McLoughlin of The Haworth Press.

"About three years ago a major company tried to sell us a bill of goods on a minicomputer system," he explains. "They had salesmen up here almost every week. What they were trying to unload was an obsolete machine that had a cassette tape, but no floppies."

The sales presentation was polished and persuasive. But at the last second, McLoughlin balked. "We made a decision," he recalls, "not to buy this fifty-thousand-dollar thing, but to get into computing a little bit first to see what was going on." When McLoughlin did buy a computer a few months later, it was a $3,500 Apple II.

"It was the right decision," he says. "We'd still be paying off that damn thing, and not have a fraction of the computing ability we have now. If we had bought it, we could seriously have been out of business. It wouldn't have been functional. To get anything from it we would have had to put in a great deal of energy and effort that should have gone into the business."

Don't Neglect the Business for the Sake of the Computer

"Small companies do that with a minicomputer," he points out. "It's a new toy and they put so much energy into it because it's not going to work for six months anyway. But in the meantime they neglect their business: the product development, the marketing, the general operations."

In your small business, it's possible that a mainframe or a minicomputer may be just the thing you need, but that isn't very likely. And it grows less likely every day as inexpensive microcomputers become more and more powerful, more and more friendly, and more and more useful.

How can you avoid getting burned? If you have the luxury of time, you can follow Pat McLoughlin's lead and "get into computing a little bit first" with a personal computer. It will cost less than the sales tax on a minicomputer system, and will probably prove more functional to boot. If the need to computerize is urgent, then consider a third-party opinion, namely, a microcomputer consultant.

Using a Consultant

The alternative to a learn-as-you-go approach to personal computing is the paid computer consultant. Ideally, a consultant will review your objectives, recommend a combination of hardware and software to meet your needs, help modify the programs to your specific requirements, and show you and your staff how it all works. But hiring a computer consultant is like buying a yacht. If you need to ask how much, you can't afford one.

The going rate for established computer consultants ranges from $50 to $100 an hour, with $65 about average. If your objectives include automating such tasks as inventory, accounting, or mailing-list management, expect to see an invoice of anywhere from $2,500 to $5,000 for a consultant's time.

Consultants justify their fees by pointing to the costly mistakes they can help the businessperson avoid and the productivity gains the well-deployed personal computer can deliver. The higher the stakes, the more important a skilled professional becomes. Any manager computerizing a medium-sized small business will need the expert assistance of a computer consultant.

But in the small firm many managers are understandably reluctant to spend as much in consulting fees as for computer hardware and software. Will the services of a high-priced expert prove cost-effective for your small firm in the long run? Once you've explained your objectives, this is the first question to put to the potential consultant. The answer you receive can reveal a great deal about their integrity—and how well they really understand the nature of your business.

Finding a number of microcomputer consultants is not difficult. The Independent Computer Consultants Association (Box 27412, St. Louis, MO 63141) will provide a list of names in your area. Bankers, lawyers, and accountants are also good sources for recommendations. And most retail computer stores offer consulting as part of their services, with the fee built into the price of your purchase.

But narrowing those recommended down to just the right one requires additional effort. It means locating two or three computer experts with proven track records in your industry or professional specialty. It means asking for and then checking out their references. It means interesting them enough in your firm so that they are willing to take the time to hear your objectives, study your existing systems, and work up a proposal or presentation. Finally, finding the right consultant means evaluating their proposals, not just for the wonderful things they promise, but on the basis of how well the consultant has understood your problems and your business.

Like Radical Surgery

Microcomputer consultants hail from diverse backgrounds. Some have been computer salespeople. Others have worked as programmers, accountants, lawyers, or even forest rangers. A few, like Peter Lawson, have experience in general management. Most will take your interests to heart. A few, whether from avarice or inexperience, may not. Furthermore, computer consultants, like physicians, may even offer differing diagnoses.

One diagnosis that requires a second opinion is when a computer consultant suggests that the only way to solve your problems is by buying custom software. Writing custom software for the small firm is like radical surgery: It's expensive, risky, and sometimes unnecessary. In today's world of powerful off-the-shelf microcomputer programs, any proposal that includes creating extensive custom programs is suspect. It's possible that no programs exist for your particular application. But it's also possible that your consultant doesn't understand your business well enough to suggest how to compromise your objectives slightly to accommodate an existing software package.

As a very general rule of thumb, if your consultant's computerization plan calls for spending more than five thousand dollars per workstation for hardware and software, then you ought to shop around for another estimate. It is a peculiar irony of the "economies of scale" in personal computing that low-cost hardware and off-the-rack software are frequently better suited to small-business applications than elaborate custom programs or even mini and mainframe systems selling at ten times the price.

U.S. BUSINESS AND PROFESSIONAL FIRMS WILL BUY MORE PERSONAL COMPUTERS THAN ANY OTHER TYPE OF OFFICE AUTOMATION EQUIPMENT BY 1987

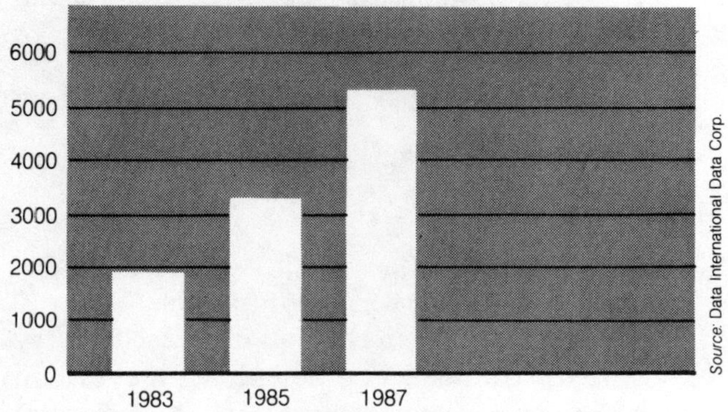

THOUSANDS OF PERSONAL COMPUTERS SHIPPED TO U.S. BUSINESSES AND PROFESSIONAL OFFICES

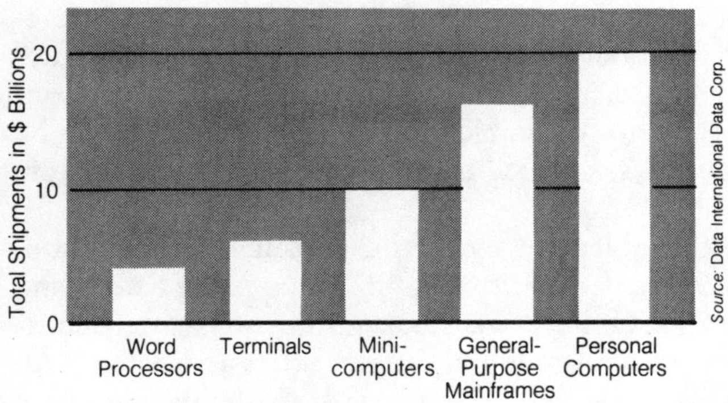

ESTIMATED SALES OF OFFICE AUTOMATION EQUIPMENT IN 1987

Technophobia

Among the most common obstacles to overcome in the computerization process is technophobia, the fear of technology.

"Almost anyone who sits at a computer for the first time has two fears," says former IBM researcher Dr. Truman Hunter, " 'Will I hurt it? Will it hurt me?' "

An hour at the keyboard usually alleviates this first worry. Unless you physically attack it, damaging the computer is nearly impossible. "After 1,500 students," reports a Boston computing instructor, "the worst we've seen is a couple of blown chips." The second apprehension, "Will it hurt me?," is more complex.

Health Worries

First of all there is some concern about the video display terminals (VDTs) used with personal computers. Over 60 percent of office workers in one recent poll expressed worry about daily exposure to computer equipment, with eyestrain heading the list of concerns. After reports of cataracts, dizziness, and even deformed babies among operators of video display terminals during the 1970s, the Food and Drug Administration (FDA), the National Institute for Occupational Safety and Health (NIOSH), and the Occupational Safety and Health Administration (OSHA) undertook investigations of the potential health hazards created by the computer industry's video display terminals. All three investigations concluded that no verifiable health hazards are posed by computer displays, at least as far as radiation emissions are concerned.

As for the problem of eyestrain, explains Dirk Hanson, "The New York Committee for Occupational Safety and Health (NYCOSH) has suggested a number of ways to mitigate the chronic eyestrain and fatigue often associated with prolonged use of computer terminals. Bad lighting, very small VDTs and screen glare are the major culprits. The ideal VDT should be equipped with a nonreflective glass screen, and the bigger the better. Indirect lighting, which further cuts glare, is preferable to direct sunlight or fluorescent lighting. NYCOSH proposes that the optimum screen-to-eye distance be two feet or more, and favors VDT systems with detached keyboards, so the user has more latitude in adjusting viewing distance. Characters on the screen should be at least 3⁄16 of an inch high, and there should be some provision for brightness adjustment."

These recommendations were set for full-time VDT operators, but they make good sense for any personal computer installation. One further technique for reducing eyestrain when working for long periods with a personal computer is to focus on a distant object at periodic intervals, say every fifteen minutes or so, to give your eye muscles adequate exercise.

Job Fears

Another fear concerns the effects computers have on jobs. Employees frequently worry, sometimes with justification, that the computer will eliminate their job, or radically alter the nature of their work. But even people who aren't worried about their health or their jobs dread computer technology.

Resistance

As director of computer services for the Columbia University Business School MBA program, Tony D'Amato has seen thousands of graduate students grapple with computer literacy. "Fifty percent of the entering MBA classes at Columbia are really enthusiastic and are pleased to see how easy it is to learn," he says. "Twenty-five to thirty percent find computer technology more difficult because they have a liberal arts background. And twenty-five percent are just resistant to learning about computers in general."

This observation holds for business managers as well as business students. "The 'self-image' sets the boundaries of accomplishment," asserts human-potential writer Dr. Maxwell Maltz. "It defines what you can and cannot do."

Some can easily envision themselves as accomplished, or at least competent, micro-power executives. Others reject the possibility.

Managers and professionals from technical backgrounds—

accounting, economics, engineering, math, the "hard" sciences—seldom have difficulty with personal computers. In general, they are analytic thinkers accustomed to logical progressions, ratios, averages, trend lines, and indices. If anything, they perceive the personal computer as a natural friend and ally.

But, what about those people whose livelihoods involve human relations—salespeople and entrepreneurs, authors and artists, personnel managers, ministers, social workers, teachers, therapists, retailers, architects, politicians, dentists, diplomats, or district attorneys? What about those whose decisions are premised on gut instinct as often as cold statistics?

To them the computer is usually, at best, an unknown quantity. What little they know is often colored by personal misconceptions and fantasies. They may suspect a treacherous HAL—the paranoid computer from Stanley Kubrick's *2001*—within the soul of every new computer. From the Luddites, the quixotic nineteenth-century English textile workers who destroyed over one thousand mills rather than acquiesce to the mechanization of handcrafts, to the tragicomedy of Charlie Chaplin's *Modern Times,* the distrust of "dehumanizing technology" runs deep.

But it is a mistake to paint personal-computer technology with the same brush used for the big institutional computers of the 1960s and 1970s. Unlike the massive mainframes that encouraged the centralization of power in vast and economically destabilizing bureaucratic institutions, the personal computer represents potential liberation and decentralization. Liberation from the kinds of manual computation and paper shuffling that leave you too weary for creative thought or decision making. Decentralization, because with personal computers, more and more people at lower and lower levels can have access to pertinent facts and the micro-power to analyze them.

But perhaps technophobia is not an issue with you. There still remains one other powerful deterrent to computer literacy. It is the fear that in your efforts to master micro-power you simply may not succeed.

Fear of Failure

"Fear of failure has many dimensions," says New York management consultant John Budd. "To the corporate manager, failure carries with it the spectres of dismissal, ego damage, and the contempt of friends, family, and business associates. Always the fear is far disproportionate to the realities." What is true for corporate managers also goes for successful pediatricians, critically acclaimed novelists, NFL quarterbacks, bankable actors, and brilliant criminal attorneys. In many careers the fear of failure is the driving force behind success.

Debbie Green teaches personal computing to senior executives in Phoenix, Arizona. "They arrive in Mercedes', Cadillacs, Continentals, and, in one case, even a Rolls Royce. But they all have the same fear: that a little machine is going to be smarter than they are, that they'll end up looking like fools."

One answer is to remove the novice from his colleagues and competitors during the training period. "Clandestine computing" helps keep professional pride out of the learning process. "Knowledge is power," said Ethel Watts Mumford, "if you know it about the right person." So, what colleagues and competitors *don't* know about you can't hurt you.

Henry Lee, the CEO of Lee Pharmaceuticals, a small business with annual sales in the $15 million range, is computer literate. It was not always so. Lee's disenchantment with the "style, frequency," and "even the data" in the reports from his chief programmer prompted his decision to buy a personal computer. But Lee's new TRS-80 went atop his dining room table, not the desk top at his office. "You don't want to show off your ignorance if you can help it," Lee told *Inc.* magazine. Not until completing a month of clandestine practice sessions that convinced him he was on the path to computer literacy did Lee inform his staff about the computer.

Fear of failure produces anxiety enough without compounding it by making personal prestige an issue in the learning process.

You may even want to reduce the financial pressure by starting out with a low-end computer model such as the Timex/Sinclair 2000 or Atari 400. These rudimentary machines will provide you with a basic familiarity with personal computing at bargain-basement prices, and the skills you acquire can be transferred to a machine capable of serious business applications. But don't be deceived into thinking that a one-hundred-dollar computer with a membrane keyboard is going to be the answer to your accounting, word-processing, or spreadsheeting needs. It won't.

Panic-Stricken

Not everyone does succeed with personal computers. Many systems purchased with the best intentions of automating the office remain attached to the family TV where "Astrosmash" is their primary activity.

There is more to operating a personal computer than turning on the power switch. "The advertising makes it look like all you have to do is press a couple of buttons and your troubles are over," says Dr. Hunter. "That's not the way it works at all. Personal computers are great at doing calculations and repetitive tasks, but they can't *do your thinking for you.*"

"I don't know who is more naive," says a San Francisco microcomputer consultant, "the salesmen or the customers. I get four or five calls a week from people who saw an article about micros and rushed out to buy many thousands of dollars of equipment for their business. Now they are panic-stricken because they have all this stuff and they can hardly figure out how to turn it on.

"The sad thing is, most of them are going to need fourteen to forty hours of training before they know what is happening. And they thought they were just going to turn the key and drive away. Half the time they've got a system that can't really do what they want anyway, at least not without sinking another grand or two into expansion boards and software. But how do you tell that to a guy who's just bought himself a fantasy machine?"

The sensible way to begin is to take micro-power one step at a time. *Do* begin with a hands-on course that provides experience with a microcomputer, not a chalkboard or textbook. Or if you haven't the time for a formal course, arrange for some lessons from a friend, a business associate, or even a computer consultant. But *don't* spend several thousand dollars on hardware or software until the full implications of its operation are crystal clear. "The first step toward knowledge," said Lord David Cecil, "is to know that we are ignorant."

Status Symbol or Social Stigma?

Preoccupation with status is yet another potential deterrent to computer literacy. Even in small firms, status is a powerful managerial lever. Top managers have the power to profoundly influence attitudes toward personal computing within their organizations. "Reality," points out John Budd, "usually ends up being what those in power say it is." This is a crucial consideration because, although the personal computer may be essential to your firm's competitive stature, the desktop computer itself remains viewed as less than an unequivocally positive symbol of professional and managerial status.

At Lee Pharmaceuticals, where CEO Henry Lee now expects all top executives to be computer literate, the microcomputer *has* become a sign of managerial authority. Upper management at American Can Company, one of the thirty blue-chip firms that comprise the Dow Jones Industrial Index, also actively promotes computer literacy among executives. At the firm's Connecticut headquarters, a "Micro Center" demonstrates personal-computing equipment and even provides executives with a personal-computer consulting service. McGraw-Hill is another major corporation that promotes computer literacy for its managers through "Micro Computer Resource Centers." As with American Can's Micro Center, they offer hardware and software demonstrations and assist executives in finding micro-power solutions to managerial dilemmas. Other *Fortune* 500 firms where the personal computer tends to be perceived as an executive tool include Procter and Gamble, Ciba-Geigy, Olin, *Reader's Digest,* Texaco, Pepsico, and Nestlé. "Microcomputers are already a fact of life in nearly every executive office of the major financial institutions," says a Bank of America data-processing manager. "Before the decade is over I guarantee you'll find the same is true of most manufacturing industries and small businesses as well."

Even so, the possibility of losing status is a disquieting concern for senior managers and professionals embarking on the course to micro-power. And there's a good reason: "Computing," says organizational psychologist Dr. Evan Peelle, "has traditionally been the job of a person in a lower position, like a secretary or a clerical worker." Jim McMullen, head of Apple's New York user's group and a leading microcomputer consultant, points out an unfortunate side effect of this "secretarial stereotype." "With the personal computer, senior managers are starting at ground zero with something they have been told is a tremendous tool, a device that increases productivity by orders of magnitude," says McMullen. "But don't forget the majority of male executives over forty were brought up thinking the keyboard is something only a secretary uses. As soon as they sit down to this new thing there is the added intimidation of social stigma."

Dr. Lee Frederiksen, psychologist at Virginia Tech, suggests keyboard stigma is a "temporary attitude that is rapidly dissipating. Even as we talk," he says, "keyboarding is becoming a fragmented issue. One reason is the growing perception of the personal computer as the new high-technology-based supertoy. The other reason is purely technological: Keyboarding and typing skills are becoming less of an issue as we get closer to alternative forms of data entry such as speech recognition and optical scanning systems."

Today Dr. Frederiksen sees *how* you use the desktop computer, not *whether* you use it, as the central status consideration. "It is no longer a status issue for an executive to have a personal computer on his desk," says Dr. Fredericksen. "Instead, what you do on your computer becomes a status thing. Doing your memos with word processing may still be seen as a low-status job in some firms. Spreadsheet analysis of financial data, on the other hand, is now widely regarded as a high-status activity."

Fear of Losing Managerial Control

Closely associated with status is the concept of managerial control, and the fear of losing it.

A fundamental benefit of the personal computer is heightened control over critical management data. But some managers resist computerizing for fear of *losing control* of their subordinates, and perhaps even their businesses or professional practices. This is not an unfounded anxiety.

"A manager who is not aware of how to use a personal computer," points out Dennis Curtin, "can lose control of people who *do* know how to use them." Microcomputer consultant Jim McMullen agrees. "The computer creates problems for those senior executives who don't understand it," he says. "Take a young fellow out of graduate school who has been using a microcomputer as a routine tool. Now put him and his computer in a small firm where he may be junior to people who have been there fifteen or twenty years. These managers are bound to feel threatened. Why? Because the computer countermands their authority. It takes away an aspect of their seniority."

The personal computer can give junior employees access to information even the boss doesn't have. "It should always be a concern to a manager when he gets cut off from a source of information," points out Dr. Fredericksen. "With greater access to information, there will be more opportunity for people on lower levels to assume more responsibility. This is partly because they are freed up on a time basis and partly because they have new tools available to them." But are managers ready to share their authority? If not, they had better be prepared for political struggles likely to test both executive skills and endurance.

Does the small-business executive have any alternative to sharing his authority? Dr. Frederiksen thinks not. "The personal computer is an essential business tool. You're simply going to have to have one."

Losing Control to the Computer

Some managers fear losing control, not to their subordinates, but to the computer itself. In fact, at firms with expensive computers and rigid data-processing procedures, it is often questionable who does control the firm—top management or the computer. Where one hears the refrain "the computer won't let me do it that way," chances are that management *has* lost control. In the eyes of workers, it is the computer, not management, that is running the business.

Such bureaucratic rigor mortis is unusual in small businesses, at least until the business has grown, and grown overly dependent on its computers. More common is the misdirection of micro-power in the firm so that employees become so enthralled with the machine that they expend much time and energy in finding new problems to solve, rather than focusing on primary job assignments. Work does not exist for the sake of the computer, the computer exists for the sake of the work. This is a common trap small firms (and large) fall into, and a cause for justifiable concern. It is also the kind of a problem a computer-literate manager can avoid.

Covert Action

Another reason managers fear the personal computer is for a larcenous, but not uncommon, business practice. "I have yet to work for a client," confesses a Manhattan CPA, "who doesn't keep two sets of books—one for himself so he knows what's going on, and one for the IRS." Where the boss controls the information systems, there is less chance of an employee getting wind of the irregularities. If part of your business is off the books, you have a good reason for keeping your books off the computer.

Political Resistance

In the final analysis, anxieties over the personal computer fall into two main categories. Fear of the unknown is one, political anxiety the other. "There are a few people for whom fear of the computer is pathological in scope," says Dr. Frederiksen, "but for most it's basically the fear of something new, a fear that dissipates quite easily with experience. This kind of fear is really a pseudo issue, a transitional stage that is going to pass."

Political anxiety may prove more tenacious. "Where the personal computer means jobs will be changed and power redistributed, that's where you encounter political resistance," explains Dr. Frederiksen. "Managers realize that if they give their people personal computers, it is going to alter the organizational power base. Questions concerning the distribution of power tend not to pass without notice."

Happily, recognizing the source of anxiety is usually the first step toward overcoming it. In chapter 4, we will discuss ways in which you can make the computer switch run smoothly for your employees.

WHAT APPROACH TO LEARNING?

"As an educator," says Columbia University's Dr. Eugene Galanter, "I'm a firm believer that John Dewey knew what he was talking about. We learn things by actually engaging in their operation. I don't think you can learn to run a computer at a chalkboard any more than you could learn to play a piano, or use a typewriter, or a telephone. Imagine going to class to learn how to use a telephone without having a telephone."

Finding introductory courses that sit students at computer terminals, not empty desks, is no longer the effort it once was. Colleges, high schools, even elementary schools now have personal-computer workshops. Computer clubs and societies offer introductory programs, as do retailers, consulting firms, and private computer schools. Some cost sixty dollars, some cost six hundred dollars. Some are taught by bright-eyed computer science majors on leave for a semester from Yale or Stanford. Some are taught by salespeople who have yet to master the fundamentals themselves. The main thing is to get your hands on the keyboard.

At the Computer Club, Inc., in Stamford, Connecticut, program director Rosemarie Gabriele tries to help businesspeople "qualify their needs" before they sign up for instruction. "I believe it's best to begin with a course in introductory programming," she says. "Not only do you learn how to operate the personal computer, you also learn the logic that is going to be used when running programs like VisiCalc or data-base management. But when an executive comes to us with a specific task he wants solved, for instance computerizing the payroll for a small business, he may not have time to go through introductory programming. For his purposes he may be better off going directly into an applications course such as VisiCalc." There are three approaches you can take for your computer education: survey classes, programming (in class and out), and applications.

Survey Classes

Survey courses, particularly those taught in the academic environment, are usually too general for business and professional people looking for answers to specific problems, not careers in data processing. Survey courses inundate you with details, but don't provide the one thing essential to building confidence—extensive hands-on experience at the keyboard. They may be helpful, but they're usually a last resort.

Learning by Programming: In the Classroom, With a Guru, or On Your Own

If possible, begin with an introductory programming course. A gifted instructor can teach a motivated student the mechanics of operating a microcomputer in under an hour, and the fundamentals of a programming language such as

BASIC in about eight hours. But not all students are motivated; not all instructors are gifted.

Many businesspeople have mastered programming by simply buying a microcomputer and a manual. Henry Lee was one. He learned the mechanics of running his computer from a Radio Shack salesman before he left the store. "I asked the salesman to take me through a complete dry run," he says. "It's so much easier to be shown."

Initially his objective was modest. "At first," Lee remembers, "I just wanted to get a feel for what modern computing was all about." That part came quickly. "To see the way it would crunch the numbers on tables of data had me giggling hysterically," he says. "I soon began to grasp what it could do on real problems."

Having discovered micro-power, Lee set out to harness it, spending "several hours a night" with his computer and exercise manual. "In the early months so much of the language and the techniques didn't make sense." He would get stuck and have to call Radio Shack for help "maybe once a week." But even after one month, he felt confident enough to bring the computer to work. Within a year Lee had bought twenty identical microcomputers for his firm.

When it came to learning programming, however, Henry Lee had a lot going for him, including a doctorate in physical chemistry and previous job experience as a technical writer with Rockwell International. Unlike Henry Lee, most micro-power novices need a guru.

"In one sense computer programming is the ideal subject for self-instruction," says Chicago computer teacher Bob Anderson. "The computer is the teacher. It responds instantly and has infinite patience. You break down the problem, write the routine, and enter it into the computer. Bingo. If the program works you have instant positive reinforcement. You're a success. The problem is—what happens when your routine doesn't work?

"A human teacher can look at your work and say, 'Hey, Bob, look you left out a semicolon in line 55.' Fix it and everything's fine. But all the computer will tell you is `'SYNTAX ERROR IN 55.'` You may spend the rest of the day trying to rewrite a program that's perfectly fine, except you forgot one semicolon."

Dr. Truman Hunter likens programming to building a patio. "I can drop a couple of palettes of brick and a few bags of cement in your yard. If you know something about laying a foundation and mortar work you'll have no problem. Most people, however, need to be shown."

Computer Languages

Computer **languages**—BASIC and Pascal are among the easiest to learn—consist of "vocabulary" and **syntax.** As with natural languages, BASIC and Pascal favor certain images, metaphors, and ways of thinking. However, compared to natural language, computer vocabulary is delightfully terse. In BASIC there are only about one hundred "statements" and "commands"—IF-THEN, LET, GOTO, PRINT, LIST, and END are among the most frequently encountered—and useful work can be done after learning only a dozen or so.

At the Children's Computer School on Manhattan's Upper West Side, ten-year-olds learn to write a simple BASIC program during their first class. It takes between thirty-five and fifty hours of BASIC, however, before most adults are writing serious programs. And for sophisticated business applications such as graphing sales, charting cash flow, calculating profit margins, or running critical path analyses it's not uncommon to take weeks, or even months, of full-time effort to write a modestly effective program.

In the early days of personal computing there was little choice but to try to develop your own software. But today few of us working under the daily pressure of deadlines, appointments, and meetings have the time, inclination, or compelling reasons to become programmers. True, in about eight hours (eight in this case being a minimum number given optimum conditions) you can learn the basics of BASIC. And even if you never use the language to write a single program, understanding a language like BASIC offers a glimpse into the logic and workings of the microcomputer "mind" and "memory." But for serious business tasks, most applications today can be handled by off-the-shelf applications packages such as VisiCalc and WordStar.

Still, there is one good reason to study the basics of computer programming. "It's been my experience," says Mrs. Gabriele, "that the businesspeople who take the time to learn a little about programming are also the ones who are most successful with the applications software."

Applications

Applications courses, the third type of introductory course, teach how to use off-the-shelf software packages for fundamental small-business and professional tasks such as word processing, electronic spreadsheeting, and data-base management. The enormous commercial success of such productivity and decision-support tools as WordStar, VisiCalc, SuperCalc, and dBase II can be attributed to one simple fact: Off-the-shelf programs put micro-power in the hands of people who are virtually ignorant about programming. In fact, applications packages offer the novice powers that are far beyond the abilities of all but a few of the world's most gifted programmers. Most of us could never create a word-processing package with a fraction of the capabilities of WordStar, any more than we could sit down and compose an orchestral symphony. Luckily we don't have to. Not when programs like WordStar and VisiCalc can be purchased for less than the cost of a three-piece suit.

With hundreds of millions of dollars to be earned from off-the-shelf programs, software writers have, as one might expect, been working overtime. Tens of thousands of packaged programs have been devised—most of dubious merit. But a rare few combine operating simplicity, or what programmers like to call a "transparent" structure, with enormous power and speed.

One point about applications software is so important that it bears repeating often: Good software is more precious, frequently more expensive, and invariably harder to find than good hardware.

Documentation—and Its Problems

Software packages come with instructional manuals called **documentation.** As anyone with a passing acquaintance with personal computers will affirm, much software documentation is, in a word, incomprehensible. "Most of the documentation in the field of personal computing is poor," says Osmo Wiio in *Creative Computing*. "There are a few exceptions, but very few. Documentation is an integral part of a computer system. And documentation must be designed for the intended user, not for the producers themselves."

In some cases, publishers such as Howard W. Sams, Osborne/McGraw-Hill, and Spectrum Books offer "primer," "power of," and "made easy" manuals that are a significant improvement over the software writer's own documentation. They are a major assistance in learning, say, VisiCalc. But since significant variations exist between versions of software developed for different brands of computers, these books supplement rather than replace the manufacturer's documentation, poor as it usually is.

I learned WordStar and SuperCalc from the documentation. (It was a struggle.) So have thousands of others. Still, a four- to eight-hour applications course would have saved us all many hours of confusion, anxiety, and effort. Perhaps even more important, an applications course would have introduced some of the finer points of these programs such as "dot commands," "look-up tables," and other subtle, yet powerful aspects of off-the-shelf programs overlooked by hurried learners. As with the human mind, it is common to utilize only a fraction of micro-power's true potential.

Unhappily, technical inadequacy is but one reason personal computers may not be used to their full potential. Another, equally important reason computers may not be used effectively has to do with the way they are introduced into the workplace. As we will see in the next chapter, when it comes to computerization, good politics often paves the way to productivity.

Chapter Four

Tactical Deployment

I want every officer up front at least once a day. You will never know what is going on unless you can hear the bullets.
—General George S. Patton

Strategy defines the long-range mission and its objectives; tactics achieve them. Tactics, by nature, are prescriptive. They deal in "oughts" and "ought nots." Like computer programs, tactics are logical sequences of individual steps designed to solve problems and attain goals. In computer programming a single error—or **bug**—may not become apparent until considerable damage has occurred. No one is immune to bugs. Months after its personal computer went to market, IBM was still "debugging" major programming errors. One caused mistakes in simple arithmetic. Another could "lock up" the entire system, destroying data that happened to be in the central processing unit.

In time, such programming errors are discovered and rectified. But avoiding undetected program bugs is one argument for eschewing computer products that are fresh off the drawing board. Software especially, like wine, needs time to mature. Unless you are willing to offer up your business as a test site—and pay for the privilege—avoid programs that have not been on the market for six months to a year.

Tactical errors. Far more common than program bugs, however, are tactical errors in the way managers deploy and use their personal computers. Tactical errors can be benign, like using the computer at only a fraction of its potential. "My son showed me how to run a simple job-cost program on a TRS-80 the summer before he left for college," says the owner of a Connecticut design studio. "I knew which buttons to push, but that was all. It wasn't until two years later when computer ads began appearing everywhere that I realized I could use the computer for the accounting, word processing, and even some of our graphic design projects."

But tactical bugs can also be more sinister. A snafu in the newly computerized receivables system at a Florida medical center posted dunning letters to hundreds of patients. "In one day," says the center's founder, "the computer cost us fifteen years of good will." The benefits of automation are anything but automatic. Careful tactical planning can help avoid careless computerization.

Tactics and people. This means coordinating your three basic resources: software, hardware, and people. All are important, but for small-business and professional firms the most costly tactical errors usually involve people. Software and hardware bugs may be inconvenient, even expensive. People bugs can be explosive. Software and hardware can be handled with logic and reason. People can be irrational and destructive.

The smaller your group of people, the easier personal-computer deployment will be. In the one-person firm, computerization is usually a joyful process. With a personal computer on-line, most one-person businesses discover that hiring a full-time secretary or assistant can be postponed even as business volume doubles, triples, and perhaps quadruples. Typically, the self-employed person finds that as haphazard business systems are automated, nonproductive paperwork and anxieties decrease and productive opportunities increase. The risks are minimal, the benefits often stupendous.

Harter Williams, for instance, is an independent Washington, D.C., transportation cost analyst. Among his clients Williams lists the Interstate Commerce Commission, the Federal Maritime Commission, and numerous other federal, state, and private organizations. Williams first computerized with an Apple II in the late 1970s; more recently he has switched to an Osborne portable.

"For cost analysis," he says, "it's the greatest thing since bottled beer." And because it's portable, he takes the computer with him to railroad yards, shipping offices, and clients such as the ICC. He has even brought it to the witness stand. "It took a while to hook it up in the courtroom though," Williams recalls.

How does Williams feel about using the personal computer in his business? "It's just gorgeous," he says. "Unquestionably, the personal computer is changing my life and my consulting business for the better. I'm so tickled that at the age of sixty-eight, thanks to the personal computer, there's going to be life in me for quite a while longer."

TACTICS FOR THE SELF-EMPLOYED

There are six fundamental tactics for computer management in the one-person firm.

1. *Strike early for full effect.* Pioneers become heroes. Everyone knows the Wright brothers and Charles Lindbergh. Almost no one remembers who followed in their wake. Yes, computerization can double, triple, or, in come cases, quadruple business volume without substantial risk or overhead. But the computer literacy needed for that doesn't happen overnight. It takes up to six months or even a year before most small-businesspeople feel genuinely confident with the personal computer. Meantime, while you're thinking it over, the competition is doing it.

2. *Find a guru.* A teacher, a salesman, a computer hobbiest, a paid consultant—anyone who knows more about it than you. Don't be deceived by age. In Los Angeles, 20th Century-Fox paid their microcomputer consultant, Eugene Volokh, twenty dollars an hour for his assistance. At the time, Eugene Volokh was fourteen years old.

3. *Attack problems sequentially.* There is legitimate disagreement among computer consultants whether it is best to com-

puterize your entire business at once or to proceed step by step. For some larger firms, where the activities of numerous departments must be coordinated, simultaneous computerization makes sense. But for the very small business, my advice is to master one program at a time. Start with the most serious obstacle standing between you and your strategic mission. In nine out of ten small businesses this is cash flow. Identify the worst offender—receivable collections, obtaining working capital, inventory turnover, etc.—and apply micro-power to solve it. Professional practitioners face specialized demands, whether text editing for authors, clinical simulations of myasthenia gravis for medical school professors, or Fourier analysis for acoustical engineers. There are prepackaged programs for these applications, as well as for swine rotation, stock option analysis, production scheduling, warehouse location, real estate analysis, property management, and thousands of other tasks. Many are useless, a few are invaluable. You know your requirements; your guru should know the software to implement them. Together you can sort the grain from the chaff—one problem at a time.

4. *Find software first, then the computer it runs on.* I've discussed this before. It's crucial. You shouldn't have to spend more than five thousand dollars, and it's depreciable, with an investment tax credit as well. But there's no write-off for the hours you waste with a dog of a word-processing or spreadsheet program because the hardware you bought won't run WordStar or VisiCalc or SuperCalc or whatever program gets the job done best. Find good software, then choose your computer.

5. *Remember your job.* The personal computer is a means, not an end. Lawyers should concentrate on the law, doctors on medicine, retailers on selling. Let computer programmers do the programming. The microcomputer is your tool, your personal strategic weapon. It is not your vocation.

6. *Exploit your advantage.* As a pioneer in personal computing you are building a mystique among your allies and your

adversaries. You are a pathfinder in a new world where many still fear to tread. Don't underestimate the value of micro-mystique. Until your competitors have caught up, they'll never know how far ahead you really are. If you control the pace, it's your competition that's most likely to stumble.

THE SMALL FIRM

The Micro-Power Vacuum

The small company with no existing computerized systems is operating in a micro-power vacuum. If the vacuum is filled intelligently and with compassion the small office can attain new levels of prosperity. There is a leap of an order of magnitude in efficiency between manual and computerized clerical procedures. Overall office productivity gains of between 15 and 50 percent within the first year are not uncommon. Productivity in certain tasks, such as bookkeeping and word processing, can increase by 100 percent, and even as much as 400 percent in some cases. Company morale can soar, particularly if computerization is linked to increased responsibilities and perhaps even a share of increased profits.

On the other hand, businesspeople who are unaware of or insensitive to the nuanced effects of micro-power on their superiors, colleagues, and subordinates may find the personal computer creating a backlash of counterproductive resentments, jealousies, and resistance. Unless you are careful to consider the volatile dynamics of office politics and other human factors, computerization can have serious consequences as well as benefits.

Deskilled Workers

Harvard's Shoshana Zuboff points out that "the purpose of the intelligent technology at the core of a computer system is to substitute algorithms or decision rules for individual judgments. This substitution makes it possible to formalize the skills and know-how intrinsic to a job and integrate them into a computer program. As decision rules become more explicit, the more they are subject to planning, and the less they require a person to make a decision at each stage of execution. For some jobs the word 'decision' no longer implies an act of human judgment, but an information-processing activity that occurs according to rules embedded in a computer program."

The result can be the "deskilling" of jobs through a reduction or even elimination of worker discretion. Here's how one collection manager describes the impact of the computer in his department: "It gives us a tighter lock on the collector, and we can hire less skilled people. But there's a real loss to the job of skills and know-how. You are being told what to do by the machine."

When Work Becomes Abstract

Another danger: "When information technology reorganizes a job, it fundamentally alters the individual's relation to the task," says Dr. Zuboff. "Usually, this means that a person accomplishes a task through the medium of the information system, rather than through direct physical contact with the object of the task." The problem? Computerized work may demand the manipulation of data without any real understanding of what the data represents.

When work becomes abstract, the manager may end up with a labor force that is both incompetent and disgruntled. Incompetent because the computer has co-opted the employee's judgment and basic understanding of his or her job; disgruntled because without any sense of spirit or purpose, work becomes an exercise without meaning.

Social Interaction

Resentment also brews when the computer reduces social interaction on the job, or increases the sense that one's work is being watched and measured. "Decades of research have established the importance of social communities and the lengths to which people will go to establish and maintain them," says Zuboff. When the computer transforms a job that once required extensive interaction with fellow workers into solitary days at a keyboard, even the most personable employee may grow sullen and resentful.

Big Brother and Employee Initiative

Networked computers such as the IBM-PCs at The A. T. Wall Company, which can monitor other workstations, have great appeal for small-business owners and managers. But there are potential side effects as well. Too often management employs such monitoring systems "without sufficiently considering the potential human and organization consequences," says Zuboff.

"With remote supervision many employees limit their own risk-taking behavior, such as spotting an error in the data and correcting it, developing a more effective approach to the work than the procedures established by the information system, or trying to achieve quality at the expense of keeping up with production standards." Remote supervision, in other words, can stifle individual initiative.

"Sometimes I have a gut feeling I would rather do something another way," explains a banker who works on a supervised computer system. "But, because it is all going to be in the computer, it changes your mind. If somebody wouldn't listen to the reason you did it that way, well, it could cause you quite a problem."

The Path of Least Resistance Is Resistance

Unless you've laid careful plans in advance, when the computer arrives, your employees see themselves facing one of three choices. They can acquiesce, resist, or quit. Most take the middle road. Duffy Goodrich of Cleworth Conditioning, Inc., in Roselle, New Jersey, computerized his firm's administrative functions over a three-year period with a pair of Radio Shack TRS-80s. "The computing system," he says, "has let us do five times the business we did before. Our profits have grown steadily, even during the economic slowdown."

In the beginning, however, Goodrich found "massive resistance to machines in the office." As long as employees were handwriting cost estimates, orders, and invoices there was tangible evidence of the importance of their jobs. But the transition to computerized recordkeeping frightened the employees at Cleworth. "Most," says Goodrich, "didn't want *not* to handwrite, thinking the computer would put them out of work." It didn't. At Cleworth the computer created more jobs by allowing business expansion. "The personal computer is something new," notes Duffy Goodrich, "and since humans tend to resist change they are afraid to move with the new way and the new routines it necessitates."

Even managers, especially those in their fifties or sixties, share this fear. For them, too, the computer often represents unwelcome, disruptive change. It is something they don't understand and don't want to understand. It may not threaten their jobs, but it definitely threatens their status, self-image, and personal influence. It is a visible symbol and persistent reminder of their own inadequacies and inability to keep up with the times.

Two Tactics for Computerizing Small Firms

There are two basic tactical approaches for computerizing in a micro-power vacuum. "The first," notes computer scientist Ron Reisman, "is the 'bottom-up' approach. This is not really an approach as much as a haphazard series of bumps and lurches, ending with a company that uses computers in all its various departments. Typically, one department gets a computer, say accounting or payroll. Eventually, this department becomes the 'computer department' as other employees try to share in the computer's efficiency. The top brass hears about this and may be persuaded to buy personal computers for the whole company. But in the meantime a computer fiefdom has been set up within the business, and resentment has cropped up among employees because of the disproportionate efficiency displayed by the computerized department."

The alternative? Reisman calls it the "top-down" method. "This amounts to a reasoned decision by management that the business should computerize. A manager is assigned to implement the computerization. Ideally, this person is not the most knowledgeable about computers, since if he is he will probably set up a fiefdom of his own. But if computerization is accomplished according to a rational plan, everybody will have computers and the power structures will stay relatively intact. The top-down versus the bottom-up method is usually a critical factor in the success or failure of an attempt to computerize."

But not every firm will welcome the personal computer with open arms. In some cases managers and professional specialists may find that bottom-up computerization is the only way to surmount top-level indifference.

Bottom-Up Computerization in Detail

Some firms will actively support their employees by helping to pay for computer training and equipment. Others are not so enlightened. In the long run, however, your career may depend on staying abreast of contemporaries who *are* acquiring computer literacy. Bottom-up tactics are often the *only tactics* available to salaried managers and professionals concerned with career growth. As an employee in the small firm where computerization is being ignored, your objective is "managing upward," a subtle exercise in which both the risks and the rewards are significant. Here are the guidelines:

1. *Sound the waters.* If a micro-power vacuum exists, there must be a reason for it. Does the boss feel that computing is a low-status activity? Is he fearful of losing control? Are there some behind-the-scenes financial shenanigans? Or is the firm essentially forthright, but slow to adapt to new technology? Learn as much as you can, but don't make proposals that can be formally rejected.

2. *Learn the political terrain.* Who holds the real power? What are the power cliques? Who are your direct competitors? Who makes promotion decisions? Most importantly, what is your boss's attitude toward his subordinates, particularly you? "The individual orientation of Western culture," observe the authors of *The Art of Japanese Management,* "encourages people to look out for themselves, stay separate, and regard boss-subordinate relationships as primarily task oriented." Ask three central questions: Is your boss willing to impugn your credibility to advance his own? If you trust him, how can you best help him? If you don't trust him, what is your best defense against him?

3. *Learn the informational terrain.* What information is vital to your job, your boss's job, the survival of the firm? The higher you ascend, the more essential information becomes, and the further removed you become from its source. Since information is valuable only when it is needed, speed is second in importance only to access. The person controlling the information flow controls the levers of power. Which computer applications can help you attain key information faster and in a more useful form than your present systems?

4. *Prepare for the transition to micro-power.* Identify the applications software that will best help with your job assignment. Take at least one good course in either BASIC programming or in operating an applications program such as spreadsheeting or word processing. Find your guru and together locate the software you'll need on the job. Stick with off-the-shelf packages. Also, remember, you may not be with this firm forever. Most headhunters estimate that twenty hours of basic computer training is worth a minimum of one thousand dollars a year to job-jumpers.

5. *Sign on the line.* A personal computer isn't *personal* unless you own it. Buy your own hardware, even if you don't have to. Sometimes the less a machine *looks* like a computer, the fewer people it is likely to upset. Remember, micro-power

is a *personal* resource. "Having seen other space reps on the road with small computers," says an advertising space salesperson, "I could see that the potential of a portable machine with a built-in screen as a sales tool was almost limitless. First there was the novelty of the machine itself. Then there is the psychological impact. People have been conditioned to think of computers as infallible. But I also knew my publisher was not about to buy portable computers for six regional reps. So I took the leap myself and charged a Kaypro II on my Visa card. That was nine months ago; I'm now number two in our force and still gaining. My annual bonus last year paid for the machine three times over."

6. *Timing is crucial.* Particularly in offices where there is an undercurrent of disparagement toward new technology, it is essential to precede the computer with a convincing demonstration of micro-power. Don't bring your computer to the office until you've proven its ability, preferably in a way that significantly advances your boss's cause within the organization. Wait until the computer is perceived as a hero, not a potential troublemaker.

7. *Move into the spotlight.* In any hierarchy, business or otherwise, the appearance of reality is often more important than reality itself. Executive and professional superstars are propelled not only by their tangible successes, but by the mythology they generate. Once you prove the value of micro-power in solving key business problems, then bring your machine to the office. With the only operational computer in the firm it is inevitable the curious will descend. The senior vice-president who was previously indifferent to personal computers may start dropping by with visiting dignitaries as if the whole thing was his idea. The purchasing agent will stop in to ask about forms generation and the comptroller about payroll systems. These visits and requests for advice may seem distracting, but they can help forge new alliances. Even more crucial, they give you the opportunity to become a consultant in the computerization projects of other departments. From this perspective you can begin to

see how the business works, who is doing what to whom, and participate in deciding the all-important question of how the new information channels flow. Along the way your reputation is growing, and with it your credibility and *functional* power within the firm.

8. The final step is positional power. In business, real power is seldom bestowed: rather it must be attained. New titles and responsibilities (positional power) are won, not granted. Usually, it might be added, at someone else's expense. If your interest lies in being the best you can be at what you are already doing, your colleagues will doubtless be much relieved. If, however, success has given you a taste for power, then you have a strong ally in the personal computer. John Bell is a twenty-eight-year-old vice-president and senior account executive in a $10-million-a-year sunbelt ad agency who successfully made the transition from functional to positional power. "I've always been very competitive," he notes, "and very prepared. I was the first person in the agency with a personal computer and there's no doubt it's helped me. The computer analysis is a rigorous discipline. How can the guy with a desk calculator and a couple of yellow scratch pads compete? People are very reluctant to challenge your ideas if they know you have a thorough computer analysis backing you up."

Avoid Premature Announcements

The early "upward management" phase is the most delicate. One needn't conceal an interest in computer technology or your having a personal computer at home. Hobbies don't intimidate. On the other hand, avoid divulging your real plans. Prematurely announced intentions can lead to resentment and they can even boomerang if original expectations prove unrealistic. "A premature announcement of what you're *going* to do," notes Robert Townsend, "unsettles potential supporters, gives opponents time to construct real and imaginary defenses, and tends to ensure failure." Master the basics of micro-power, then strike swiftly. "The thunderclap," wrote one of the twentieth century's great guerrilla tacticians, Mao Tse-Tung, "leaves no time to cover one's ears."

Computerization by Fiat

It is entirely possible to computerize the small firm through fear and fiat. "In this company," says the president of a small Saint James, New York, firm, "employees either go on-line with the computer or off-line with their job."

This approach is typical of the method invoked by many computer manuals, corporate consultants, and vendors. Their procedures are based on underlying assumptions common to most western large-scale technologies: that most employees are interchangeable cogs, and that productivity is wholly independent of superior-subordinate relationships and worker morale. But as the Japanese have demonstrated, employee motivation is not irrelevant; it is essential. And in the information economy, people frequently are more important than machines.

War of Nerves

Unfortunately, even managers who do not share such views may unwittingly provoke worker hostility simply because these antilabor attitudes are deeply ingrained in every step of the traditional computerization process. The established tactics of office automation as practiced in the United States, in fact, amount to little more than an unvarnished campaign of employee intimidation. The war of nerves begins with the very first step, known as the "base-line analysis" or "audit."

On the surface, the base-line analysis makes good sense. The CEO rallies his key managers, announces he is automating burdensome office procedures, and requests each manager to itemize his department's tasks including who is doing what, how many hours are being spent at it, and how much it all is costing. There is no denying the logic of this approach. From the base-line information the CEO or his consultant can then develop a cost/benefit analysis, decide how many machines to buy, where to put them, and can then request price quotations for competitive vendor bids.

There is also no denying the adverse impact of the base-line analysis on staff morale. In the first place, no one likes to justify his own existence, or job—which is what a base-line audit is all about. Managers may feel a slight quiver of resentment; clerical workers are likely to respond with open hostility. Bureaucracies move slowly, but their antennae are finely tuned. Supervisors rummaging through times sheets and interrogating workers on job procedures will, at the very least, fan the flames of office gossip. Work may progress as usual, but beneath the surface, resentment is building. The approach virtually assures labor polarization and resistance even before the actual decision to computerize has been made.

The base-line audit and similar analytic approaches are the usual and, perhaps, unavoidable approaches in businesses where central mini or mainframe computer acquisitions are made. But for the small firm whose basic computer needs can be met with a microcomputer and a few off-the-shelf software packages, the cost of a thoroughgoing cost/benefit analysis may actually exceed the price of the computer. And the hidden cost, in human terms, may be incalculable. One shouldn't throw an entire firm into turmoil to discover that a $5,000 microcomputer system can save time and increase productivity. And the CEO who doesn't know where his firm's greatest inefficiencies lie is blind, incompetent, or both.

TACTICS FOR OWNERS AND TOP EXECUTIVES

As the owner or CEO of a small firm, how do you computerize in a sensible, compassionate, and profitable fashion? This is one battle only quiet diplomacy can win.

1. *Get literate.* Despite the pressures of running multi-million-dollar companies, Carl Griffin (chairman of the board

of Touche Ross & Company, one of the "big eight" accounting firms), Henry Lee, and Fred Frost all mastered the personal computer while serving as their firm's chief executive officer. Like Henry Lee, you should take your computer home and work clandestinely until you are confident of your abilities. This way you'll be computer literate when the time comes to install equipment and software. If custom programs are necessary, you'll be better able to communicate your needs, and better equipped to recognize someone who is trying to sell you unnecessary programming.

2. *Set the example.* Take the lead in demonstrating the efficiencies of computerization. Use word processing and spreadsheeting to turn out your own reports and memos. Give employees a few weeks to *see* how the boss is using his personal computer before you begin proselytizing.

3. *Make employees feel indispensable.* Praise work requiring ingenuity, creativity, human relations, and skill. Let every worker know individually that his or her skills can't be replaced by a computer. Hone your sensitivities toward your workers' insecurities.

4. *Reward your bookkeeper.* Offer the person in charge of your financial records a fully paid "scholarship" for a course in BASIC programming, and arrange the necessary time off. Once the course is under way, ask them to analyze some specific accounting packages to see whether, for example, computerizing the accounts receivable might not be worthwhile. Then move diplomatically but swiftly to computerize your bookkeeping system.

Spend some time talking about specific computer programs with employees you think can benefit from them. Tell your best salesman, for instance, how you recently saw a couple of computer programs that are supposed to make price quotes a breeze. Then give him the afternoon off to visit the computer store and see what *he* thinks. He may find that the programs in question won't work at your business; he may decide they will. Avoid vague statements about the computer, and concentrate instead on how particular application programs may lighten the employee's burden.

5. *Establish a demonstration center.* If computerization involves more than one or two employees, hire a teacher to give regularly scheduled classes in computer literacy *on company time.* Be sure managers and key employees have a chance to break the ice. Encourage personal computing by helping employees finance home computers through low-interest loans, preferably for purchasing the same models used at work. Post listings of computer courses and users group meetings.

6. *Offer incentives.* Reward workers for increased productivity. A number of firms have found that linking computerization to a gainsharing plan adds a significant boost to both profits and computer acceptance. Unlike profit sharing, which usually rewards certain individual employees, gainsharing sets company-wide goals such as reducing the payroll-to-sales ratio. Targets are set by an employee-management committee and funds for gainshare bonuses are drawn from a percent-of-the-increased-profits pool. All employees, not just star performers, receive gainshare payments when targets are achieved, usually on a monthly basis. Another potent source of incentives, particularly for management personnel, is recognition. One study of American managers found that 49 percent cited recognition for their work as the *most* important reward. Use all public forums at your disposal—including memos, local press, luncheons, association meetings, and trade shows—to recognize achievements of managers and workers who are making outstanding progress.

7. *Computerize humanely.* Keep the drawbacks of computerization in mind as well the benefits. The computer can deskill workers by eliminating judgment and making tasks abstract and repetitive. Try to structure work assignments to include both computer activities, such as word processing, and tasks requiring human relations, judgment, and creativity.

KEEPING THE COMPUTER PERSONAL

The personal computer offers opportunities for career advancement and business growth that are unlikely to be repeated in our lifetimes. But successful automation is far from automatic.

The real success or failure of computer management has little to do with the hardware, and a great deal to do with attitudes and motives. The secret of successful computerization lies in compassion, understanding, and diplomacy. "If you want productivity and the financial reward that goes with it," Peters and Waterman advise in *In Search of Excellence,* "you must treat your workers as your most important asset." Keeping the personal computer *personal* is the key. In the end, success will demand more art than science, more tact than muscle.

Chapter Five

Traversing the Hardware Maze

The little I know I owe to my ignorance.

—Sacha Guitry

For the beginner, especially the impatient beginner, the micro-world, like the Minotaur's maze, is a vexing conjunction of false starts and dead ends. Finding the continuous passage may at times seem to be futile. This is particularly true of microcomputer hardware.

Because hardware and software are so intimately related—as the song goes, you can't have one without the other—it is necessary to have at least a rudimentary understanding of micro hardware before plunging into the software world in Chapter Six. What route takes us through the maze with the fewest digressions?

For this chapter, I have collected the four vital hardware issues that more than any others are necessary for understanding the software discussions that follow. On paper these topics—compatibility, **memory capacity, bits** and **bytes,** and **disk operating systems**—appear technically formidable. Fortunately, the ideas behind the jargon are not nearly as forbidding as they look. Master these basic hardware concepts now, and you will find yourself well along on the path to computer literacy.

HOW'S A PERSON TO CHOOSE?

As a publisher of *Desktop Computing,* Wayne Green reads most of the microcomputer journals and attends thirty to forty international trade shows each year. "The fact is," he says, "that though I've been with the microcomputer industry right since it started—and I know most of the people who made it grow—the profusion of desktop computers now available is far beyond even my grasp."

Today more than three hundred companies are building over four hundred different microcomputers. How's a person to choose? It's a funny thing about personal computers, but once you've identified your strategic objectives *and the programs to help attain them*—word processing, financial modeling, accounting, inventory control, project scheduling, or whatever—selecting the right microcomputer can be almost simple. In personal computers, software dictates hardware, and software programs are compatible only with certain computers. This is extremely important, since it can vastly limit the usefulness of the computer you buy.

On the other hand, incompatibility has its hidden benefits. For one thing, once you've decided, for example, that WordStar, SuperCalc, dBase II, and Accounting Plus are the best software packages for your needs, you've automatically narrowed your hardware options. Out of four hundred personal computers, perhaps only forty or fifty machines can run this combination of programs without expensive modifications. Eliminate the off-brands and models with no track record, and you're down to a handful of choices. It can be that simple.

More likely, however, you'll discover that some of the programs you want will work with one machine, say an Apple IIe, but not with any other model. This compatibility puzzle is one of the unhappy characteristics of life in personal computing.

DISK OPERATING SYSTEMS: WHY THEY ARE CRUCIAL

Why will software programs run on one computer, but not another? For business applications, the major factor determining software compatibility is the disk operating system, or DOS (it rhymes with floss).

The disk drive and the floppies that go into it are the microcomputer's data bank. Without disk drives to load programs and store large quantities of data, the personal computer is useless for business tasks. And without DOS software, there is no way to control the flow of data between the disk drives and the computer.

How does the DOS work? Even a simple task, for example printing a 200-word memo you've written using a word-processing program, involves thousands, sometimes millions, of individual steps within the computer's circuitry. As far as you're concerned, instructing the computer to make a printout is easy. You just flip the power switch, load your word-processing program, and then type the letter "P" followed by the arbitrary "file name" you've used to label your memo, let's say "MEMOTOJR." Almost before you've finished keyboarding, the words "PRINTING MEMOTOJR" will appear on the "status line" of your video monitor and, assuming you've remembered to turn your printer on, a letter-perfect copy of your memo to JR is being typed out for you.

Simple for you, but extraordinarily complex for your computer. For starters, the computer must read and recognize the command "P MEMOTOJR" and display it on your video screen. Then the command must be analyzed and its validity ascertained. Finally, it must be executed, a process that involves coordinating the transfer of data from the disk drives to the central processor and printer. What supervises all this activity, making certain the right data gets to the right location at the right time? The DOS does.

CP/M—The First Industry Standard

In the early days of personal computing, when Apple and Radio Shack dominated the market, it seemed as if most programs were written to run on either APPLE DOS or TRS DOS. The introduction of the IBM Personal Computer added another major DOS to the alphabet soup, called Microsoft DOS, or MS DOS. But while these computers and their disk operating systems became media superstars, still another DOS was quietly winning favor with business users and personal-computer manufacturers alike, the Control Program for Microcomputers, or simply CP/M.

CP/M was developed in 1973, several years before the Apple and Radio Shack personal computers were invented. The original CP/M, Version 1.0, has over the years been upgraded by Versions 1.3, 1.4, 2.0, and 3.0, among others. The newer versions ironed out bugs and allowed CP/M to operate on a greater variety of microprocessors, and hence a greater variety of personal computers, then any other disk operating system.

As the popularity of the personal computer snowballed, so did the number of models running CP/M and the universe of compatible business programs. Today CP/M is the closest thing there is to an industry-wide DOS. In fact, CP/M compatibility is so important that it has become the first software product that computer industry leaders, including IBM, NCR, DEC, Hewlett-Packard, Xerox, and Wang, have all agreed on, although they carefully differentiate all their other products.

In the personal computer arena, at this writing, the market leaders—Apple, Radio Shack, IBM, and Commodore—continue to sell their own disk operating systems. But they have also made certain their machines can be easily adapted to run CP/M as well. So have the makers of over three hundred other personal computers. "You couldn't offer a computer system today without a CP/M base," says Fred Gibbons, president of Software Publishing. "It would be suicidal."

Suicidal because more business applications programs are compatible with CP/M than any other DOS. If your computer runs CP/M, or can be modified to run CP/M—and most of the major personal computers can—thousands of software programs are available to you. If your personal computer can't be adapted to run CP/M, you have the wrong computer. In personal computing, CP/M is the "compatibility window" onto a universe of powerful business software.

CP/M Cards

How do you go about modifying an Apple, Radio Shack, Commodore, IBM Personal Computer, or other model to run CP/M, and hence the thousands of CP/M–compatible business programs? Usually all you do is plug a "CP/M card" into one of the "expansion slots" inside the computer. But since the CP/M card is often a computer within a computer containing a microprocessor chip, it seldom comes cheap. Adding CP/M can cost hundreds of dollars for the hardware components and CP/M software. Also, although CP/M is not a computer language, you will still need to devote an afternoon to learning its basic commands for such functions as copying, erasing, and renaming your electronic files.

Many, but not all, of the programs recommended in this book run on CP/M, meaning they can be used on most of the business-oriented computers using the CP/M DOS, including the North Stars, Victors, Kaypros, Otronas, Cromemcos, Zeniths, and DECs, as well as modified Apples, TRS-80s, and IBM-PCs. In an industry where incompatibility is the rule, CP/M is the one sane and eminently practical exception.

Second Standards—The IBM-PC

There are, of course, numerous worthwhile business applications programs for disk operating systems other than CP/M. Apple DOS, TRS DOS, and MS DOS all support a wide selection of practical business applications software. The Apple and Tandy Radio Shack computers achieved a mass audience of business users during the late 1970s and became the first low-cost computers to develop a significant repertoire of business programming.

Since 1981, however, the IBM-PC—backed by IBM's enormous technical resources and market prestige—has eclipsed all other microcomputers, particularly in the area of small-business computing. As a result, the IBM-PC, with its MicroSoft disk operating system, has become the second standard of the microcomputer industry.

Dozens of copycat computers that claim to run IBM-PC software are now available. And it is estimated that 60% of all new software programs today are being written for the IBM-PC, while existing software programs are being adapted to run on it. As a result, software available for the IBM-PC and IBM-PC compatible computers will soon rival, or even exceed, the universe of CP/M programming in terms of the range and usefulness of available business applications.

Looking even further ahead, many experts foresee an increasing role for two other disk operating systems, UNIX and Smalltalk, in the new generation of 16-bit and 32-bit (see **bit mode**) personal computers that will become dominant in the late 1980s. Smalltalk, in particular, will become a major factor in business computers, because, unlike CP/M and most other disk operating systems that expect commands to be typed, most commands in Smalltalk can be accomplished merely by pointing.

For the time being, however, unless you have very good reasons for doing otherwise, stay with well-established software programs and hardware models. Buying the IBM-PC or a brand-name computer that can run CP/M is your safest play.

PROVEN SOFTWARE

As for the programs you will find recommended in this book, the majority are available in CP/M, and the remainder are available in at least one other major disk operating system, notably Apple DOS or MS DOS. They may not be the newest and sexiest software around, but they've been used with considerable success. If you like what you hear about a software package, either here or elsewhere, call the distributor's customer service department for an updated list of personal computers that run it. There are enormous financial incentives to make programs available for as many disk operating systems as possible. As a result, programs that aren't offered for a NEC or a DEC or a Televideo personal computer today may well be available tomorrow. Three excellent sources of recent software compatibility reports are the weekly tabloid *InfoWorld* published in Palo Alto, California, and the monthly periodicals *Personal Computing* in Rochelle Park, New Jersey, and *Popular Computing* in Peterborough, New Hampshire.

COMPROMISING SECONDARY OBJECTIVES

If, after winnowing down your software options to a handful of stellar selections, you learn that the programs you want won't run on the same DOS, there is still hope.

You can often compromise your secondary software needs without ill effects. If your primary objective is, say, computerizing your client files, then find the best data-base management program you can and settle for a second choice in the other application areas such as word processing or spreadsheeting.

As a rule, however, if you are planning to computerize your accounting system—even if it's in the distant future—make accounting software your pivotal selection. There is an abundance of good word-processing, spreadsheeting, and data-base-management programs in CP/M, Apple DOS, TRS DOS, and Microsoft DOS. But good accounting software to match the needs of a particular business and bookkeeping system is still rare. Thus, when in doubt give priority to accounting.

BRAND NAMES AND HARDWARE COMPATIBILITY

The personal-computer market is not the place to look for no-name bargains. Aside from the obvious reasons of avoiding off brands—questionable support, service, and quality—there is the all-important question of future software development. Unless a personal-computer model is selling very well, it is unlikely to attract the attention of software authors. Not when programmers know that a mass market for their products already exists among Apple, Radio Shack, or IBM-PC owners.

What about bargain models that run CP/M? Yes, there's a vast selection of CP/M software awaiting you. But even CP/M programs may have to be slightly modified to accommodate the idiosyncracies of a particular model. If your bargain brand becomes an Edsel, how many software houses will bother to stock programs for it? Nobody needs an orphan computer.

"Almost all of the firms that made microcomputers three years ago are out of business today," says Wayne Green. That means no service, no support and, worst of all, no software. Unless your bargain model is *fully compatible* with a major brand of personal computer, my advice is don't buy it.

THE COMPATIBILITY QUESTION

What does "fully compatible" mean when applied to computer hardware? More and more, new manufacturers are attempting to ride the coattails of top-selling machines such as the Apple II and IBM-PC. They do this by building new machines that are similar, and in some cases virtually identical, to popular models. Sometimes these clones offer new features that are actually improvements. Sometimes they don't. The Franklin Ace, for instance, is an Apple II look-alike that has done well—legal issues aside—by enticing buyers with extra features such as a built-in CP/M card and expanded memory. The Compaq and Eagle are among the many computers that claim to be compatible with the IBM-PC.

Full compatibility, i.e., disk *and* software compatibility, means that the clone computer will "read from and write to" any disk intended for use on the big-name machine. Hence, you should be able to purchase programs formatted for the IBM-PC and run them on an IBM-PC-copycat model. You should even be able to swap disks between a real Apple II or IBM-PC and the model that claims to be fully compatible with it.

Some fully compatible computers are outstanding values. Others aren't. The chief problem? There are varying degrees of compatibility. Very few computers that claim to be compatible with well-known machines are actually *fully* compatible. They run some programs, but not others. Such computers look terrific in the showroom, but they may not run the programs you expect.

How do you determine if an allegedly compatible model microcomputer runs the programs you need? You *could* take the maker's word for it. But as I write this, two major lawsuits against computer manufacturers, alleging fraud, are pending. In both cases, the defendants are accused of disguising someone else's computer as their own for the purpose of luring customers and distributors. "There are just so many examples of these sorts of things I just don't know where to begin," says Ken Bosomworth, president of a Norwalk, Connecticut, computer consultancy.

Grapevine

So how do you find out if Brand-X is *really* fully compatible with the IBM-PC or Apple? Check *InfoWorld, Personal Computing,* and other computer magazines for reviews. Such publications review programs in each major application area—word processing, spreadsheeting, accounting, etc.—at least once a year. And you'll find that most retail computer stores stock back issues. Also check with computer dealers in your area for a list of regional users groups. If, for instance, you have a specific IBM-PC–compatible model in mind—say the Compaq, Corona, or Hyperion—chances are someone in the IBM-PC user's group already owns one. Word of a new computer's benefits, as well as its flaws, travels swiftly on the user grapevine.

Venturing into the world of personal computing provokes anxiety enough without the added risk of buying a pig in a poke. Unless you have excellent reasons to do otherwise, stay with proven hardware.

BUNDLED SOFTWARE

In 1981 a well-known microcomputer author and industry critic named Adam Osborne offered the business world its first portable computer. Like many of the microcomputer industry's once-bright stars, Osborne Computer Corporation has fallen. But the factor that helped propel the ugly little Osborne I to center stage during the early 1980s was not so much the convenience of portability, but the economy of "bundled" software.

Along with the hardware elements of the computer—disk drives, central processing system, keyboard, video monitor, and various "output ports" for a modem and printer—Osborne generously included a software bonanza. Among the programs bundled into the Osborne I were the computer language MicroSoft BASIC, the WordStar word-processing program, a SuperCalc spreadsheet, the CP/M operating system, and a variety of other goodies. At full retail, the software alone was nearly worth the $1,795 price of the Osborne computer.

Today, bundled software deals targeted for business users abound. If, as with the Osborne I, the software is useful stuff of first-class quality, the bundled package can be an attractive opportunity.

Lisa—Integrated Programs

The release of the Apple IV computer, or Lisa, in mid-1983 gave the notion of bundled software a new twist. Not only does the Lisa come complete with software for word processing, spreadsheeting, data-base management, graphics, and several other basic business applications, but the software is both integrated and makes use of a control device known as a "mouse."

Integrated software has three advantages: First, the user need learn only one set of commands to operate several different packages. Second, multiple tasks such as word processing and spreadsheeting can be performed simultaneously. Third, data can be easily transferred from one program, say a spreadsheet, to another, such as the graphics package for plotting bar graphs.

Lisa's mouse further simplifies operation by allowing you to perform many commands merely by pointing the cursor at various pictures on the video monitor, instead of typing complex instructions into the keyboard. In a sense Lisa is the prototype of other personal computers based on the Smalltalk disk operating system, which will become increasingly available at sharply reduced prices during the late 1980s.

If you are buying a computer primarily for one specific application such as word processing or accounting, or several applications that are to be performed by different people, then integrated software is mostly likely a luxury for which you have little need. If, however, you envision using your computer more as an executive workstation for multiple applications such as preparing reports from spreadsheet analyses or data-base records, integrated software is a convenience well worth the extra cost.

MEMORY POWER

In part, innovations like integrated software are made possible by the increasing **memory capacity** of each new generation of computer hardware. What is computer memory, and when do you have enough of it? The answer to these questions is found in **bits** and **bytes,** the microworld's equivalent of mile-per-gallon ratings and horsepower.

Within the human brain, the relationship between brain cells, memory, and consciousness remains an unsolved riddle. Computer memory, by contrast, is child's play.

Bit Talk

The memory cells in the personal computer's brain are electrical circuits that have been painstakingly designed and etched on silicon microprocessor chips. Each circuit, or bit, has just two positions, on or off, symbolized by the digits

1 and 0. One fascinating thing about 1s and 0s is that if you organize enough of them into a code, you can reproduce almost anything from full-color video and stereo sound to the text of the Koran. And thanks to microelectronics, it's possible to store—and process—hundreds of thousands of these on/off symbols on a toenail-sized silicon wafer.

Practical Units

The bit, then, is the smallest discrete unit of information. Eight of these bits make up a byte. (There is a good reason why there are eight, rather than any other number of bits, in a byte, but it would take too long to explain properly, and it really isn't necessary to know.) The 8-bit byte is now universally accepted as the smallest *practical* unit of information.

Statistically, a byte can be arranged in 256 possible combinations (or two to the eighth power). For example, the 8-bit sequence 0100 0001 is used as the **binary** code equivalent of an uppercase letter *A,* while the combination 0110 0001 may stand for a lowercase *a.* One of the rare areas of agreement among computer makers is the standard code, called **ASCII** (pronounced *as-key*) for American Standard Code for Information Interchange, that assigns characters to most of these 256 possible binary combinations.

As for the microprocessor **chip,** where these 8-bit bytes are stored and processed, envision a hotel consisting of numbered rooms. Each room holds one byte of data. The first Intel microprocessor chips contained only about four thousand rooms. As microprocessors have grown more powerful, the number of memory **addresses**—like our numbered hotel rooms—has increased dramatically. Today's 256K chip, for instance, offers about 256,000 address locations.

It is customary to discuss computer memory in terms of **kilobytes** and **megabytes.** One kilobyte (K) equals 1,024 bytes—or about 1,000 **characters** of memory capacity. A megabyte is one million characters of memory storage.

When Apple, IBM, DEC, or Radio Shack offers you a *64K* personal computer, they mean a machine with sixty-four kilobytes (or 65,536 bytes, to be precise) of **random**

access memory, or RAM. Random access memory is to the personal computer what the cerebrum is to the brain. It is the electronic playground where programmed instructions meet and process the data that have been stored at various memory addresses. Each individual byte, or memory address, represents one character, and so you may prefer to think of 64K as 64,000 characters of data, all available in the random access memory.

Thirty-Five Pages

As a professional or business executive with patient or client files, accounting systems, and mailing lists, you may be wondering just how much information 64K of RAM represents. The answer is, not much. Some of the chapters in this book contain more than 64,000 characters. So does the typical 1,000-name mailing list. In terms of printed characters, 64K is about thirty-five double-spaced typewritten pages.

Not only is 64 kilobytes a meager amount of random access memory, but usually at least half of those memory cells, say thirty or forty thousand of them, may be needed to store your word processing, spreadsheeting, or other software program instructions.

The more RAM you have, the more room there is for programs and data. Fortunately, it is seldom necessary to have either your entire set of programming instructions or all of your data "in RAM" at any one time. Even so, for business tasks, 64K is the minimum amount of computer memory you'll need. Today, powerful small-business microcomputers with random access memories ranging from 128K to 500K and more are available at prices under $10,000, and in many cases under $5,000. Not long ago 500K of RAM could be had only in mainframe computers costing hundreds of thousands of dollars.

Disk Drives

How is it that a computer with only thirty or forty thousand characters of available random access memory can be used to process records containing hundreds of thousands of characters of data? The answer is found in the floppy disk drive.

If you don't know a floppy disk drive from a five iron, and most people don't, I urge you to drop by the nearest personal computer and acquaint yourself with one of the seven wonders of the twentieth century. The disk drive itself is used to spin the floppy disk or diskette at something like 300 rpm. As the disk rotates, a drive head reads data that has been encoded on the magnetic surface. Disk drives can also be used to record data, in which case the drive head is said to **write** to the disk.

Even the slowest drives can find information located anywhere on a diskette in under $\frac{1}{100,000}$ of a second. They can load data to RAM at the rate of tens of thousands of bytes per second. With disk drives, hundreds of kilobytes of data can be read from a disk, processed in the computer's CPU, and written back onto the disk to make room in the random access memory for more data—all within seconds.

Since it is not actually part of the computer's central works, the disk drive is considered a **mass storage peripheral.** Generally, the $5\frac{1}{4}$-inch disk drive is used with microcomputers, while a larger 8-inch drive operates on the more expensive (but not necessarily more useful) minicomputers and **dedicated** word processors. As for the terms "disk," "diskette," "mini-disk," and "minidiskette," there is no real consensus on their definition. Many computer salesmen and publications use all four terms interchangeably. When talking about personal computers, you can usually assume it's the $5\frac{1}{4}$-inch disk that's under discussion, regardless of the terminology. A new generation of 3- to $3\frac{1}{2}$-inch pocket-sized "microdisks" has been available for several years, but the $5\frac{1}{4}$-inch mini-disk format remains the microcomputer industry standard.

Quad Density

As with central processors, disk drive systems come in a range of memory capacities. On the low end are "single density" floppies that can store about one hundred kilobytes, or 100,000 characters, of data. **Quad density** diskettes hold in the vicinity of 500K, or half a megabyte. It would be crowded, but by using a quad-density disk drive the entire text of this book could be squeezed onto one 500K floppy.

Some small-business applications—notably accounting, inventory, and data-base management—require computerized records that run into the tens of millions or even hundreds of millions of characters. One way to handle such vast amounts of data is to spread your records over numerous floppies. But when more than a handful of disks are involved, data processing becomes physically and technically awkward.

Hard Disks

The alternative to the floppy is a **hard-disk** drive capable of storing anywhere from five to fifty megabytes—that's five to fifty million characters—of information. During its development at IBM, the hard-disk drive was given the product number 30-06, accidentally corresponding to the thirty-ought-six caliber of the popular Winchester carbine. Thus the hard-disk drive became known as a **Winchester,** a name that has since become institutionalized.

Two Disks for Safety

The minimum "peripheral storage **configuration"** you'll need for your small-business computer is two disk drives of at least 100K apiece, and preferably 200K or more. Why *two* disk drives? The main reason is security.

Floppy disks are extremely reliable, but they are not perfect. Disks have been known to mysteriously **crash,** irretrievably dumping all the information on them into the cosmic void. More frequently, human accidents happen. A few drops of coffee, a magnetized paper clip, or just plain rough handling is enough to destroy the delicate memory patterns encoded on their surface. "They're vulnerable to fingerprints, dust, coffee spills, cigarette ashes, sneezes, and maybe even dirty looks," says one disk manufacturer. "Exposing the disk to close contact with any kind of magnetic field (which you'll find in and around television sets, electric motors that run fans, typewriters, air conditioners, etc., as well as the coils in most loudspeakers) can muck up the arrangement of particles—and your disk will end up with either amnesia or madness."

Amnesia or madness in a disk, regardless of cause, is a disaster. Hundreds, perhaps thousands of hours of work can be lost. Irreplaceable data can be swept away by a mere sneeze or unseen magnetic force. Not to mention an increasingly common cause of crashed disks—disgruntled employees.

How to defend yourself? The best way is with a set of duplicate or **backup** disks of all your important files.

Duplicating a disk is a fast and easy process, *if* you have two disk drives. Duplicating a disk with one drive is possible. But it is also tedious and error-prone. Disks are generally so reliable it is easy to be lulled into a false sense of security. If, in addition, the duplication process is troublesome, it's easy to overlook making backups. Two disk drives are essential.

Most firms begin with a pair of floppy disk drives (price $250 to $700 each; disks cost between $2 and $5 apiece), and then add a Winchester hard disk ($1,500 to $3,000) when, and if, it becomes necessary to accommodate enormous volumes of data. However, if your strategic objective involves computerizing extensive files such as inventory, accounting, or patient records, you may save considerable effort and money by going with a hard disk right from the start. Certainly, if your business records are this extensive—numbering into the hundreds or thousands of patients, clients, accounts, or inventory items—you would do well to obtain the advice of an independent microcomputer consultant before computerizing.

8-Bit Versus 16-Bit

Before we end this discussion of hardware basics, there remains one additional issue to be confronted: the 8-bit versus the 16-bit personal computer.

In selecting a personal computer, not only do you need to determine which disk operating system will support the software you want, you will also have to choose between an 8-bit and a 16-bit machine. In general, 16-bit computers are faster, friendlier, and more versatile while 8-bit machines are less expensive.

Technically, 8-bit computers have a "data path" that is eight bits, or one byte, in width. This means that data is marched from the memory to the central processor one byte at a time. By contrast, the 16-bit computer's data path is two bytes wide. As a result, 16-bit machines run faster and address more memory. This increased **throughput** makes possible some fancy tricks such as "multitasking," i.e., performing two or more tasks simultaneously, that were once the exclusive province of mini and mainframe computers. Perhaps even more importantly, programmers can also use the extra memory and speed to create software that is at once more sophisticated and yet simpler to use than anything available for 8-bit computers.

Program Selection

The chief disadvantage of the 16-bit computer had been software availability. Eight-bit programs have been in constant development since 1975 and a vast selection is available. The first major 16-bit computer, the IBM-PC, was introduced in 1981. Yet, as mentioned earlier, the IBM-PC has become the focus of an extraordinary amount of programming talent, and the library of good business software for this particular model is virtually exploding.

Many 8-bit computer programs such as DB Master, WordStar, and VisiCalc have been upgraded to 16-bit computer versions, often with significant improvements in performance. The 16-bit computer has also proved capable of running programs that were originally developed for minicomputers. Thus, the 16-bit computer is establishing a significant software advantage over the 8-bit machine.

In scientific or statistical number crunching, 16-bit computers are significantly quicker. For general business users this increased speed is most noticeable in data-base programs, where searching and sorting large quantities of records can tie up an 8-bit computer for several minutes. More significantly, 16-bit machines permit the use of integrated software, where such applications as spreadsheeting, database management, and graphics are combined on one disk with the same commands, allowing easier data interchange between programs. Integration vastly simplifies the learning of new programs as well as the ability to quickly assemble crucial management information and present it in the form of charts and graphs. With more memory to devote to graphics, 16-bit machines offer higher resolution, more colors, and a broader range of visual possibilities.

The 16-bit computer is the machine of the future—well, the near future, anyway. For just as 16-bit models are crowding out 8-bit machines today, 32-bit computers will be dominating the personal computer market during the late 1980s.

So how's a person to decide? If your current files are small and your software applications modest—say, some financial spreadsheeting and word processing—the 8-bit personal computer is likely to provide all the micro-power you'll need for years to come. But if you anticipate the need for more than one computer workstation in your firm, or if you already have extensive files—the typical small-business accounting, inventory, or client records, for instance, may run into millions of characters—then the speed, muscle, and multitasking capability of a 16-bit computer will be worth the added investment. Perhaps the most common complaint among users of 8-bit personal computers is that they have outgrown their system. With a 16-bit machine, you can grow faster, harder, and longer before feeling the limitations of your system.

At the moment, 8-bit computers still hold the software

advantage, but the balance is rapidly shifting toward the newer and more powerful 16-bit machines.

And now it's time to explore the important world of microcomputer software.

Chapter Six

Executive Communications: Word Processing

I love being a writer. What I can't stand is the paperwork.
—Peter De Vries

WORD PROCESSING IN DIFFERENT SETTINGS

Lean Staff

Since a near-fatal cash-flow crisis in the late 1970s, keeping the administrative overhead down has been a prime tactical objective at The Haworth Press. One way to keep a lean staff, co-owners Bill Cohen and Pat McLoughlin discovered, is by living without personal secretaries. Instead, they use microcomputers. "My personal secretary is my personal computer," says Pat McLoughlin. Financial recordkeeping and general file management are among the jobs Haworth's top executives now do for themselves. So is word processing.

"Word processing alone," says Bill Cohen, "allows us to eliminate at least three departments." Cohen uses a word-processing program called Magic Window II on an Apple II computer. "With Magic Window II and a mailing list program I can do publicity in a couple of hours every few weeks. Normally in publishing, that's one full-time job."

Another of Cohen's duties is royalty statements. With the computer he completes twenty printed royalty statements in half an hour. "With the word processor and a few days work a year," says Cohen, "I'm doing the job for which most companies our size hire a full-time royalties person." Such publishers, of course, also use paper recordkeeping, file cabinets, and electric typewriters—office systems that, in Bill Cohen's opinion, "are a disaster for the small business." Thanks to the personal computer, Cohen estimates Haworth's six-person staff is doing the work for which his competitors need fifteen employees to accomplish.

Executive Delegation

Cohen and McLoughlin see the personal computer as the *only* way small businesses can escape the treadmill of high administrative overhead. As for the successful small firm of the future, "my prediction," says Bill Cohen, "is that we will see the rate of delegation and the type of work delegated radically change. Executives will assume more of the responsibilities normally give to secretaries, storage and retrieval clerks, and executive assistants. I don't think it will be uncommon to find one manager with a personal computer replacing several departments."

Does this mean that the quality of the work being performed is likely to diminish? "On the contrary," says Cohen. "There's a subtle factor here, but a very important one. Previously a top manager or owner didn't have the time to do all the things he would have liked. With the personal computer he can accomplish far more with his time. I see the rate of delegation decreasing not because the executive is unwilling to delegate a responsibility, but because he doesn't have to. In the small business nobody really cares as much as the owner. If you really want to get a job done right, you do it yourself."

"Without the computer," adds Pat McLoughlin, "we'd still be running on a treadmill. We'd need too many people and too much payroll." But do they have any misgivings about the increasing reliance on the personal computer they predict for executives like themselves? "I see only one real danger in the process," says Cohen, "and that's the possibility we'll witness the emergence of a new class of executive 'computerholic.' "

"But that," says Pat McLoughlin, "would be a big improvement over the traditional 'workaholic.' It's more of a pleasure working this way than in the 'good old days.' "

Professional Advantages

While Cohen and McLoughlin are publishing scientific journals, Dr. Ronald Olson is writing them. "I love research," says the acting dean of the College of Associated Health Professions at the University of Illinois at Chicago, "but publication of your findings is essential to maintaining academic credibility." To prepare his papers, Dr. Olson uses an IBM Personal Computer and a word-processing package called Spellbinder.

"Like most scientists," he says, "I compose on the typewriter anyway, so I might as well have to type a paper only once." Before word processing, Olson would type a rough draft, then turn it over to the college secretarial staff. What happened then was far from satisfactory.

Many scientific publications require camera-ready copy—a document that is literally ready to go before a camera for reproduction. "Sometimes they went through twelve or fifteen drafts before getting one that was letter-perfect," says Dr. Olson. "Of course, I would have to proofread each draft. With word processing only the corrections are retyped. There's no need to proofread an entire paper. I just have to check and see the corrections were properly made." Word processing also helps Dr. Olson compose faster. "It makes the task of writing less onerous. I hate doing anything twice, so I used to be very careful about thinking everything out before committing it to paper. Now I just get the ideas down fast, then go back and 'cut and paste' with the computer. I don't worry about form anymore, or how to best *say* an idea; I concentrate more on the substance."

One of the most troublesome manual chores involved in scientific and scholarly writing is footnoting. Along with Spellbinder, Dr. Olson uses a program called Bibliography.

"I only have to enter the titles of books and articles into the computer once," he says. "Then whenever a citation is needed, the program automatically prints it in the format I need."

Does the personal computer make it easier to write scientific papers? "Easier is not the word," says Dr. Olson. "Word processing increases my productivity by three hundred to four hundred percent. I may spend as much time writing as I did before, but I get three to four times as much accomplished."

Boilerplate

Getting more accomplished is also a top priority with California attorney Steve Guralnick, who describes the firm of Kyriakis & Guralnick as "a typical two-man suburban law partnership." Typical, perhaps, except for their commitment to word processing and the personal computer. Like Haworth's Cohen and McLoughlin, Steve Guralnick has been using the personal computer for word processing since the late 1970s. Today he owns two powerful CompuPro microcomputers tied to a hard-disk memory system that stores thousands of pages of what Guralnick calls "master text." When he needs to draft a will, a partnership agreement, or a commercial lease, Guralnick turns to these "master text" files. They contain the "boilerplate" clauses of legal documents that rarely change from client to client.

"We meticulously examine all master text before putting it on file," he explains. "When we need to draw up a document, the computer gives us back exactly what we put in, nothing more, nothing less. This saves labor and produces a degree of accuracy that cannot be matched by human beings. We only have to proofread the sections that have been customized for the client. The repetitive aspects of drafting and redrafting similar documents have been virtually eliminated. So has the need for proofreading and the possibility of errors."

As for the economics of using personal computers for word processing in the two-man law firm, says Steven Guralnick: "We would be paying an additional ten thousand to fifteen thousand dollars a year for a full-time secretary were it not for word processing."

The Great Emancipator

The word processor is an obvious boon to secretarial productivity. Unhappily, few managers recognize word processing's potential as an *executive* tool. Most businesspeople, if they think of word processing at all, consider it an activity that is not only beneath their dignity, but a misuse of expensive managerial time and talent. Nothing could be further from the truth.

Management *is* communication. "The operating work of the organization—producing a product, doing research, purchasing a part—appears to be undertaken infrequently by the senior manager," Henry Mintzberg concluded in a classic 1966 study of managerial work roles. "The manager's productive output *must be measured in terms of information.*" Much of this information is necessarily verbal, but by no means all of it. In the information age the speed and ease by which a manager can write, revise, edit, proofread, and distribute correspondence, reports, proposals, memos, contracts, and other documents is a fundamental benchmark of effectiveness.

Toward this end, the word processor is the great emancipator of the micro-power applications. For many executives, word processing succeeds where sixteen to twenty years of formal education have failed. The word processor makes writing bearable. It makes writing easier to produce, evaluate, edit, polish, and present.

The word processor—whether a $12,000 **dedicated** (i.e., an office machine designed exclusively for word processing) like IBM Display Writer, or a $2,500 personal computer with WordStar—is the logical extension of the correcting typewriter. But the word processor is to the electric typerwriter what the Space Shuttle is to a hang glider.

Word processors translate the elusive stuff of human thought into the steadfast strokes and stems, **ascenders** and

descenders of typographic composition. Word processors allow you to weave words on the page almost as fluidly as one flashing pattern of thought dissolves into the next. With the word processor you can modify written documents exactly the *way* you want, *when* you want. Revisions are fast and efficient. No need to badger secretaries. No waiting for retyped drafts. No proofreading the same document over and over. No tears. No pain.

The Jargon

Word processing has a jargon all its own, a subset of computerese. Any information entered into a word processor, be it a laundry list or the fiscal 1986 Federal Budget, becomes a "document." Documents can contain words or numbers. "Text" and "copy" are also used to describe the general contents of a word processing document. Documents are stored in **files,** usually on floppy diskettes. Many word-processing packages perform "global search and replace" operations. This is not a covert military action. Rather, it means the computer will "search" a document for every occurrence of a word, phrase, or number and automatically replace it with something else. Some word processors can use the power of the computer to produce "justified margins," that is, flush on the right- and left-hand sides, like this page. They also have the capability to execute "block moves," in which the computer transfers entire sentences, paragraphs, and even groups of paragraphs from place to place. But by far the most commonly used feature of any word processing software is its capacity to insert and delete words and phrases without the need to retype anything but the information being entered.

HISTORY OF WORD PROCESSING

Dr. An Wang's Vision

In its institutional form, word processing boosts secretarial productivity, often by a factor of 100 percent or more. On an electric typewriter, a sixty-words-per-minute typist needs about twenty working hours to complete four drafts of a fifty-page report. With a word-processing unit the same typist can handle the job in about seven hours, turning out letter-perfect copy free of white-outs or lift-off corrections.

The lure of such office productivity gains created a multibillion-dollar market for dedicated word-processing equipment during the 1970s. It also helped introduce a new era of office management in which the *personal* executive secretary is fast becoming an endangered species. Pioneering the technological drive to bring word processing to big business was a Chinese immigrant with a degree from Harvard, a Ph.D. in physics, and an entrepreneurial vision worthy of Thomas Edison. His name is Dr. An Wang.

In the early 1970s Dr. Wang's Lowell, Massachusetts–based semiconductor laboratory was among the first of the small high-tech firms to produce a profitable line of programmable electronic calculators. By mid-decade Wang had announced he was abandoning his bread-and-butter product line to concentrate on the development of equipment for the new and largely uncharted market niche of office word processing. In retrospect, Wang's timing was pure entrepreneurial clairvoyance. Just months after he conceded the calculator market to his competitors, chip prices began a devastating decline, sweeping many small electronics firms into bankruptcy. By then Wang's new course was set, his financing secure, and Wang was at work building a technological lead that to date has kept his firm one step ahead of such giants as Xerox and IBM.

After five consecutive years of 55 percent-plus annual growth, Wang Laboratories now boasts a 19,000-employee work force, two million square feet of manufacturing facilities, and revenues in excess of one billion dollars a year. During the same period, Wang Labs' common stock, which sold on the American Exchange for about $2 a share in 1977, increased almost 30-fold. "Because of An Wang's uncanny timing in the marketplace and streetwise application of technology," observed *Business Week* a few weeks before Wang Labs officially joined the billion-dollar-a-year club, "the company holds first place in the sales of word processing equipment."

What Wang had foreseen in the early 1970s was that new technologies and mass production by giants such as Texas Instruments would devastate the small semiconductor manufacturer. At the same time, the plummeting cost of microprocessor memory would open a vast new market for a small-computer system dedicated exclusively to the processing of words instead of numbers. If the dedicated word-processing machine could, as Wang knew it would, pay for itself within a year or two, the market would be virtually fathomless.

Inside the Word Processor

The device Wang envisioned in the early 1970s has become a fundamental office tool of the 1980s. The hardware components of the dedicated word processor consist of a central processing unit and memory chips capable of sorting and comparing tens of thousands of bits of information per second. Since active computer memory is "volatile," meaning it lasts only as long as electrical power is on, a storage device is necessary to retain information. The most inexpensive, yet reliable candidate for the job of mass storage peripheral is the floppy disk drive.

Next a typewriterlike keyboard is used to enter text into the computer memory. A special set of keys control such specialized functions as deleting or inserting words and moving blocks of text. A **window** into the computer's volatile memory (RAM) consisting of a video display lets the operator keep track of the text being entered since the electron beams that scan the video screen's phosphorescent surface reflect changes within a few thousandths of a second. Finally, for hard-copy printout the word-processing system can be connected to a teletype-style printer.

Two software programs are required. One program, a disk operating system (DOS, see page 115), is necessary to manage the internal computer housekeeping functions such as transferring information between the memory chips and the various peripheral devices. The second software program—the word-processing applications program—contains the specific step-by-step instructions that tell the central processing unit and the active memory chips how to edit and store the words, sentences, and paragraphs of the document.

The Immutable Barrier

From the technical and marketing perspectives the dedicated word processor was a triumph, proving beyond a shadow of a doubt the economic virtue of using a computer as a kind of supertypewriter for editing successive drafts of any document. But the cost of dedicated word processors, approximately ten thousand dollars and up, was beyond the means of most individuals and many small firms. With the arrival of the personal computer, word processors no longer needed to be dedicated, nor expensive.

When used with any one of several dozen word-processing software packages, the NEC and IBM Personal Computer become excellent word processors. So do the Kaypro II, the Compaq, the Victor 9,000, the NorthStar Advantage, the Xerox 830, the Otrona Attache, and many, many other personal computers. In general, the so-called business computers, most of which use CP/M as their basic disk operating system, make good word processors. But even the game- and graphics-oriented machines, such as the Atari 800, Apple II, and TRS-80 Model III, can be tortured into a word processor for light-duty use.

LEARNING TO USE IT MEANS NEW WAYS OF THINKING—AND WRITING

Learning word processing can be simple. While writing *The Third Wave* in the late 1970s, Alvin Toffler bought a microcomputer and word-processing software package. "To my pleasure I found I could master the machine in a single short session," he recalled. "Within a few hours I was using it fluently. After more than a year at the keyboard I am still amazed by its speed and power."

In the business environment, where thousands of messages clamor for attention, effective communication—being *understood* despite the babble of background noise—is crucial. On the verbal level, directives and discussions are adequate for day-to-day operations. But for establishing policy, proposing new ventures, or presenting technically complex concepts or information, written documents—like death and taxes—are inevitable. "Writing clear, persuasive letters and various communications both within and outside the company is necessary to job effectiveness," concludes *The Cox Report*. "Any executive lacking skill in written communication is without a prerequisite for leadership,"

An Intellectual Tool

Word processing multiplies the skill of the articulate communicator. More important, it offers the poor writer a battery of powerful communications weapons. When businesspeople and professionals learn to use word processing as an *intellectual tool* the gap between ideas and words, thoughts and actions, narrows. The mechanical drudgery, and, hence, much of the pain of writing diminishes. Writer's block is reduced. Spelling and grammatical errors are decreased. Letters, memos, proposals, and reports are finished faster and with less anguish, more verve. Word processing, in short, endows the part-time writer with many of the capabilities of the professional. With word processing your "intellectual products"—the proposals, reports, or whatever

—can change dramatically for the better. So can the person writing them.

"When the executive learns to use the word processor for himself," points out Warren Stallings, a San Francisco microcomputer consultant and author of several books, "he becomes more familiar with the flow and procedures that take place in the creation of a document. This begins with the thought process itself and continues through the various stages of communicating his ideas, getting them into a draft, revising it and checking it over for spelling and grammar."

Moral Dilemma

Effective business and technical prose is not so much inspiration as perspiration. Writing well means *rewriting* extensively. Professional writers consider the first draft as an outline to be reworked, embellished, and edited through perhaps half a dozen or more versions. Such fastidiousness is gilding the lily in business writing. But for most people rewriting a text even once is so laborious that the first draft becomes the final draft. The art of editing your work with a critical eye is never learned. And should you discover an obvious improvement then, as Peter A. McWilliams declares in *The Word Processing Book:* "What do you have? A Moral Dilemma. A question worthy of Aristotle arises: 'Is making this change that should be made worth retyping the whole page?' And if it's a long document, several pages long, the change would mean going onto another page, so the question becomes, 'Is making this change that should be made worth retyping the whole document?' "

What if you possessed a kind of "living page" on which to try out different words, phrases, idiomatic expressions, sentences, and paragraphs? A page that is always neat and tidy and shows exactly how your words will look and "feel" when typed. A page that allows the luxury of unlimited revision without the need to flatter, plead, and cajole a secretary into typing it over "just one more time."

This is what the word processor does. With most—but not all—word-processing programs, words are displayed on the video monitor just as they will appear on the typed page. Deleting and inserting phrases, reorganizing paragraphs, and even shuffling long blocks of text around are child's play. Even an incompetent typist can turn out letter-perfect copy, often in less time than a skilled secretary would take on a typewriter.

Finished by Noon

At Lee Pharmaceuticals, founder Henry Lee once wrote his letters—some of them twelve or more pages long and crammed with technical detail—longhand, and waited for his secretary to type a first draft. He would then mark up the corrections and return the letter for retyping. "Sometimes it took a week to get a long letter off," he told *Inc.* With an Electric Pencil program and a TRS-80 computer, Lee found he could do it himself and "have it done by noon." Since Lee's staff also write their reports on the TRS-80 with the Electric Pencil, Lee can electronically transfer data into his reports and letters without retyping it. "I could ask for three or four paragraphs from other specialists," he says, "borrow their disks, and pull the information off onto my own disk."

Lee spends little, if any, extra time when preparing his letters and reports on the word processor. Yet they are available almost immediately, and in exactly the form he wants. To some executives the notion of a CEO typing his own letters may seem odd, but where productivity, results, and cost-effectiveness are paramount to status, the word processor in the hands of an aggressive executive or professional is a formidable communications weapon.

Fringe Benefits

Not only does the word processor eliminate an expensive and frequently ineffective intermediary—the secretary—it also trims many of the hidden costs of written communications, including proofreading, Xeroxing, filing, express mail or messenger service, and even typesetting and mailing list fees.

Programs such as SpellStar, The Word, Easy Speller, SpellGuard, and Perfect Speller can be used with word-processing packages to compare documents against a computerized dictionary, pinpointing many typos and misspellings. Aspen Software's Grammatik is a proofreading program that provides rudimentary analysis of sentence structure and word usage. These packages are no threat to human proofreaders, at least not at the present state of the art, but they do work quickly and can catch the kind of embarrassing errors writers often overlook.

Magnetic disks eliminate the need for Xeroxed file copies. One floppy disk can serve as a file drawer for several years' worth of business correspondence. Boilerplate text, covering frequently used subjects such as product descriptions or standard contract clauses, can be lifted out of "master-text files" or even previous correspondence or reports and inserted into letters, memos, and proposals without retyping. And the **letter-quality** computer printer will churn out as many typed "originals" as needed. There is no opportunity for ruffled egos when everyone on the distribution list receives a typed document, not a Xeroxed copy.

When clients, customers, or vendors have microcomputers, letters, reports, or manuscripts can be telecommunicated across town, across the country, or across the globe for the price of a short telephone call. Specialists located in opposite ends of the country, or anywhere on the international telecommunications grid, can collaborate by "squirting" data back and forth between computers. This is exactly how writers Stephen King (*Carrie, The Shining*) and Peter Straub (*Ghost Story*) wrote their recent novel, *The Talisman*. Although King lives in Bangor, Maine, and Straub in Westport, Connecticut, the pair swapped "files" containing the novel's outline, scenes, and chapters between their word processors using conventional telephone lines.

Typesetting by Phone

Word-processing programs can be linked by phone to electronic phototypesetting equipment, eliminating the most labor-intensive step in the typesetting process—text entry. In Miami the advertising department of a $6-million-a-year discount mail-order house uses a modem and word processor to transmit approved ad copy directly to their typesetter's Compugraphic machine. The firm's ad manager estimates the technique has shaved the annual typesetting bill by $17,000. For printed materials where quality typesetting is not required, such as newsletters or instruction manuals, a microcomputer with word-processing software and a letter-quality printer can provide camera-ready type. Many word-processing programs allow justified margins. A few programs, such as Spellbinder and Peachtree's PeachText, can even produce *proportionally spaced* type, a feat that once required expensive typesetting equipment.

Small mailing lists of about five hundred or one thousand names and addresses can be integrated with a word-processing package by using off-the-shelf programs that go under such names as MailMerge, EasyMailer, and Apple Post. More sophisticated programs, such as DB Master and dBase II, can be used to construct lists that run into the thousands and even hundreds of thousands of names. Aside from automatically labeling envelopes and letters, these programs will also personalize documents by inserting the addressee's name, town, or other information in designated places throughout the text.

Getting Started

New York Times Home Improvement editor Bernard Gladstone uses the PeachText word-processing package for his newspaper columns. "At a minimum my productivity has increased fifty percent," he says. "I turn out one-and-a-half, maybe two times as much work as I did before. Or you can look at it the other way and say I do my work in half the time."

Gladstone recommends PeachText for its ease of learning. "Everyone is a little afraid of the computer at first," he points out. "Once you get over that psychological hurdle, you can get cracking very quickly." One problem Gladstone faces is teaching typists to use his personal computer with PeachText for transcribing interviews. "Within fifteen or twenty minutes," he says, "you can teach any typist enough, as long as you are present to do some of the commands."

With the word processor, getting started with your writing is also easier. The writer using a pencil or typewriter experiences something like this, according to Bernard Gladstone: "You sit down and stare at the paper for a while. Then you go and sharpen some pencils. Stare some more. You remember a check you need to write. Then a phone call you need to make. You look for every excuse you can find not to start writing.

"For some reason, with the computer, I don't stall as much before getting started. Maybe it's the video game syndrome. I won't say it's actually *fun,* but it's somehow a lot more interesting than sitting down at a typewriter."

Because it opens an extraordinary world of new possibilities, the word processor can help expand the manager's creative awareness. But only when you are willing to enter its domain for yourself. The expansion of human potential through *personal* computing cannot be delegated.

A Model for Human Perception

Harnessing a basic computer skill such as word processing can alter how you write, even how you think. When you begin using the computer for yourself, and not through intermediaries such as a word-processing operator, the machine, in its infinite complexity and flexibility, becomes not only a tool, but, as MIT educator Seymour Papert points out, *a model* for perceiving and interpreting the world. "By providing a very concrete, down-to-earth model of a particular style of thinking," Papert agrees in his book *Mindstorms,* "work with the computer can make it easier to understand that there is such a thing as a 'style of thinking.' " Learning to use the computer changes the way you learn everything else, from how to approach a problem to how to solve it—and even whether you tackle it in the first place.

In word processing, for instance, the computer helps teach the importance of getting one's thoughts "on paper," without being much concerned about style or organization. John Ball, who won an Academy Award for the screen adaptation of his novel *In the Heat of The Night,* has trained himself to use the word processor as a direct channel between his thoughts and the page. "One of the major advantages," he says "is that you can type just as if you have a continuous line. Since the computer automatically puts in carriage returns, I can put my thoughts right into the keyboard without having to look up at the end of every line. That always held me up and distracted me subconsciously."

Electronic Proofreader

The word processor also provides greater insight, and hence, greater personal control over the various stages of document preparation. If you have, as most of us do, a fondness for jargon, wordy phrases, redundancies, vague adverbs, misused words, or trite sayings, a session or two with Grammatik will prove enlightening. Grammatik analyzes your finest prose word by word, explaining that "referred to as" is a wordy phrase better replaced by "called," that "seldom ever" is redundant, and querying whether one really means "immanent," (i.e., inherent), or whether the intention was to say "imminent" (i.e., impending).

What can't Grammatik do? Aspen Software's manual explains: "Grammatik does not know anything about the meaning of words. Anything that requires an understanding of meaning, such as subject-verb agreement, cannot be detected. Such software is technologically some years away." Even so, what Grammatik can do is remarkable.

On an intellectual level, these programs and the computers that run them teach a valuable lesson. The message is subtle, but insistent. "You *can* improve this sentence, this paragraph, this report," the machine is saying. "Just get the ideas down, that's what counts. Write naturally, don't worry about the mistakes. Don't slow up. Follow the cursor, it moves with the speed and ease of light. Be like me. Stay loose and flexible and free. Later you'll come back and revise, revise, revise."

TRENDS AND BRANDS OF SOFTWARE FOR WORD PROCESSING

Recent word-processing programs such as Spellbinder, WordStar, PeachText, Select, Easy Writer II, Super Scriptsit, Perfect Writer, SuperWriter, VisiWord, Volkswriter, and Final Word allow the business executive to use the microcomputer to transfer information, say a profit and loss statement, from the accounting files directly into the text of his shareholder's report. The entire procedure can be accomplished without assistance, as long as the information was available in the computer system in a technical "format" that the word-processing program can "read." Any data, from current inventory levels to a firm's financial ratios, that is located within the computer's filing system can be called up, rearranged, and edited if necessary, and then printed out. The entire procedure can be accomplished, perhaps not without some difficulty, but at least without the aid of line managers, accountants, assistants, or even a secretary.

Third-Generation Software

The lastest trend in personal computer software is the so-called third-generation program in which the boundaries between word processing and other applications such as spreadsheeting, graphics, and data-base management are eliminated altogether. "People's problems usually span several applications areas," Dan Fylstra, founder of VisiCorp, told *Personal Computing*. "So, increasingly, people really need to use what are now individual applications in combination with each other."

With the "fully integrated" third-generation package, procedures for moving a document file from one program to another are vastly simplified. Also, many of the basic **commands**—such as the instructions to delete or enter data—

have been standardized. With second-generation software it is necessary to learn a different set of commands with each applications package. As a result, third-generation software packages can be easier to learn and use.

Utilizing a technique developed by Xerox, and commercially pioneered by VisiCorp, IBM, and Apple Computer, some third-generation word-processing packages are being combined with a "hardware **interface**" known as the "mouse." This device allows keyboard-shy executives to bypass some of the complicated commands that require holding one key down while pressing one or two others in sequence.

Third-generation software programs as well as hardware/software products such as VisiOn and the Apple IV computer demand careful consideration, especially in the executive and professional setting where multiple applications—including word processing, graphics, spreadsheeting, and data-base management—go with the territory. Still, the actual use of word processing, regardless of the type, is the important step. Compared to the differences between an electric typewriter and a computerized word processor, all software distinctions pale in significance. Even so, here are some thoughts on finding the best word-processing program to fit your needs.

An Industry Standard—WordStar

Despite mounting pressure from third-generation software, the world's preeminent word processing package is WordStar—a second-generation program. Within a year of its introduction, WordStar had become the closest thing there is to an industry standard for word processing. Aside from file compatibility with MailMerge, SpellGuard, Grammatik, and other programs, WordStar's major strength is its enormous versatility. WordStar performed most of the important tricks of a $12,000 dedicated word processor, plus a few the big machines couldn't do.

As with most serious business software, WordStar requires a computer with at least one and preferably two disk drives. The WordStar diskette, or a copy of it, is inserted into a disk drive and "booted to memory." With most computers this is done by striking the RETURN key. A delay of several seconds follows as the WordStar program is loaded into the computer's memory. When the loading is complete a "file directory" listing the contents of the disk appears on the screen.

Several of these files contain the WordStar program **code.** If the diskette has already been used for word processing, other document files will be listed. These files can be activated, one at a time, by typing a simple command—the letter *D* followed by the name of the file you want to edit. There is a momentary pause, a faint humming as the disk rotates about ten times faster than an LP record, and then the first twenty or so lines of your file flash on the screen, ready for editing. To use a paper-and-pencil analogy, the video screen represents the sheet of paper, while the cursor is the editor's red pencil.

Files

If the "file name" you enter is not found in the disk directory, WordStar automatically opens a new file for you. The maximum number of pages of text a file will hold is determined by the storage capacity of the disk drives. With a pair of inexpensive 100K disk drives, about twenty-five double-spaced pages is the limit. With souped-up quad-density disk drives, a WordStar file can hold over one hundred pages. But putting one hundred pages in a single file is akin to putting all your eggs in one basket. If it's accidentally erased, or if it perhaps mysteriously vanishes—which can happen—it may take days, even weeks, to replace. Thus, the WordStar manual advises, "it is best to keep files as small as possible."

As soon as a WordStar file is opened, you can set margins, line spacing, justification, tabs, and dozens of other text **formatting** features. Or format can be ignored and typing begun immediately. There are **default** settings within WordStar to automatically adjust margins, line spacing, tabs, and other features to predetermined settings, should you happen to be more concerned with getting your ideas down than with how the words appear on the screen. The default capability is an important feature. It means you can boot the diskette and be working in WordStar almost as quickly as a yellow pad and pencil can be dug out of a desk drawer.

Exceptions

Writing on a WordStar file is much like using an electric typewriter, with three notable exceptions. First, as the keys are stroked, the characters appear not as printed words, but as phosphorescent images upon the computer's video monitor. Second, when the cursor reaches the right-hand margin in WordStar there are no bells or buzzers. Instead, the cursor automatically jumps to the beginning of the next line. In computerese this is known as "word wrap." There are never any stranded syllables. If the last word on the line won't fit at the end of the line, word wrap automatically pulls it along with the cursor. Third, it is possible to **scroll** to any point in a multipage document. "I find one of the big advantages of word processing," says *Oregonian* editor Phil Adamsak, "is the ability to jump to any point within a document." If a change is needed in page 10, one merely pushes the scroll button, stopping when the "status line" at the top of the page indicates that page 10 has been reached.

Reformatting

Like John Bell, many writers prefer to "pour" their ideas into the word processor, not even pausing to correct typos or break for new paragraphs. Once a sizeable block of copy has been written, with WordStar it takes only a few keystrokes to "reformat" the text by setting new margins, line spacing, adding paragraph indentations, and perhaps even shifting a few sentences around.

Changing the width of a margin, for instance, requires pressing the **CONTROL** key and simultaneously typing two characters—"O" and "R." A "prompt" appears at the top of the screen asking for the 'RIGHTHAND COLUMN NUMBER.' For a typical business letter one might answer "65." Within a few nanoseconds (one nanosecond equals one billionth of a second) a new margin sixty-five characters wide is established. If double spacing is desired (or triple, or more) the **control** key is depressed along with the characters "O" and "S." Another prompt appears asking for your line-spacing preference. By typing in "2" you establish a double-space format. Pressing the **CONTROL** key plus the letter "B" will then reformat your document into a double-spaced block of text sixty-five spaces in width.

Ninety-seven Commands

There are ninety-seven different commands in WordStar. Some control the cursor movement around the screen. Some delete text, others insert it. Some add headings or page numbers, others keep track of page numbers so that an entire book written over dozens of files can be automatically paginated. But whatever commands are given in WordStar, the text—with just two or three minor exceptions—appears on the video monitor exactly as it will look on the typed page.

This last point is an essential feature, and one that is not common to all word-processing packages. Some word-processing programs rely on what are known as "imbedded commands" to format text. These commands *appear on screen* as various symbols, some familiar, others not. When using "character-oriented" word-processing packages, one sees a block of text interspersed with hieroglyphic notations. Not until a test printout is made do you really know how the typed pages will look. Character-oriented programs are fine for full-time word-processing personnel, but they can be cumbersome for managers, salespeople, lawyers, teachers, and anyone else who uses word processing intermittently.

WordStar is a screen-oriented program. However, it does have some drawbacks of its own. While WordStar is a joy to use, not only is it among the most difficult word-processing programs to learn, it is widely regarded as one of the most difficult of *all personal computer* packages, including spreadsheets and data-base managers. WordStar's great strength—its vast array of commands for solving almost every text-editing challenge conceivable—is, paradoxically, a great weakness. The complexity and variety of WordStar commands make it far more difficult to learn, and relearn, than its less powerful cousins.

Spellbinder

Spellbinder (from LexiSoft in Davis, California) is without qualification the most powerful microcomputer word-processing program I have encountered. As with WordStar, Spellbinder is no picnic to learn. But what would you expect of a program that will do almost anything you can dream of doing with the printed word? Not only does Spellbinder offer virtually all the features found in WordStar—insertion, deletion, block moves, search and replace, centering, justified margins, and more—Spellbinder has a few tricks of its own.

One common complaint of WordStar users is the inability to jump the cursor forward or backward one sentence, or one paragraph, at a time. With Spellbinder you can do that. Or perhaps you don't trust your spelling. Spellbinder has a spelling-check program built-in. Do you need to alphabetize a mailing list, or sort by zip code, or age, or dollar volume, or any other characteristic you care to define? Again, you can do it with Spellbinder. Spelling check, mailing list, and data-management capabilities are all included in one admission price—about three hundred fifty dollars at a discount software house. The combination of WordStar, Mail Merge, and SpellStar by contrast, discounts for about five hundred fifty dollars, and still lacks some of Spellbinder's features.

Select

For light-duty word processing such as letters and memos, you should consider Select. Like Spellbinder, the Select package includes a spelling dictionary and mailing-list manager. But Select also comes with a self-teaching tutorial that has many users up and running in ninety minutes. The authors of Select have done a better job than most in keeping the commands simple and mnemonic. Typing an "E" followed by the **RETURN** key, for instance, tells the program you are ready to edit. To proofread with the spelling-check program, the command is "S."

Select is also a screen-oriented program—what you see is what you get. Text appears on the video monitor just as it will in the printout. This is Select's second greatest advantage, the first being its ease of learning. Unfortunately, Select lacks Spellbinder's ability to enter and edit text simultaneously. You must use a *text entry* screen for composing, then switch to a second *text editing* screen for making corrections and revisions. This is a constraint that casual users may never notice, but that the full-time writer or word-processing operator can find immensely annoying.

Perfect Writer

Between the power of Spellbinder and the simplicity of Select there are dozens of word-processing packages to consider. One that gets high marks from users is Perfect Writer, the word-processing program bundled with the Kaypro portable computer.

Perfect Writer is considered one of the easier word-processing packages to learn, yet it still has all the basic capabilities for text editing. Moreover, Perfect Writer offers several intriguing features. Perfect Writer includes subroutines that facilitate indexing and footnoting. And when a disk becomes full when using Perfect Writer, your text is automatically saved. With many programs, including WordStar, the text you are working on can be lost if you fail to keep accurate track of your remaining disk memory. Also, with Perfect Writer there is a *split screen* feature that allows simultaneous editing of two documents, something you can do with only a handful of word-processing programs. The only major thing that's missing from Perfect Writer is automatic hyphenation, a convenient software routine that spontaneously suggests where to break words that are too long to fit on one line. You *will* find hyphenation available on WordStar, Spellbinder, and PeachText, among others.

Other Word-Processing Programs

Additional word-processing programs worthy of note include Apple Writer II, Easy Writer II, Magic Window II, PeachText, SuperScriptsit, SuperWriter, Volkswriter, and VisiWord. None of these have quite the power and flexibility of Spellbinder or WordStar, but many of them are easier to learn and all of them have large and devoted followings.

OTHER CONSIDERATIONS

Before buying a computer for word processing you will also want to consider several important hardware features, including the quality of the keyboard, video monitor, and printer. These issues are discussed in detail in chapter ten.

One final word on word processing: The moment a floppy disk or diskette enters your disk drive it is at risk. A power failure or surge in line voltage can crash a disk beyond repair by scrambling the electronic code written on its magnetic surface. More likely, operator error—usually one human error compounded by another—can destroy this fragile magnetic code that represents the document on which you've worked hours, days, or even weeks to create. And sometimes, although thankfully not often, even the computer makes a mistake.

People who use word processing extensively make duplicates of their important disks, and keep a hard-copy backup as well. Even so, accidents happen. During the past 2,500 hours of operation, I've had three documents mysteriously vanish into the maws of my starboard disk drive, never to be seen again. The first was a piece for *Newsweek* that dematerialized when, instead of copying the diskette, I erased it. It's true that I was new at word processing and slightly confused. I should have **write protected** the disk by covering the tiny slot on its side with a piece of tape. But I didn't. By typing "A" instead of "B," I copied the blank diskette onto the one containing my story. Having seen the error of my ways, I began write protecting everything. This was no panacea either, as I discovered with my second mishap, having beamed part of chapter three of this book to wherever it is that disembodied word-processing documents go. Disappearance number three, however, I blame on the computer. How else do you explain a message that flashes on the screen saying your "ADDRESS HAS FALLEN IN A HOLE" an instant before the screen, and the afternoon's effort, fade to black?

Yes, these things happen. All you can do is take consolation that, with your vastly increased productivity, rewriting will only take you half as long. Or you can always think of *Time* Magazine Senior Writer Frederick Golden. After weeks of researching a *Time* cover story, Golden's computer inexplicably erased the contents of his diskette. Golden's topic? Would you believe . . . personal computers?

Popular Word Processing Programs Compared
GRAMMATIK

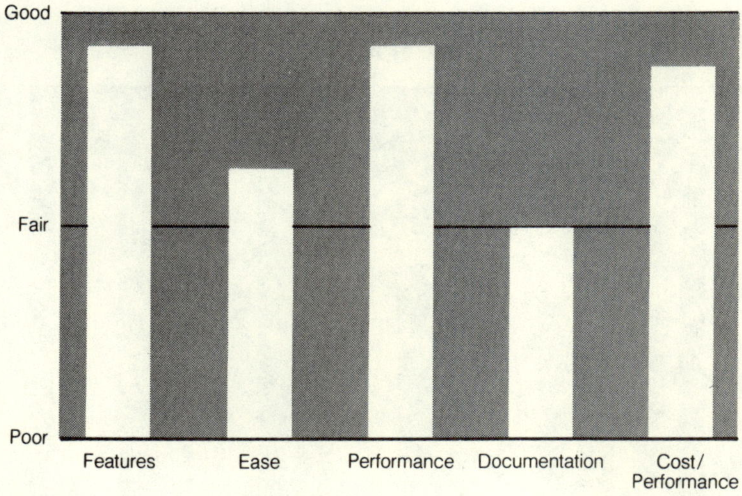

Popular Word Processing Programs Compared
APPLEWRITER II

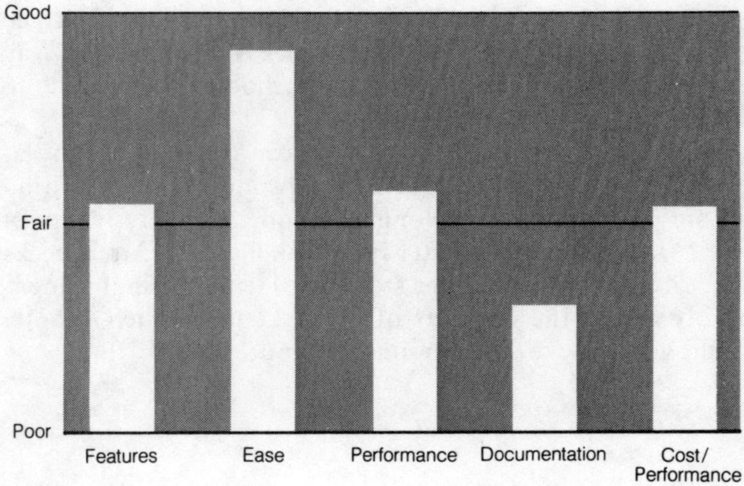

Popular Word Processing Programs Compared
PEACH TEXT

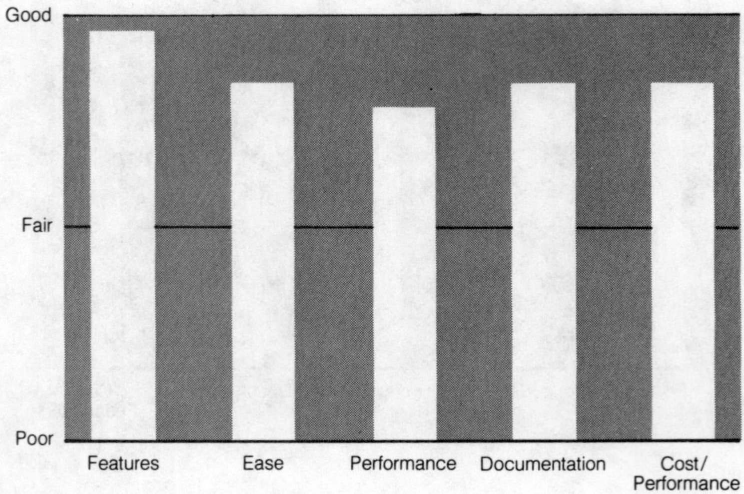

Popular Word Processing Programs Compared
SPELLBINDER

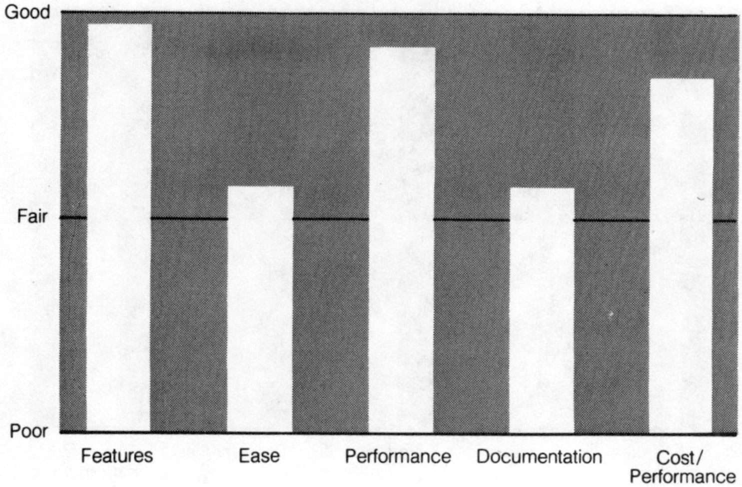

Popular Word Processing Programs Compared
SELECT

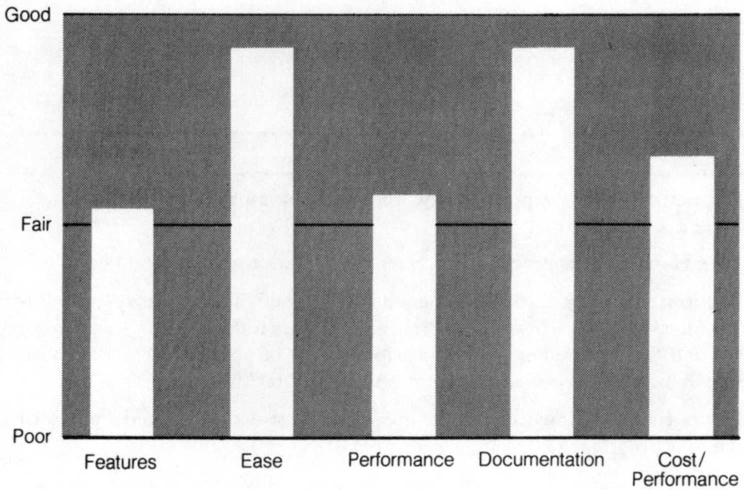

Popular Word Processing Programs Compared

WORDSTAR

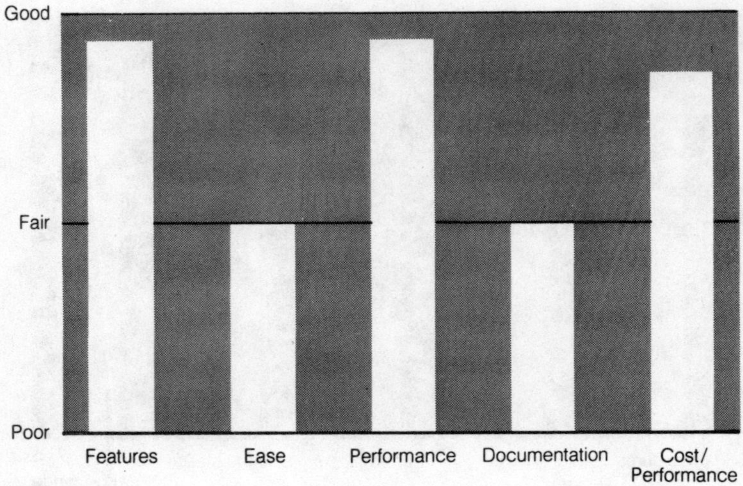

KEY

Features: How do the program's word-processing capabilities rate for general office and personal use?

Ease: How does the program rate in terms of learning and operating ease?

Performance: How does the program rate overall? This category considers "features" and "ease" as well as "reliability" (does it do what it's supposed to do) and "error handling" (does it help you out of your mistakes and, most important, does it prevent you from making a "fatal" mistake)?

Documentation: How useful is the manual and instructional material provided with the program?

Cost/Performance: Based on suggested list price, how good a value is it?

Chapter Seven

Scenarios for Success: Electronic Spreadsheets

The electronic spreadsheet acts like a zoom lens. You find the best economic strategy to follow, then zoom in for a close-up of the details.

—***Barry Hugh Miles,***
Senior Lecturer in Accounting,
Polytechnic of North London

HOW JIM GASTON TRANSFORMED HIS BUSINESS

Gaston's White River Resort sits near the spine of the Arkansas Ozarks, just south of the Missouri border and about one hundred fifty miles north of Little Rock. Good roads are rare in this corner of Dixie and many guests arrive by plane. For their convenience there is a private landing strip as well as a boat dock, boutique, and the more common amenities of a secluded four-star luxury retreat. At the height of the season, 112 employees run Gaston's, serving an upscale clientele that, in a good year, generates gross revenues of $2.5 million.

Rate Structure

Traditionally, January is the slowest month: This is the time of year that owner Jim Gaston sits down with his accounting journals and adding machine to calculate the new season's rate structure. How much should he charge for aviation fuel at the landing strip? For an air-conditioned cottage by the water? What about a hamburger lunch platter? A six-course poached salmon dinner? A half-day boat rental? A mint julep? "In the past," says Gaston, "figuring rate structure took the bulk of thirty days."

For each of the resort's "products" and services—from a week's lodging to a fifth of Kentucky bourbon—Jim Gaston must prepare a detailed cost analysis. Starting with a sheet of ruled paper he itemizes the hundreds of goods and services offered at each of the "profit centers." Across the top of the page he enters his various expense categories—projected wholesale prices; percentage of fixed overhead including equipment and property depreciation, insurance, utilities, maintenance; finance charges; operating costs; projected sales volume; taxes; profit margin; and any other variable that may affect his costs during the year.

Using a ruler, Gaston draws vertical lines down the page, creating a separate column for each category. He now has what accountants are fond of calling a "spreadsheet"—a reference table with data systematically arranged in rows and columns.

The Tedious Way of Spreadsheeting

Once Gaston has scoured his ledgers for figures, queried his managers and vendors, and penciled in the expense data, he can begin. As for the hours of manual calculation that follow, says Gaston, "it's probably the most tedious aspect of resort management." Unfortunately, the tedium does not end when Gaston gets his totals. If, after adding, subtracting, dividing, and multiplying his way across the columns and rows, the final figure is unrealistically high—as often happens—Gaston must begin juggling numbers and experimenting with alternate scenarios. What if he trims a few hundred dollars here? Or cuts back 5 percent there? What about volume discounts? What if the restaurant serves cherries jubilee in place of baked Alaska? "There are a thousand and one variables to change," he says. "And changing the one means recalculating the thousand others. Somewhere I knew there had to be a better way."

The VisiCalc Difference

Two years after he started his quest for a personal computer, Jim Gaston went on-line with a TRS-80 Model II and the "spreadsheet processing" program known as VisiCalc. Instead of setting up his rate structure analyses on paper spreadsheets, as he had done every January for years, Gaston booted his VisiCalc program into the computer's memory from a 5¼-inch floppy diskette.

Road Atlas

What Gaston now saw on his video monitor—or, more precisely, what he had *trained himself to see*—was one corner of an enormous electronic grid divided into columns and rows, much the same way that a page in a road atlas is sectioned off into imaginary squares, with Centerville located at C-7 and Colorado Springs at J-13. But the VisiCalc spreadsheet was potentially far larger than any atlas map. VisiCalc's designers had intended their spreadsheet to be used for complex financial models. Across the top, if one needed them all, sixty-three columns were available. Along the left margin were 254 rows. Enough room, as one economist had discovered, to accommodate the annual budget of a small Caribbean nation.

There is no penalty, however, for using only a small corner of the VisiCalc spreadsheet, which is all Jim Gaston's work requires. But since even a few columns and rows exceed the eighty-character-by-twenty-four-line **window** of the typical video monitor, it is necessary for him to **scroll** the monitor across the spreadsheet's surface.

To visualize this, imagine that the active area of the spreadsheet is, indeed, a page from a large road atlas and that the video screen is a magnifying glass. When laid on the map, the magnifying glass reveals Centerville at C-7 and all the surrounding territory for three or four squares in every direction. To see more, slide the magnifying glass across or up or down the page. Or, with the VisiCalc spreadsheet, scroll the screen north or south, east or west by using special function keys that are equipped with arrows to show in which direction the video window will travel.

Data entry is accomplished at the keyboard. At cell C-7, for instance, Gaston might type in "1.27," representing his projected cost per gallon for aviation fuel. At J-13, in place of Colorado Springs, Gaston could enter a simple equation to multiply last year's expenditures for margarine by 5 percent. With the pencil-and-paper spreadsheet, entering this data is only the beginning. With the electronic spreadsheet, once his data is in place, Jim Gaston's job is almost over. With just a couple of keystrokes, the computer automatically calculates the rows and columns. Painlessly. Effortlessly.

"This year," says Jim Gaston, "we completed all our rate structuring in one eight-hour day." For Gaston that translates into a productivity leap of about twenty-five or thirty to one.

Impressive Productivity Gains

Even including Gaston's $4,000 investment for the computer and software, as well as the forty to fifty hours he spent learning VisiCalc ("it was the first program I ever did on a computer so a lot of that time was spent getting used to terms like **backup** and **format**"), Jim Gaston's productivity gains are still impressive. Consider, also, that he uses the same program, VisiCalc, for over "thirty different record-keeping and reporting jobs, from daily cash and tax reports for each of our profit centers to keeping track of inventory, accounts payable, workmen's compensation information, and occupancy rates. It even saves us money with our CPA," he says. "We used to have to send him a voucher every time we wrote a check. Now he gets one printout at the end of the month, and it's already been totaled."

Has the computer cut overhead in other ways? "We haven't fired anybody because of the computer," says Gaston. "But to do everything manually that we are now doing on the computer I would have to hire at least four or five more people. Even then, I still wouldn't be getting what I call the 'free information.' That's the data I can get from the spreadsheet files that simply isn't available from any manual system."

Jim Gaston is not alone in his esteem for the powers of

spreadsheet processing. Over a million businesspeople and professionals are using spreadsheet-processing programs. Only one micro-power application—word processing—enjoys greater popularity.

The Original—VisiCalc

VisiCalc, the original spreadsheet-processing program, continues to rank among the best-selling personal-computer software. But dozens of new rivals, promising greater speed, power, and convenience, now crowd the marketplace. Heading the list of new spreadsheet software is the enormously successful SuperCalc, as well as CalcStar, MultiPlan, T/Maker III, 1,2,3, and over forty others.

"Spreadsheeting," observes Bob Korngold, publisher of *Spreadsheet,* a bi-monthly newsletter, "has become a religion with many cults. There is a MultiPlan cult. A SuperCalc cult. A '1,2,3' cult. But the first and the foremost is the VisiCalc cult." (*Spreadsheet* contains advice and tips for users of VisiCalc and other spreadsheet programs and is available for $52 a year from InterCalc, P.O. Box 254, Scarsdale, NY 10583.)

VisiCalc was *the* spark that ignited the personal-computer explosion. It is estimated that VisiCalc was responsible for 40 percent of Apple's sales between 1979 and 1981, the years when VisiCalc ran only on the Apple II computer. "Give me VisiCalc and whatever computer it runs on," was the refrain that built the Apple empire. Spreadsheet processing gave the personal computer legitimacy as a business tool.

The specific applications of the spreadsheet proved nearly as complex and varied as the spectrum of human commercial endeavor. Farmers learned to use the computerized spreadsheet to foretell crop and livestock yields. Wall Street investors used it to anticipate securities performance. Real estate developers, contractors, and architects used it to predict when and under what circumstances a new project would be profitable. Retailers and wholesalers used it to plan inventory levels. Accountants used it to keep books and figure taxes.

Product managers had uses for it. So did marketing, sales, and production executives in virtually every field.

Jon Nackerud, a data-processing professional who is now president of a California software company, recalls the pre-VisiCalc era. "It was the stage when we referred to 'those dumb users,' " he says. "In those days you needed to know *exactly* what you wanted the computer to do. But the executives we'd talk to would want to do one thing one day and something else the next. We used to ask ourselves: 'How can this company make any money if these people are always changing their minds?' " What the executives knew, and what the data-processing professionals couldn't understand, is that decision making and analysis are creative processes that often cannot be defined in advance.

Programming without the Priesthood

With the arrival of the microcomputer, professionals and executives gained direct access to computer power without the intercession of the data-processing priesthood. But there remained the question of programming. A few modeling and analysis programs had been written for the personal computer before VisiCalc. These were useful only if you could bend the problem to fit the program. Like the big-business software packages they resembled, the early microcomputer modeling programs handled specific applications. Until 1979 you had two choices for "what-if" modeling: Hire a programmer, or devote a few months to learning a computer language. Either way the process was costly, time-consuming, and there was no guarantee it would work. Then came VisiCalc.

Even in the supercharged world of computer software the new program that Dan Bricklin and Bob Franksen cooked up in Cambridge during 1978 was a bombshell. The execution was brilliant, but the concept behind it was even better.

For openers, Bricklin and Franksen wrote a program that *eliminated the need for a computer programmer.* This alone went contrary to thirty years of data-processing tradition. Bricklin and Franksen's VisiCalc package allowed the total neophyte to construct what amounted to an infinite variety of complex data-processing programs without knowing one word of BASIC, ASCI code, or the other esoterica of computerland. "With VisiCalc you can do it for yourself," financial planners and research analysts told each other so often it became a cliché.

What would immortalize the authors of VisiCalc, however, was the concept behind VisiCalc. After thirty years of computer software development it seemed logical that someone would have written a computer program that would let the user draw some rows and columns, insert a few labels, numbers, and simple equations into the boxes, and then calculate the results. But no one had. At least not in such a way that it could be displayed on a screen and look like a real spreadsheet and not a list of disembodied calculations.

Even more important than the possibility of dispensing with the programmer was the fact that professionals and executives no longer had to solve problems according to the rigid logic of software designed and written by "code pounders" whose business assumptions were often ill-founded. With the spreadsheet program, executives and professionals could bend the software to fit their problem. No longer were they obliged to make the problem fit the program.

Scenarios Projected with the Aid of VisiCalc

Take Boston general contractor and land developer Claude Comeau. His problem—cost analysis of complex land deals. "In my business," explains Comeau, "we usually don't know what the financing rates or land costs will be. Yet we still need to look at deals to see if they might work for us. And since we're also a general contractor we have at least four or five variables that go into any potential deal." Enter Comeau's TRS-80 and VisiCalc.

"Even if I don't specifically know what the financing rates and land costs will be, I do know their probable range. With VisiCalc I enter this range for each variable and come out with about ten or fifteen scenarios. It gives me an intuitive feel for the problem, even without tangible figures.

"The great thing about spreadsheeting," says Comeau, "is

that you are really molding the program to the way you think. You don't just get 'one answer.' You get a range of answers. As you crank them out you get an intuitive feel for what's behind the numbers. You sense which scenarios will work, which won't."

In Comeau's business, even when figures are available, they are frequently subject to change. "By the time a potential client arranges financing or clears up a zoning problem, six months or a year may have gone by. But with a spreadsheet we can just go in, update our cost factors, and . . . poof! we have a new estimate."

The Magic of Cells

In the parlance of spreadsheeting, the boxes formed by the intersection of a row and a column are "cells," "matrix locations," or "coordinates." Into each cell one of three things may fall: a numeric quantity, a descriptive label, or a mathematical relationship that adds, subtracts, multiplies, or divides. For most spreadsheet work no advanced mathematics are required. "Perhaps a little high school algebra," says *Spreadsheet* copublisher Korngold. "But very little."

This much, of course, can be done on any sheet of yellow paper. But not the next step. After the various cells have been filled in with the basic data for a marketing plan or cost estimate or balance sheet, one merely nudges a couple of keys and *the electronic spreadsheet does the calculating*.

"The beauty of it," notes microcomputer consultant Jim McMullen, "is that once you change a number in any cell, the whole spreadsheet changes with it—percentages, subtotals, totals, everything." Having set up a VisiCalc spreadsheet, say, for an annual budget, all it takes to see the impact of an unexpected, but possible, decrease in sales is to insert the new figure and command VisiCalc to go to work. Deep within the central processing unit, bundles of electrons race down microscopic highways at the speed of light, performing hundreds of thousands of calculations in a twinkle. When it is over, perhaps in two or three seconds if it is a complex annual budget with a few hundred figures in it, a new set of numbers has taken shape amid the gloaming havoc. Even with that previous marvel of semiconductor engineering—the pocket calculator—you might need the afternoon, the evening, or, perhaps, the better part of next week to do the work that has just been done in a few seconds' time.

Impact of VisiCalc

The implications of the VisiCalc concept for small businesses and professionals are profound. Bricklin's inspiration for VisiCalc had come during a finance class at Harvard Business School, and Bricklin himself thought of his VISIble CALCulator program primarily as a tool for simplifying the laborious number crunching of intricate financial models by manual methods. What neither Bricklin nor his coauthor clearly realized was the infinite flexibility and problem-solving potential of VisiCalc.

"Anything you can do with columns and rows," says Jim McMullen, "you can do better with VisiCalc." What no one in the computer industry had realized, at least not until after VisiCalc had gone to market, was that the spreadsheet format is the way most people keep track of data, not only in their professions and businesses, but also in their personal lives. Bank statements. Sales journals. Cash disbursement diaries. Sales tax records. Scientific tabulations. Job and cost estimates. Profit-loss statements. Media plans. Break-even analyses. Expense diaries. Production projections. Manpower assignments. Payroll records. Efficiency analyses. Strategic plans. Loan amortization schedules. Stock and bond portfolio analyses. Inventory control records. Statistical surveys. Baseball box scores. Accounts receivable. Accounts payable. Crop rotation schedules. All have one thing in common: columns and rows. "I'm still amazed at the things people are doing with VisiCalc," says Bricklin.

"Once VisiCalc was out," notes McMullen, "it was obvious to anyone who understood data processing that there should have been a product like this long ago." Since VisiCalc there have been significant improvements in the power and convenience of spreadsheet processing. Super-

Calc, for instance, was a quantum leap. So was Advanced VisiCalc. Second- and third-generation packages such as T/Maker III, 1,2,3, and VisiOn add new dimensions, such as automatic chart and graph generation, word processing, and even company-wide file management systems, to the basic spreadsheet capability. "But they are only refinements of the power and convenience of the original VisiCalc," says McMullen. "There hasn't been a *new concept* since VisiCalc."

USING SPREADSHEETING FOR DECISION SUPPORT ANALYSES

In the small firm with a modest inventory and limited financial transactions, the spreadsheet can be programmed to keep the books, write the checks, and even calculate the UPS shipping charges. But spreadsheeting's most dramatic, and most profitable, applications are in decision support analysis. Which deals will work, which deals won't? Which plans offer an acceptable rate of return, which plans don't? With spreadsheet processing the micro-power novice can muscle through more what-if scenarios in an afternoon than an MBA with a slide rule can solve in a lifetime.

During the early 1980s, when "creative financing" became an unwelcome reality in California's San Joaquin Valley, real estate agent David Greeley turned to his CompuPro microcomputer and SuperCalc for help. "Even sophisticated buyers," recalls Greeley, a second-generation Manteca, California, realtor, "were being overwhelmed by the complexity of the 'creative financing' arrangements. Usually these involved two or three alternative combinations of owner financing, deferred loans, assumable mortgages, and conventional first and second mortgages. All at different rates and periods." Greeley soon discovered no one really understood how to compute the true cost of the various alternatives. Not the sellers. Not the buyers. Not even the banks. "We saw people making financing agreements because their father-in-law or neighbor had a 'feeling' one arrangement was better than the others." With SuperCalc and the aid of an engineering friend from Livermore Laboratories, Greeley went to work on a spreadsheet program that could replace guesswork with the hard facts.

Templates

Today Dave Greeley uses over thirty different SuperCalc "templates," i.e., master spreadsheets he has devised using SuperCalc, to help clients analyze their financial alternatives. Typically, Dave Greeley's SuperCalc programs save anywhere from $2,000 to $45,000 over the life of a mortgage agreement. Greeley's most impressive case, however, was a Lodi, California, farmer seeking to refinance his land. "He had the feeling one plan was better than the others," says Greeley, "but he couldn't put his finger on the reason. We ran it through the computer and he was right. One plan was less expensive than the other. About $70,000 less expensive."

While SuperCalc has helped save his clients tens of thousands of dollars, what is it doing for Dave Greeley? "I'm selling more," he says, "because I can show my clients exactly where they stand. We don't lose deals anymore because buyers are apprehensive and confused."

An Eye-Opener

In suburban Chicago, restaurant owner Mike Maxwell thought he knew where he stood, until a spreadsheet model proved otherwise. After three years of flagging earnings, Maxwell's business was clearly headed in the wrong direction. But should he attempt to rejuvenate his business through an ambitious project requiring a large second mortgage? When Maxwell attacked the problem with SuperCalc he made an unwelcome discovery.

"I'd been using SuperCalc on a North Star personal computer for about two years to keep daily running totals of our sales, taxes, major inventory items, and expenses," says Maxwell, who had been a high school science teacher before opening his restaurant in 1974. "I developed about twenty spreadsheets in all," he says. "Together they gave me the foundation for a mathematical model of my business. But until the ad agency recommended some major changes, I never had an incentive to try it out."

An advertising agency study had suggested extensive renovations around a "Baker Street Pub" theme to attract a more affluent clientele, and Maxwell found the idea appealing. "Everyone wants to see their business prosper," says Maxwell. "The agency's concept was exciting, and had the added lure of franchise potential. But to finance the alterations—and they were very extensive—would require a large second mortgage." Along with its intriguing possibilities, the proposal raised a host of unanswered questions. How much business would be lost during the renovations? How much new business, and at what margins, would it take to recoup the construction and finance costs? What about increased operating expenses? Parking facilities? Property tax assessments? Insurance? Promotion costs? Staff? "It was obvious," says Maxwell, "that if the renovations didn't attract the new customers, my entire equity position would be in jeopardy. I needed more information to make a decision. And I needed that information structured in a way I could use to make valid comparisons. Which is what the spreadsheet does best."

Defining the Problem

The spreadsheet model Maxwell had hoped to work up over a weekend turned into a four-week project. "Setting up the spreadsheet format was the easy part," he says. "Defining the problem, identifying the variables—things like population base, and the quantity, quality, and price structure of our geographic competiton—and entering the categories on the screen took only a couple of hours. Establishing an objective rating criteria, on the other hand, was tough, and researching the information was even tougher." So was the bottom line of the fifteen different what-if scenarios Maxwell tried out. "About halfway through I started to get an inkling which way this thing was heading. Even so, the result was a shocker."

Maxwell found that not only was expansion a risky gamble, but "even the 'best case' numbers showed I'd get nearly as good a rate of return on my investment in a money market fund as staying in the restaurant business." What Maxwell learned was that some of his basic business assumptions were dead wrong. "For instance," he says, "I had always taken for granted that the population growth in our area would automatically generate new business. What I discovered from my model was that while the population had increased about twenty-five percent, local restaurant capacity was up over one hundred percent."

Was there an advantage to doing the analysis himself? "If I'd hired a consulting firm, I never would have believed the figures," he says. "Because I had developed the model, I knew exactly where the numbers came from and what they meant."

Mike Maxwell did not renovate his restaurant. But neither has he sold it. "There's an emotional factor involved," he says. "I happen to love what I'm doing. It's just that now I have no illusions about why I'm doing it."

SPREADSHEETING FOR ROUTINE DECISIONS

Spreadsheeting also has powerful applications in *routine* decision-making situations. Piloting a small firm through a troubled economy demands constant fine-tuning. But the business manager faces a dilemma. Information from manual records, or even large-scale computerized accounting systems, is seldom available in time to help resolve daily operational problems. Yet only when armed with timely reports on daily sales transactions and cash-flow activity can managers make day-to-day decisions based on fact, not guesswork.

Small-businessman Pete Eversole refers to this kind of up-to-the-minute decision support as an "operational management record." And in La Crosse, Wisconsin, Eversole has found that spreadsheet processing is not just the best way to keep up a day-to-day operational record in the small business, it's the only way.

Eversole Motors, a Chrysler and Toyota dealership with

annual gross sales of $7 million, may not be entirely unique among auto dealers, but it is nearly so. Even at the depths of the worst U.S. auto slump in over two generations, the family-owned firm could report steady profits. One reason Eversole Motors has stayed in the black while hundreds of other car dealers were closing their doors is a micro-power technique pioneered by Pete Eversole. The basic recipe calls for a personal computer, a spreadsheet processing program, a dash of ingenuity, and about fifteen minutes a day.

Useful Comparisons

"I find the spreadsheet lends itself very readily to a number of useful comparisons in our business," says Eversole. "Comparisons that other companies normally wouldn't put together except on an annual basis." Eversole, however, does put these comparisons together. And he does it daily.

"What I like to do," he explains, "is pick up the daily sales totals *before* they get into the accounting system." To do this Eversole collects the previous day's sales figures from cashiers at each of his profit centers—new car sales, used car sales, service, parts, and the body shop. "I keep these dollar figures in SuperCalc on a daily running basis."

The spreadsheet-processing program allows Eversole to generate a daily report for his profit center managers. On the printout each manager finds a running total of his actual sales-to-date compared to his monthly projection and figures for the past month and year. "It gives our managers a pretty good idea where their month is going," he says. "If there is a problem, they know it before it's too late. It also helps them make informed decisions on everything from scheduling the service bays to spending their promotion budgets. The spreadsheet gives us an *operational* record, while our accounting system, as good as it is, only provides a historical record."

How time-consuming is this kind of recordkeeping? "The averaging and summing and all those things are easily accomplished once the spreadsheet format is set up," explains Eversole. "It's really just a matter of collecting the numbers and plugging them in at the keyboard. Maybe ten or fifteen minutes a day."

Up-to-the-Minute Working Documents

As far as Eversole is concerned, spreadsheet processing with a personal computer is the only way for a small business to produce accurate data for making day-to-day operational decisions. "We've been totally automated with a mainframe computer and very sophisticated accounting software for about eight years," he says. "But like anything big, it takes time to get information into and out of the system. By using spreadsheet processing and a personal computer you can get a working document that is almost up-to-the-minute. It gives us a far better handle than we can obtain from the mainframe accounting system."

Over the years Eversole has used three spreadsheet programs—VisiCalc, SuperCalc, and his first program, a package marketed by Lifeboat Associates called T/Maker. When he purchased an IBM Personal Computer, he was forced to switch to VisiCalc "because at the time I got the IBM, VisiCalc was the only spreadsheet-processing program the computer would run." Later, he upgraded to SuperCalc when it became adapted for the IBM-PC. Of VisiCalc and SuperCalc he says, "if you know one, you know the other." Which is the best? "There are little operating features that make SuperCalc more convenient."

ADVANTAGES OF SUPERCALC

One feature of SuperCalc that Eversole appreciates is "total flexibility over column width. You can set column A at nine characters, column B at sixteen characters and column C at six." This allows him to fit an entire daily report on a single sheet of 8½-by-11-inch paper—something he couldn't do with VisiCalc. Another frequently mentioned advantage of SuperCalc is its ability to "look up" information from previous spreadsheets. When building a new spreadsheet model, say for analyzing the net present value of a potential business investment, it is not necessary to reenter information that is already on file. Instead, you enter the coordinates of the cells in which the information can be found. SuperCalc then automatically finds the data and transfers it into the new model.

But Eversole says that for his purposes, his favorite program is T/Maker. "Once you learn it," he explains, "T/Maker is the wildest. It encompasses a form of word processor that can store sentences or paragraphs which you can then maneuver within the spreadsheet. It's much more flexible."

CASH-FLOW SOLUTIONS LEAD TO EXPLORING ASSUMPTIONS

Rising costs and stagnant sales are two familiar problems of businesses, big and small, in the 1980s. Dennis Curtin's tiny Somerville, Massachusetts, publishing firm is no exception. After three years of steady growth, Curtin & London's annual sales plateaued at $700,000 during the recession of 1980–1983. Instead of waiting out the lean years, Curtin is fighting back with a new weapon, the personal computer.

"I was losing control of what was going on," he recalls. "I had to increase the productivity of my company." Curtin's first micro-power objective was cash-flow management. "The typical small company has cash-flow problems," he says. "You're always worried whether you'll have enough money next month." He began with an Apple II and VisiCalc. Curtin was prepared to spend a great deal of time learning about computers. Instead, he found himself learning about his business.

"The only effort involved in using VisiCalc," he explains, "is learning how to build the model. But you can't build a model until you understand your problem. So you're forced to learn more about the problem. Which means you have to learn more about your business."

Crisis-Reaction Versus Planning

Before VisiCalc, Curtin's approach to cash flow was typical of most small firms. He ignored it until a serious problem forced him to do otherwise. Even then, his attempts at cash-flow control were not impressive. "With ledger sheets I would only do cash-flow planning when I had a problem. It would take me three or four days to finish. Then I'd have so many errors that two weeks later we'd run out of cash. I'd go back and find out I'd made an arithmetic error."

By building a cash-flow model on VisiCalc, Curtin made two discoveries. First, there was no rule of thumb he could follow in projecting cash flow for Curtin & London, intuitive benchmarks for sounding the depths of the cash-flow problem simply wouldn't work. "I had to build the cash-flow model from the bottom up," he says. "In my business there was no way I could say our costs average forty percent overhead, forty percent for costs of goods, and that therefore I could count on a twenty-percent gross profit, or whatever." Cash flow at Curtin & London, in other words, was too erratic for generalized prediction. To make an accurate projection, Curtin found it necessary to work his way through the entire operating system, including such factors as product mix and production schedules.

A Creative Tool

Curtin's second discovery was that once he had developed a cash-flow model, not only could he create a detailed cash-flow statement, but *he could update it with minimal effort.* Now I revise my entire cash-flow statement monthly," he says, "and it takes me no more than one hour to do it. With the spreadsheet model I spend one-tenth the time doing cash flow as a regular planning tool that I used to spend doing it only on a crisis basis. The productivity gain has been enormous."

In the process of bringing his cash flow under control, Dennis Curtin developed a fundamental insight into the role of the personal computer in the small firm. "What happens when you get the computer," he explains, "is that you realize the tool is much more powerful than your understanding of the problem. If you're going to sit down and do business analysis in the same way as you always have, then you're probably wasting your time. There's absolutely no point in approaching financial analysis that way. You might as well use a calculator."

In Curtin's experience the personal computer and its spreadsheet programs are *creative tools* for breaking new ground in business analysis and control. "I began by transferring the same analytical techniques to the computer that I was doing with a paper and pencil," he says. "Then I started thinking that I could add to this model. I could expand it. I could answer this question that had never been answered. I could enter this information that had never been entered."

What began as a cash-flow model "gradually got bigger and bigger and more complicated in terms of what it would do for me." After two years of working with spreadsheet models, says Curtin, "the typical end model is one where I plug in the production and manufacturing cost and the computer automatically calculates all my first printing costs, it calculates reprinting costs, it calculates gross margins in each of the markets, it calculates author royalties."

By publishing industry standards, Dennis Curtin's spreadsheet models are highly sophisticated. But Curtin is quick to point out that the learning process he has been undergoing has less to do with computers than with his own business. "Yes," he says, "the model has become very, very sophisticated. But in the process of building that model I've learned more about my business in the last two years than I learned in the first fifteen. That is what the spreadsheet lets you do."

Exploring Assumptions that Defied Analysis

Specifically, Curtin's spreadsheet models allow him to quantify and explore assumptions that previously defied analysis. "I used to have these very simplistic beliefs," he says, "about how things worked in publishing. You might call it an intuitive understanding. But I'd never sat down and quantified my ideas because the calculations would be too much. With spreadsheeting, once the basic model is built, you can ask what-if questions to your heart's content. What does a certain dollar price increase mean? What if I cut my paper costs? What if I cut royalties? What if I do this? What if I do that? All the calculations are done instantly."

Has this what-if capability had a tangible impact on his decisions? "I've completely changed my thinking on how to publish a number of books," says Curtin, "as a result of the spreadsheet models."

False Confidence—A Possible Danger

What if the what-if model is wrong? What if you've programmed a false assumption into the equation? "If you build a template wrong," says Curtin, "and you're getting wrong answers, you tend to trust them anyway. The chances are you will only discover that some of the assumptions are wrong after the damage has been done."

In Curtin's case the false assumptions were built into a model he used for pricing book-club sales. "I underpriced books to book clubs for six months," he recalls, "before I found the error in my template. I knew what their formulas and guidelines were and what they can afford to pay for a book. So I built that calculation into the gross-margin-analysis spreadsheet I use. Unfortunately, I made an error. So for six months I was underbidding what the book clubs could really afford to pay."

Since his original investment in the Apple II, Curtin has added more microcomputers to his office, including an Osborne portable and an IBM-PC. "During the start-up phase," he says, "when I was the only one who had a computer, I was doing a lot of things I shouldn't have been doing. It became a serious problem at one point. I would come into the office and for two hours I'd sit and plug in numbers, which is strictly a mechanical function. You need more than one computer, and you need more than one person who knows how to use it."

Other Dangers of Computerized Information

In addition to building false assumptions into a spreadsheet template, Curtin foresees other dangers for the small-business manager when computerizing crucial business information. The manager who does not understand the machines runs a potential risk of losing control of his employees.

At the other extreme, Curtin sees that managers who fail to delegate basic computer tasks will reduce their own productivity and effectiveness. "Executives who try to do everything for themselves—and I've seen managers who actually file their own correspondence—are misusing their time. The personal computer is only going to compound their problem."

Not only is Curtin training his staff in how to use the personal computer, he looks forward to the day when his employees will be setting up and expanding his financial analysis models. "Then," says Curtin, "I'll revert to my managerial role where I sit back and evaluate what's being done, instead of having to do everything myself."

What's the Bottom Line?

After two years of computerization, how does Curtin feel the personal computer has influenced his productivity? "The productivity increase," he estimates, "has probably been on the order of magnitude of four or five hundred percent. I don't even deal with traditional office machines anymore, they're just too time-consuming. IBM Selectrics, for instance, are gone from the office; and my productivity has increased by three, four, or even five times in those areas of my job where the computer can be applied."

But Curtin & London's work force has also increased since the arrival of the personal computers. "We're adding employees from growth," he says. "I know I've actually eliminated the need for one person I probably would have needed to hire. We used to publish ten books a year tops. Now we're publishing twenty books with an addition of only two employees. Next year I think we can add another ten books with only an additional one or two people.

"If I was trying to do these books in a traditional way," he explains, "we'd be adding five, six, or seven people. I'm not even sure the books could be done in a traditional way."

ALTERNATIVES TO VISICALC AND SUPERCALC

VisiCalc and SuperCalc are the classics of electronic spreadsheeting, dating back to the late 1970s and early '80s. They are practical, economical, effective, and available for a wide variety of personal computers. SuperCalc, in particular, can run on most computers equipped with CP/M. Still, there are other spreadsheet programs offering "enhanced" features that deserve consideration. Chief among these are Lotus Software's 1,2,3; Microsoft's MultiPlan, and a pair of more familiar names—VisiCorp's Advanced VisiCalc and Sorcim's SuperCalc2.

The most powerful of the lot is 1,2,3—a third-generation, or integrated, software program that includes data-base management and graphics capability as well as a top-flight electronic spreadsheet. 1,2,3 is available for the IBM-PC, certain IBM-PC–compatible machines, the Texas Instrument Professional Computer, and other 16-bit machines. For a detailed discussion of this powerful business package see the next chapter on data-base management.

MultiPlan

As a software product, MultiPlan has the twin advantages of a thoroughbred pedigree—Seattle's Microsoft Corporation is one of the microcomputer industry's oldest and most illustrious software houses—and several years of development time during which it has improved on the basic features of VisiCalc and SuperCalc. MultiPlan offers a number of refinements not found on the original versions of VisiCalc or SuperCalc that are appreciated by novices and sophisticated spreadsheet users alike. Chief among these is ability to assign English language descriptions to the spreadsheet cells.

With MultiPlan, for instance, the computer can recognize and perform the equation,

Gross Margin = Revenues − Cost

as written in English. With MultiPlan's predecessors it is necessary to use the road atlas–type coordinates such as "JJ210 = AZ4 − QQ67" to express the same equation. English language descriptions permit a speedier, more intuitive creation of spreadsheet templates.

Business users will find that MultiPlan contains a number of built-in functions that can be executed without having to create your own formulas. These include net present value, standard deviation, average, index, minimum, maximum, look-up, mid, round, sum, and value, as well as the logical operators true, not, or, and, if-then, and false.

MultiPlan also contains a built-in "sort" function that lets you list the results of your calculations in both alphabetical order and numerical ranking. With MultiPlan, a sales manager, for example, can create a spreadsheet template to automatically print out sales districts by alphabetical order in one column and then rank them according to performance in a second listing. MultiPlan, like SuperCalc, runs on almost any CP/M–based personal computer. In addition, MultiPlan is available for Apple DOS or MS DOS (such as the IBM-PC) personal computers. One limitation is that Microsoft recommends that computers running MultiPlan have a minimum RAM of 128K.

Advanced VisiCalc and SuperCalc2

While VisiCalc and SuperCalc have become the no-frills programs of the spreadsheet marketplace, VisiCalc Advanced Version and SuperCalc2 now offer enhanced versions of these original spreadsheet classics.

Both programs automatically perform the basic business calculations similar to those available in MultiPlan. The advanced version of VisiCalc, for instance, offers net present value, future value, internal rate of return, annuities, and interest-rate calculations as built-in features. Moreover, advanced VisiCalc is designed with "macro" commands, while SuperCalc2 has a similar ability called the "execute" command. Macro and execute commands permit users to assign an entire series of operations to a single keyboard symbol such as the character "A." As a result, cumbersome repetitive procedures that once required extensive typing can be reduced to one or two keystrokes.

Also included in these programs are extensive enhancements that make it easier to set up, edit, and reshape your spreadsheet templates. What's more, both advanced VisiCalc and SuperCalc2 allow several spreadsheets to be linked together, updating one another, even if they are placed on separate disks.

What is the advantage of linking spreadsheets together? Consider an inexpensive set of templates marketed by Modular Tax (BOX 3361, Stamford, CT 06905). Put the Modular Tax program in one disk drive and SuperCalc Version 1.12 (an upgraded version of the original SuperCalc with some, but not all, of SuperCalc2's features) or SuperCalc2 in the other. With a few keystrokes you will have an electronic version of IRS Form 1040 on your video monitor. Modular Tax can also supply you with most other federal income tax forms and schedules. What you will see is a facsimile of Schedule A '(Itemized Deductions"), Schedule B ("Interest and Dividends"), Schedule C ("Profit/Loss from Business"), etc. What you won't see is a complex set of underlying equations that link all related schedules to one another as well as to Form 1040 and the tax tables.

What is the net effect of taking a short-term capital gain on 500 shares of IBM this summer, as opposed to waiting until December for the long-term rate? Enter your anticipated short-term profit on Line 1, Schedule D ("Capital Gains and Losses") and stroke a few command keys. You'll find your new tax liability automatically calculated on Line 71 of Form 1040. Now repeat the procedure entering your anticipated long-term capital gains on Line 2. Presto, once again your total tax liability is calculated and displayed on Form 1040. The whole process takes about three minutes.

The income tax templates happen to have been designed by a professional programmer. But the point is that with the enhanced versions of VisiCalc and SuperCalc the *potential* exists for the small-businessperson to build some highly sophisticated planning tools.

As with most computer programs, the price one pays for enhanced features is complexity. A 300-page manual, for instance, accompanies VisiCalc Advanced Version. Another possible drawback of these powerful programs is that they require powerful hardware. The prerequisite for VisiCalc Advanced Version is at least 128K of main memory.

LEADING SPREADSHEET PROGRAMS COMPARED

Relative Problem-Handling Power

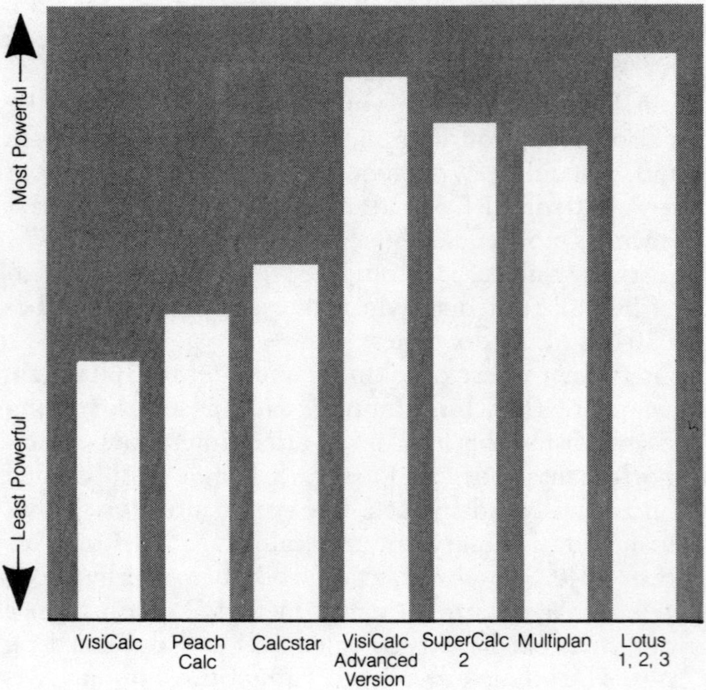

Chapter Eight

The "Magic Bullet" Data-Base Management

"If they want five-foot-eight blondes with twenty-five-inch waists, a size seven dress and six-B shoe, I just punch that up on the keyboard, and the names and phone numbers will flash up on the screen.

—Leil Lowndes,
modeling agent

THE THIRD STRATEGIC COMPONENT

Word processing and electronic spreadsheeting are micropower tools that endow small firms with the same computer advantages that have helped big businesses achieve international dominance. Both offer significant benefits through increased productivity, enhanced decision support, and reduced administrative overhead.

In an effective decision-making environment, however, a third strategic component is vital—accurate and timely information. In business and the professions, information is energy. Without hard facts, word processing and spreadsheeting are useless. They are weapons without ordnance.

Once again, the personal computer offers the solution—a concept called data-base management. It is an idea not well understood by most small-businesspeople or professionals. It will be soon. Such is the power of data-base management that within the next five years several million people who never heard of it before will be using some form of a computerized data-base management system as a central part of their daily office routine.

In essence, the data-base management program is a "magic bullet" that homes in on crucial information located within an electronic filing system. Do you need to find every customer to whom you shipped a five-fingered widget in February? Some data-base management systems will not only search your invoices for all of February's five-fingered widget buyers, they will print out the names and addresses in alphabetical order on adhesive labels. Should you want to take advantage of bulk postage rates, you may prefer to have your widget owners organized by zip code. Perhaps you need to find the total sales of left-handed widget models for the past six months. Or maybe you want the computer to automatically merge the invoice number, buyer's name, and the widget model number into a personalized letter reminding your customers it's time for their annual widget cleaning and preventive maintenance. No problem at all for the right data-base management program. Once aimed at the information you need, the data-base program is the magic bullet that strikes home, regardless of how deeply buried your target may lie.

What Is a Data Base?

For our purposes the data base is simply a collection of records: records for customers, employees, policyholders, vendors, clients, or patients. Financial records of invoices, accounts receivable, payables, sales tax receipts, or payroll. Records for case histories, budgets, property listings, job estimates, resumes, contributors, marketing plans, projections, price lists, pension plans, inventory. Data-base management is the use of the personal computer to store, sort, and retrieve the information contained in such records.

Limits and Limitations of Pre-Computer Methods

In an earlier era, paper ledgers and file folders were adequate for most recordkeeping. Not in the information age.

Today the family doctor may have medical records for as many as 10,000 patients in his files. The two-person law firm serves thousands of clients. Local insurance agents, if they are doing well, write up to three or four thousand policies a year.

It is fashionable to argue that the personal computer will replace the electric typewriter, the adding machine, and the file cabinet. I think not. The IBM Selectric still has its advantages—addressing the occasional envelope or label, completing a printed form, knocking out a brief note—limited as they may be. And I keep a pocket calculator taped to the keyboard of my computer. The arrangement is inelegant, but practical. One small irony of the information age is that it is far quicker and more convenient to perform simple computations on a $6.95 pocket calculator than on a $3,500 computer.

Likewise, a data-base management program will not replace that piece of office furniture everybody hates—the filing cabinet. For small firms, the index card and filing cabinet are necessary and important. Like the pocket calculator I use, manual filing systems have certain advantages over the personal computer. For retrieving client telephone numbers, for instance, the Rolodex beats out the personal computer every time. And certain documents—court transcripts, case histories, incoming correspondence, and all manner of proposals, reports, or printed articles—defy electronic filing, although the computer can be used effectively to index their whereabouts.

But index cards and file folders also have severe limitations. Retrieving, updating, and correlating large numbers of paper records is an enormously ineffective and labor-intensive activity. By the time that data is collected and posted throughout successive revisions of paper documents, it is often outdated and riddled with errors. As a source of useful management information—as opposed to archival storage of documents, say, for tax purposes—manual filing systems are awkward, costly, and inefficient. But for the small firm, there has been no economically feasible alternative until the personal computer.

The Need for New Methods

Not so for big business, of course. A major factor in the economic domination of giant corporations has been the efficiency of mainframe and mini computer systems in streamlining the management of business records. According to one estimate, corporate bureaucracies would need about three trillion clerical workers—750 times the earth's population—to duplicate the work being performed by big computers. But in the entrepreneurial eighties, big business's advantage is waning.

By the late 1970s a few small firms were discovering that the first generation of microcomputers—the Apples, TRS-80s, and Commodores—were capable of storing and organizing surprisingly large quantities of business records. With the advent in the early 1980s of the 16-bit central processing unit (first introduced on the IBM Personal Computer), high-density floppy disk drives, and the Winchester hard disk for microcomputers, the distinction between the micros, minis, and even mainframe computers ceased to be one of function. Says Jon Nackerud, the president of Relational Technologies, Inc., a Silicon Valley software company: "We have our own definition of what 'microcomputer' means. The 'micro' refers to the cost. The microcomputers of today look very much like the minicomputers we ran a couple of years ago."

With the new generation of powerful microcomputer hardware available, software writers have created electronic data-base management programs at all levels of sophistication, from low-power "personal filing systems" to high-power "relational data bases." Most of these programs are written specifically for the personal computer. Some have been adapted from minicomputer technology. Either way, today's software priced from $100 to $3,000 is duplicating the electronic recordkeeping tasks performed by mini and mainframe computer programs costing tens of thousands of dollars.

What Was Formerly Prohibitive Is Now Possible with the PC

By computerizing paper filing systems with data-base management software, small-business executives and professionals find that they, like their big-business counterparts, can make decisions based on accurate, relevant, and timely information. And such information, as one executive points out, "allows us to see the business more clearly and to free ourselves to think more logically." Also, electronic systems release clerical staff for more productive work in areas such as marketing, sales, or research. With data-base management, the small firm reduces administrative overhead, often dramatically, by eliminating the physical retrieval and retyping of documents, as well as the need to store and maintain similar information in multiple sets of files.

An Accountant's Nightmare Brought to Heel

In San Francisco, the Robert Henri Travel Agency has seen its revenues double over each of the past three years. "We couldn't have done it," says travel agent Bill Dias, "without our computerized data-base management systems."

Like many travel agencies, the Robert Henri Travel Agency leases a mainframe terminal for booking reservations. But for maintaining his schedules, rates, accounting, and client records, Dias uses an Apple computer and an inexpensive (list price: $229) data-base management program known as DB Master.

"The travel agency business is an accountant's nightmare," says Dias. "Fares and schedules are constantly changing, meaning that our rates and procedures are subject to constant revision." The computerized data base, however, allows Dias to revise his files almost as quickly as changes occur. "It lets us keep up-to-the-minute information on prices and schedules," he says, "as well as standing balances on any aspect of our business. A human being would go out of his mind if he had to keep track of all that."

Does the electronic filing system cut overhead at the Robert Henri Travel Agency? "We'd have had to hire two to three additional people to do what we now do with one person and the Apple," says Dias. "We estimate the Apple costs about $225 a month. To hire two or three employees would cost ten times that."

Data Tamed

With a computerized file management system, once records are placed on a floppy diskette or another mass-storage peripheral such as the hard-disk drive, a profound transformation occurs. Instead of becoming so much dead weight in the bottom of a filing cabinet—unread, unused, unwanted, and costly to revise—data entered into an electronic file-management system can lead a useful life in the mainstream of managerial activity. By capitalizing on the personal computer's power of absolute recall, files can be searched, compared, combined, and manipulated in ways no sane man or woman would contemplate with paper records and manual systems. And once a file—containing words or numbers—has been entered into the computer's memory, it can be expanded or contracted, rearranged or disarranged. But it never needs to be typed again. With some data-base packages, information from one set of records can be electronically transferred and integrated into many different documents or reports, eliminating the possibility of errors as well as the need for repeated proofreading and data verification.

VARIETIES AND VOCABULARY

Data-base management programs are now available in several dozen varieties. Three packages, however, have achieved preeminence in the marketplace. They are PFS, DB Master, and dBase II. The first two, PFS and DB Master, have proven remarkably user-friendly, yet powerful and versatile enough to handle all the file management, mailing list, accounting, and inventory-control needs of the very small company or professional office. The third program, dBase II, is touted by its distributor as "the most powerful information-handling tool you can get for your microcomputer." The use of the superlative may be arguable, but dBase II is indeed very, very powerful.

The language of data-base management is necessarily precise. The terms **record, file,** "form," and **field,** for instance, have narrowly defined meanings. A field is an individual item of information such as an invoice number, client's name, or part number. A group of these fields is called a form. Once the actual information has been entered into a form it becomes a record. All records using the same form are then combined and stored together in one file.

The data-base management file is well suited for maintaining mailing lists, inventories, and even performing many accounting fuctions. Unlike dedicated applications packages such as EasyMail, Peachtree Inventory, or General Ledger, however, the data-base programs are not specifically constructed for these jobs. Instead, they allow you, the user, to create records according to the specific parameters that you define. Then, the data-base program lets you update and search your files (and the records your files contain), and create reports or lists based on your criteria. The contribution of PFS and DB Master to the very small firm can be profound, but they do have one significant limitation.

In the previous chapter we observed a key reason for the spectacular success of electronic-spreadsheet programs: For the first time, a computer could be used as a decision-support tool without the need to define the problem in advance. Not so with "simple" data-base management packages such as PFS and DB Master. They require the user to carefully define how his records are going to be used and what questions will need to be answered *before* his forms are designed. Adding new parameters once a system has been established is sometimes possible, sometimes not. If a lawyer wants to search his case files, for instance, to find out how many hours he worked for each client during the month, it can be easily done with PFS or DB Master. But only if the program has been set up for this function at the time the lawyer originally designed his records. With these programs, in other words, you must know the *exact questions* you want answered *before* you design your electronic records.

This constrains the decision-support capability of the simple data-base management packages to solve problems that are known and can be defined before you create your electronic forms. Also, while easy to learn and operate, most simple data-base programs do not conveniently integrate with other applications software such as word processing or spreadsheeting. Although it is technically possible to electronically transfer information from PFS or DB Master into WordStar, SuperCalc, or other programs, the process can become so involved it is often easier to simply reenter the data through the keyboard.

In many small firms such limitations are unlikely to be noticed. For managers and professionals whose decisions have been premised on intuition and instinct, merely having access to accurate and relevant information on sales, cash, clients, customers, receivables, inventory, production, and other key factors will in itself be cause for celebration.

PFS—PERSONAL FILE MANAGEMENT

Not a Clowning Matter

He clowns around for a living, but when it comes to managing his business, George Zoorhis is nobody's fool. In twenty-two years as a professional clown, Zoorhis has performed with Ringling Brothers and other big-name circus acts. But only as a sideline. George Zoorhis, it seems, prefers to work free-lance. "For a clown," he says, "there's no money in circuses."

Since the 1960s, Zoorhis has appeared throughout Southern California in the role of Ronald McDonald, as well as a character of his own invention, Mr. Pockets, the clown-magician. A typical week's schedule for Zoorhis entails a dozen performances, many involving extensive logistical preparations. Weekends and holidays find him organizing two or three crews to deliver and operate his trains, floats, and other parade equipment.

Paperwork Mushroomed with Success

As his popularity grew, so did the amount of time George Zoorhis devoted to paperwork. A personal secretary was one alternative. A personal computer was another. Zoorhis's solution was the Apple III and PFS (for Personal Filing System) distributed by Software Publishing Corporation (Mountain View, CA). He uses PFS "to keep track of where I'm going, who the people are, what type of show I'm doing, what kind of equipment is needed, and who's going to get it there." He concedes these are all tasks he could accomplish with paper records. But Zoorhis estimates that PFS cuts the amount of time he spends on paperwork by half. And the time he does spend on business administration "is a lot more fun." That's an important consideration when you make people laugh for a living.

Two Minutes to Be Up and Running

Zoorhis programmed PFS to generate three basic reports: one for his work crews, one for his customers, and one for himself. Having set up the system for the kind of data he needs to retrieve, Zoorhis then transferred his paper records —names, addresses, equipment lists—onto a floppy diskette. How difficult was it to get started with PFS? "I'd say it took about two minutes to get PFS up and running," he says.

With his electronic filing system operational, Zoorhis produces his reports with little more time or effort than it takes him to enter the name of the parade or performance site, the driving instructions, and a brief description of the act he'll be performing. The PFS program automatically sorts and correlates the information and prints the results. For his crews there is a list of the equipment as well as instructions for its delivery. For himself, Zoorhis has an inventory of the costumes and props he'll need to take, where he should be, what time he should get there, and whom he should contact. And for the customer there is yet another printed statement confirming the financial and logistical arrangements. "It lets everyone know this is a real business that I'm running," he says. "It relieves the customer's worry about whether I'm going to show up or not. They appreciate getting something in the mail that shows this guy knows what he's doing. And it forces me to organize myself a little better." Not only does the computerized filing system give George Zoorhis more time to clown around, it also helps him find more business. "The system builds customer confidence. As a result they recommend me more often." And that, says George Zoorhis, "is the best kind of advertising there is."

Five-Foot-Eight Blondes

Three thousand miles away on Broadway in Manhattan, Leil Lowndes has a different kind of information management problem. As owner of Offstage, a theatrical modeling agency, her job is matching actresses and models with roles in plays, TV commercials, and print ads. Requests can be extremely specific. "It's not at all unusual," she says, "for a producer to need a girl who is blonde, five-foot-seven or eight, has a twenty-five inch waist, and wears a size-seven dress and six-B shoe."

At Offstage, such requests once meant rummaging through filing cabinets and narrowing down candidates by gradual elimination. Then Leil Lowndes purchased an Apple II Plus and PFS. "If they want five-foot-eight blondes with twenty-five-inch waists, a seven dress, and six-B shoe, I just punch that up on the keyboard," she says, "and the names and phone numbers will flash up on the screen."

How does it work? "You start with a blank screen," she says. "Then you create a standard form that will be used for every girl. Within the form you designate as many individual fields as you need for things like height, weight, hair color, eyes." Once these forms have been filled in with the appropriate data—thus becoming actual records—useful information can be retrieved by matching any combination of fields. Five-foot-eight blondes, for instance.

PFS Report for the Financial End

Software Publishing Corporation also distributes a program called PFS Report. "You can use PFS report," Ms. Lowndes says, "to add, subtract, multiply, divide, or take percentages of any particular field." She uses the report program to "keep track of the financial end of things." She can, for instance, generate a weekly statement on what each of her models has earned, who the clients were, and what the agency commissions should be.

For a more "intellectual" application of a PFS, Leil Lowndes points to a data-base system she has designed for her husband, Barry Farber, a late-night New York City radio commentator. Farber uses PFS to maintain what he calls his "humor file." "When Barry hears something he thinks is especially precious," she says, "he jots it down and gives it to his secretary to enter in the PFS system. When he does a show on a particular individual or issue he punches in the topic and the computer prints out all the related jokes, sayings, and little phrases that he has been saving up." Has the computer improved the radio show? "I can tell you this," says Leil Lowndes, "he would need at least one more full-time person on his staff to replace it."

Helping Keep Track of Weird Provisions

In Willingboro, New Jersey, general law partner William J. Kearns, Jr., has found that PFS is changing the way he practices law. "What used to take a day," says Kearns, "now takes fifteen minutes."

Kearns is referring to the preparation of reports for major clients, some of whom have as many as thirty cases pending. "PFS is enabling me to produce and retrieve information in ways I couldn't do before," he says. "With a little bit of updating on a weekly basis I can prepare a status report for my clients in about fifteen minutes. Before I would have to plow through each individual file, dictate a report, have it drafted, proofread it, have it typed, and probably proofread it a second time." And that, says Kearns, used to take "anywhere from three hours to a day." How much time did he have to invest in mastering PFS? "It took about thirty minutes to learn," he says.

Not only does he get out his reports faster, Kearns also finds PFS helps make his records more useful as well. He does not store the entire contents of every case in the computer, but Kearns does use PFS to index the important characteristics of every case. "With PFS I can search by type of case, such as matrimonial or personal injury, as well as by client name. If I know we drafted a partnership agreement including some really weird provisions, but can't remember the client's name, I can go to the computer and hit 'PARTNERSHIPS.' It pulls them all out for me. Then I can either scan them on the screen or list them on the printout until I say, 'damn it, that's the one I want.' " He then goes to his paper file records and digs out a copy of those "really weird provisions."

Kearns is clearly impressed by the power of PFS in the law practice. "Quite frankly," he says, "I foresee the day when we have a personal computer on the desk of every attorney and secretary, both in the office and at home."

DB MASTER—LIST POWER

Similar in operation, though more powerful than PFS, is the data-base management package known as "DB Master," distributed by Stoneware Publishing Microcomputer Products in San Rafael, California. Businessman Barry Wolkon began using DB Master to maintain mailing lists at this $3-million-a-year sports complex, the Rockland Sport-O-Rama. Later, when he founded a second business to distribute industrial chemicals, Wolkon adapted DB Master to handle the firm's entire information needs, including inventory, accounting, payroll, and billing. "I just took DB Master and designed my own programs. There are very few restrictions on it," he says. "Although I think the people at Stoneware would be very surprised to know some of the applications I'm using it for."

DB Master Instead of $50,000 in Programming Fees

Wolkon was originally attracted to DB Master's versatility in maintaining and sorting mailing lists. "I dealt with mailing lists many years ago on large IBM computers," says Wolkon. "I can safely say that the $175 I spent on DB Master bought me the equivalent of what once cost $40,000 or $50,000 in programming fees."

Wolkon keeps approximately five thousand names on the Sport-O-Rama mailing list that he "uses extensively throughout the year for promotional mailings." His records are coded so mailings can be broken into interest and age groups such as men's tennis, racketball or high school ice hockey. The same records also serve as Wolkon's master membership list. "Once a month," he says "we run a sort and pull out the names of everyone whose membership will be expiring six or seven weeks down the road. We send them a mailing, then turn the list over to our salesmen to follow up with telephone calls.

300,000 Alphabetized Records

One feature that makes DB Master so useful for maintaining such records is, in the words of Stoneware's Frank Colin, "that DB Master allows the user to keep alphabetized records that are spread over many volumes of floppy diskettes." When the memory capacity of one diskette is exhausted, DB Master automatically "pushes" records located at the end of the alphabet onto a second diskette. This process continues to a limit of 200 diskettes for any one file. This leaves Barry Wolkon approximately 295,000 more records to fill before he is obliged to open a second mailing list file for the Sport-O-Rama.

Wolkon feels his mailing list capability gives him a significant competitive advantage. "Nobody else in the rink business in my area has been able to figure out how to do it," he says. "I know of people who have tried to duplicate my system manually, but they've always dropped it after a short while. It's just too overwhelming. I don't think it's possible to do these things clerically."

Peripheral Uses of DB Master

Along with his mailing list, Wolkon soon developed what he calls "peripheral" uses for DB Master. "We maintain our plus-or-minus inventory records and our dollar inventory records for the snack bar using DB Master," he says. About one hundred items are included. Wolkon also developed a maintenance directory with DB Master for his engineering staff. All equipment used in the skating rink and health club is cross-referenced by vendor name and part number.

The real value of data-base management, however, became apparent to Barry Wolkon the year he founded Bowmark Industries, a regional distributor of industrial chemicals. The new business allowed Wolkon to start from the ground up, designing forms to meet all of Bowmark's recordkeeping requirements. Wolkon has built himself an order-driven inventory-, accounting-, and sales-reporting system. Based on salesmen's orders, Bowmark's one-woman staff uses the computer to create invoice records. "Out of that invoice file," says Wolkon, "I can generate all the financial, sales, and inventory reports I need to run the business."

For his salesmen, Wolkon creates a monthly sales report "with a full commission report showing every invoice that was billed, who the customer was, what commission rates apply, and how much the salesman is owed." The computer automatically generates a monthly sales journal totaling all receipts, including sales tax. There is a monthly receivables list of open accounts and the amounts due. Every two weeks the computer supplies Bowmark's bookkeeper with an aged receivables report of accounts thirty, sixty, and ninety days past-due. And for his sales manager, Wolkon generates a monthly statement comparing each salesman's projected sales volume against his actual total. "Last quarter, DB Master even did my full New York State Sales Tax Report."

Set It Up and It Runs Itself

Surprisingly, designing the system and generating his reports proved "fantastically easy. Just follow the instructions on the machine. Unlike PFS, the report generator is included as part of the DB Master software package," Wolkon says. One add-on Wolkon did purchase, however, was a package known as Utility Pak #1. With it he can change the fields in his records. For instance, he can add a new category to his mailing lists such as "occupation" or "education" without having to reprogram—and reenter—an entire file.

Wolkon sees that the primary advantage of his computerized data-base system is in enhanced managerial control. "Most small businesses go bankrupt," he says, "because of poor controls. When they start out they have some good salesmen, some good ideas, a good product. But they don't really have any control." With the system he has designed, Wolkon points out, "we can do our receivables aging every week if necessary." And that, he says, "can be essential for cash flow in the new business."

But isn't there a price to be paid for such up-to-the-minute information? Wolkon thinks not. "I've been in comparably sized firms where they have four or five women making up reports, doing billing, and keeping track of everything." At Bowmark there is "one woman who spends maybe twenty hours a week on the bookkeeping." About the reports he uses to manage his new business he says, "Once you set them up, they run themselves."

dBase II—RELATIONAL POWER

Barry Wolkon's DB Master programs are ideal for monitoring and controlling routine business functions. But what happens to these simple data-base programs—or a paper record system for that matter—when an unanticipated inquiry is necessary?

Consider the dilemma of one family doctor. A revolutionary new treatment for hypertension has been approved by the FDA. This physician can wait for patients with a history of high blood pressure to come to her, which may take a year or longer. Or she can attempt to notify high-risk cases that the new treatment is available. But with 7,500 records in her files how does she sort out which patients to notify? The answer is . . . she doesn't. The task is too overwhelming to consider. A manual search of 7,500 records would take about two hundred fifty hours and cost thousands of dollars. Even simple data-base systems such as PFS and DB Master won't help, unless they have been specifically designed in advance to sort and list records on the basis of blood pressure readings.

Unforeseen Problems

The ideal file-management system, it seems, should have the flexibility to provide the retrieval of data from records that can help to solve *unforeseen* problems. In addition, these electronic files should be capable of being transferred directly into other software applications packages for word processing, spreadsheeting, and perhaps even the computerized generation of charts and graphs. Such features do exist, in the form of a type of file-management software known as the "relational data-base management program." But while relational data-base programs are immensely powerful, they are not for the novice, as one look at the over-300-page manual for the popular program dBase II will confirm.

At the Galleria Clinic in Houston, Texas, Dr. Don Winston and computer programmer Charles Mitchel are using dBase II to devise a system that utilizes patient records as a tool for practicing medicine *and* administering a medical practice. With their system, for instance, patient names can be sorted and listed according to certain variables, including diagnostic criteria. Finding all occurrences of high blood pressure is simply a matter of entering a computer command such as "LIST PATIENTS WITH BLOOD PRESSURE >160-90."

Not only does the computer search every patient record to extract the right names—the "inquiry" function—but the dBase II program can also be combined with other applications packages such as word processing and accounting. Thus, the names of the hypertensive patients can be automatically merged into personalized letters and printed out on a roll of **tractor feed** stationery. What was an impossible manual task for the family practitioner and her paper records requires only an hour or two of secretarial time at the Galleria Clinic.

The capability to search and "capture" patient files by variables such as clinical history, prescribed medicines, or demographic factors is not all the Galleria Clinic's program can do. The program also has the ability to spot the kind of potentially troublesome details the harried doctor is prone to overlook. Physicians using the Galleria Clinic system can enter dosage instructions, adverse reactions, warnings, and contraindications for their most frequently prescribed medications. Each time a drug is prescribed, the patient can be given a hard-copy printout of the proper dosage instructions. The computer alerts the doctor to potential allergic reactions or other complications that may be buried in the fine detail of the patient's medical record.

Central Records

The Galleria Clinic's system also schedules appointments, keeps track of doctor and laboratory fees, and even types up bills and fills out medical insurance and workmen's compensation forms. Yet, behind these many tasks lies one simple idea: By centralizing all the clinic's records in one set of electronic file drawers, as it were, Winston and Mitchel have created a highly efficient recordkeeping environment. Once a patient's name and address has been entered at the keyboard it will never need to be typed or handwritten again. Whenever it is necessary to address a letter, send a bill, or fill out a medical insurance form, the computer automatically looks up the appropriate information in its memory, executes any mathematical calculations, and prints out the results on standard forms. Such tasks are possible because the centralized data-base program can be hooked into specific applications packages such as accounts receivable, word processing, or doctor scheduling. By maintaining just one set of central files —a true data base—information can be retrieved and processed with maximum efficiency, both for the people who are entering the data and for the computer.

Relational

The data base at the Galleria Clinic is "relational" in that each variable entered into the computer—patient names, dates, medical procedures, drugs, billing data, therapies, family medical history, blood types, disease, diagnoses, etc. —can be sorted, correlated, and listed according to a vast number of criteria. 'LIST ALL CASES OF HEPATITIS TYPE B BETWEEN 10-1 AND 11-1.' Or perhaps, 'LIST ALL PATIENTS CURRENTLY UNDER TREATMENT WITH AMPICILLIN.'

Because they can sort, correlate, and analyze data in ways not previously foreseen, relational data-base programs emulate a key step in the decision-making process. And relational data-base management programs such as dBase II use the computer's unfailingly precise memory to discover relationships between pieces of information. The art of thinking, says science writer Michael Harwood, "demands an exceptional ability to concentrate, to remember, to make connections between ideas." Remembering and making connections between pieces of information is precisely what the relational data-base program does best. Programs like dBase II, in short, are helping managers and professionals think faster, more efficiently, and more effectively.

VERTICAL APPLICATIONS PACKAGES

Within the software industry the Galleria Clinic's program belongs to a category known as the "vertical applications package." Vertical applications software has long been available to institutions able to afford a mini or mainframe computer. The notion of using such packages on personal computers, however, is still novel. But it is an idea whose time has come now that personal computers from companies like IBM, Apple, Hewlett-Packard, and DEC are eclipsing all but the most powerful minicomputers.

For many, perhaps most, small firms in which computer know-how is limited and managerial time is precious, even superfriendly systems such as Apple's Lisa may not be the final answer. What are really needed are tried-and-true software packages *tailored to solving the problems faced in a specific profession or industry*. Especially if this software can be presented in a low-cost, easy-to-use "turnkey" package that is ready to crank up and run.

Use of Vertical Applications in Insurance

Few small-businesspeople have a greater need for such a vertical applications package than the typical independent insurance agent. "In the insurance business much of the premium cost goes into paper shuffling," says Jim Cappell, a Princeton, New Jersey, insurance industry consultant. "Some lines of insurance are more than fifty percent overhead."

Early in the microcomputer revolution, insurance agent Jay Gillis of Holyoke, Massachusetts, recognized the potential of the personal computer for cutting overhead in his business. Gillis, with a background in data processing, set out to develop a system to automate his basic recordkeeping needs. For several years, however, he was frustrated by the inability of his programs to cope with the 3,500 active policies he needed to manage. Then Gillis found dBase II. "The amazing thing about dBase II," he says, "is that it allows the microcomputer to take the place of the minis and mainframes."

Using dBase II as his foundation, Gillis developed an applications package that "does the insurance systems, the accounts receivable, the accounts payable, the general ledger for the independent agent, and concatenates them all with WordStar." Does *what* with WordStar? "In addition to doing all the accounting and data-processing work," Gillis explains, "the system incorporates WordStar to perform many marketing and sales functions as well." And it can do it for up to 8,000 client accounts on any one of over forty personal-computer models.

Gillis, for example, can ask a computer to list all clients who have an automobile policy with his firm, but do not have home-owner, personal-liability, or life insurance. Not only does the computer produce a list of names, but built in to the system is a collection of pithy sales letters. The computer automatically selects one of these standardized letters from its memory and merges it with personalized information from the policy records. A secretary merely has to tear the letters off the printer as they are typed, slip them into a window envelope, and deliver them to the post office. The letters, of course, are printed out in zip code order to take advantage of bulk postage rates.

Gillis has programmed the system to search policy records for other variables with potential sales applications, including age, occupation, and marital status. One letter, for example, reminds registered nurses of their vulnerability to job-related legal suits, and suggests they protect their careers with a professional liability policy.

Gillis also used WordStar to build a dunning letter into his accounts receivable system. Whenever a listing of aged accounts is requested, the program automatically generates overdue notices. Once again, pertinent data from the policy records, including the amount owed and how long it has been overdue, is merged into the text of the letter.

At one time Jay Gillis's prime incentive was to develop a program for solving his own data-management needs. But with a quarter of a million independent insurance agents looking for a similar solution, Jay Gillis now spends more time selling his applications software than insurance.

One-third the Cost

Fred Holland was among the first to buy Gillis's program. As co-owner of the Brown-Smith Insurance Agency—a $1.5 million-a-year independent, located in Macon, Georgia—Holland had made up his mind that the time to automate was at hand. "I wouldn't say the manual systems were unworkable," he recalls, "but they were terribly inefficient. Closing the books was beginning to take over a week. And with a number of different people handling the records on 2,500 accounts there were always errors."

Holland was considering a $40,000 minicomputer system offered by a major insurance company. Instead, he purchased a Zenith microcomputer and had his local computer store install both the computer and Jay Gillis's software package. "Our system will do the same thing as the minicomputer," says Holland, "but it does them for one-third the cost."

There was no special training necessary. Holland's secretaries were able to work the system simply by following the prompts on their screen. When he did hit a snag, Holland found Gillis was always available to help sort it out. "We paid for the computer and its software approximately what it would have cost us to hire a qualified person for one year," says Holland. After three months of operation Holland reports that the system "is doing the work of two full-time people." So where are those employees now? "Spending their time on things that make us some money," says Fred Holland, "like selling insurance."

A Growing Trend in Software

In the years ahead, vertical applications packages like the one developed by Jay Gillis for independent insurance agencies will become a major segment of the booming microcomputer software industry. Some vertical applications packages will be downsized from existing minicomputer software to run on powerful 16- and 32-bit micros. One sign of this trend is the recent release of an extraordinarily powerful relational data-base program, now called "Micro Ingres," for 16-bit machines such as the IBM-PC. Previously, Ingres was available only for DEC minicomputers at a cost of $35,000 per program. In the micro version it is priced at under $1,000. Like dBase II, Micro Ingres will make a potent vehicle on which micro-power innovators can build vertical applications packages selling for two or three thousand dollars that just a few short years or even months ago could not have been purchased for ten times the price.

Finding good vertical applications packages will provide the micro novice with a stiff, but by no means insurmountable, challenge. Local computer stores, unfortunately, will not be much help. "Vertical applications packages are too complex for the typical storefront operation," says Adam Green, a leading dBase II consultant. "The market is too narrow and the customers will nitpick you to death with details. I see the stores staying with general applications software like VisiCalc, but not the vertical applications packages."

The Data on Data Bases

So where does one learn about the existence of vertical applications packages? Professional and industry trade publications is one way. Contacting the distributors of relational data-base programs is another. (See David Kruglinski's *Data Base Management Systems,* published by Osborne/McGraw-Hill, for a list of distributors and reviews.) Ashton-Tate, for instance, the Culver City, California–based distributor of dBase II, provides an "applications junction" computer printout listing many of the vertical applications packages under development for use with dBase II.

Evaluating these packages may seem a forbidding task, but it can be both simple and enlightening. After speaking to the developer of a vertical applications package that suits your needs, ask him to recommend two or three firms comparable to your own that have been using the package for at least three months, and then interview them. John Klienhammer, a California contractor who is also the author of an accounting and job-costing package for a general contractor, suggests starting with the companies that are the most geographically distant. In any event, it's been my experience that the people who are pioneering in the micro-power applications are eager to discuss their experiences, and are candid with the details. A few phone calls is all it should take to find out what other users think of any specific program, and why.

INTEGRATED SOFTWARE

As we move into the mid-1980s, among the hottest topics in the micro-world is the issue of integrated software. This is especially true when the integrated software packages are combined with hardware devices such as the mouse found on the Apple Lisa and Xerox Star computers, or available as an add-on feature for other machines such as the IBM-PC by using a software/hardware package such as VisiOn.

The concept behind integrated software is excellent, regardless of whether the integrated software comes bundled with a computer, as with the various programs included in the purchase price of Lisa, or bought separately, as with Lotus's 1,2,3 or VisiOn. The basic idea is that with *one set of commands* you can do word processing, spreadsheeting, graphics, data-base management, or whatever applications happen to be included in your integrated package. With the earlier generations of software it is necessary to learn totally different—and sometimes conflicting—commands for every application. Pressing the **CONTROL** key plus the letter "G" in WordStar deletes whatever character happens to be at the cursor position. However, pushing the **CONTROL** key and the letter "G" does completely different things in other programs such as SuperCalc or DB Master.

Convenience of Integration

The integration of commands is primarily a convenience factor. Going from, say, WordStar to SuperCalc is a little like switching from a car with the gearshift on the column to having "four on the floor." You simply have to get used to different ways of telling the machine how to do what you want.

A second, more practical advantage of integration, however, is the ability to move information from program to program. With "stand alone" programs such as WordStar and SuperCalc it is sometimes possible to shift information from one program to another without retyping it through the keyboard. But working out the complex file manipulations can often be more trouble than it is worth. Colin Gilboy, a San Francisco–based sales representative, uses his personal computer on weekends to score the results of a junior sailing program at his yacht club. After finally mastering the procedure for electronically moving the number from his spreadsheet into a word-processing program, Gilboy went back to the old-fashioned way of doing it and simply retyped the numbers. "It turned out to be faster and easier," he says, "than screwing around with a bunch of complicated file transfer procedures." With integrated software, data can be easily transferred from program to program, often within seconds.

Integration on the Executive Level

When the personal computer is used primarily on the departmental level in a small firm to perform just one or two specific tasks such as word processing or inventory control, the need for integrated software is marginal. But integrated software does offer a significant advantage at the convergence of the various departmental information streams—at the executive level.

1,2,3

One integrated program especially worthy of consideration is the 1,2,3 program designed by Mitch Kapor. Kapor is a 32-year-old Cambridge, Massachusetts, programmer who earned considerable renown, not to mention over $1.2 million, by writing three successful programs during the late 1970s—Tiny Troll, the first business and statistics package for the Apple II, as well as VisiPlot and VisiTrend/Plot.

Kapor's integrated package—1,2,3—contains a spreadsheet, which in the words of Gregg Williams, Senior Editor of *Byte,* "has all the features you've ever seen on spreadsheets." Next, 1,2,3 has a graphics package that enables users to graph up to four variables taken from, say, a spreadsheet of an annual balance sheet. After a little practice, most users say they can create graphs from their spreadsheets *in less than*

THREE POPULAR DATA-BASE MANAGEMENT PROGRAMS COMPARED

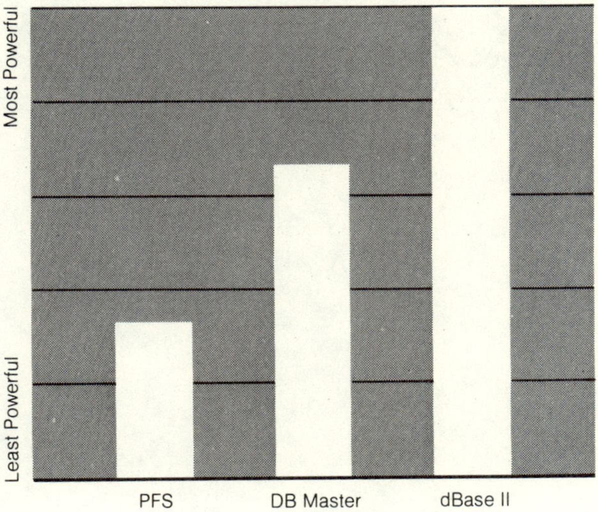

RELATIVE DATA-HANDLING POWER

one minute. And where does the data for the spreadsheet come from? Part three of 1,2,3 is a data-base program. The data base program in 1,2,3 is not as powerful as dBase II. But it seems that Mitch Kapor has taken that into consideration, too. He's designed 1,2,3 to hook into dBase II, just in case.

Phil Paul, whose Sudbury, Massachusetts–based Strategic Decisions Company is among the nation's leading microcomputer consulting firms, sees 1,2,3 as the software centerpiece of a powerful executive workstation. As a spreadsheet, he finds 1,2,3 unbeatable. "I've worked with VisiCalc, Advanced VisiCalc, SuperCalc, and MultiPlan," he says, "and clearly 1,2,3 does more than anybody." Paul is also extremely impressed by the graphics and data-base capabilities of the program. His one criticism, a common complaint about most of the powerful software programs, is that "it may be harder to learn. There are more nooks and crannies in it," he says, "than in a Thomas's English Muffin."

Attempting to master all of 1,2,3's capabilities at once, however, is neither wise nor necessary. "It is the kind of package," points out Phil Paul, "that, if you bought it today for $495, would last you a long time. You could forget there are graphics and a data base in there and just use it for a spreadsheet. It's just $95 more than somebody else's spreadsheet. Then, when you're ready, you'll have an integrated data-base and graphics capability just waiting for you."

Chapter Nine

The Big Five of Small-Business Accounting

We were not organized before we went with computerized accounting. The computer organized us. It told us that we must send purchase orders out. It told us that we had to maintain a chart of accounts. It told us that we had to do things in a certain systematic way, and that's the way we do them.

—***Maurice Maio,***
Maio Plumbing, Heating & Solar

SOME SCENARIOS WITH AN AUTOMATED ACCOUNTING SYSTEM

Balancing Flamingos

The basis of all modern accounting is the double-entry balance sheet where debits go on the left, credits on the right. "Debit-left, credit-right *by hand*" is how Tom Collins describes the manual accounting system that served Flamingo Homes Sales during its formative years. But by the early 1980s, the Collinses' "ma and pa" mobile-home dealership had become a $4-million-a-year business. With "debit-left, credit-right by hand" Peggy Collins was devoting "better than thirty days working until three or four in the morning to close the books every year."

Mrs. Collins still keeps Flamingo's books. But the all-night marathons are ancient history. Today Flamingo's accounting is done in "no more than a couple of hours a day" using a personal computer and a set of off-the-shelf software packages for general ledger, accounts receivable, accounts payable, payroll, and inventory. The personal computer, says Tom Collins, "has transformed that job from absolute drudgery to something that is fairly much of a pleasure."

Crossing Curves

Manual bookkeeping *is* dull, boring, and oppressive. Massachusetts publisher Dennis Curtin speaks for small-businesspeople and professionals alike when he says of the bookkeeping system at his firm: "I don't *want* to go down to that level of the way the company is operated. I pay a bookkeeper good money to keep my entries in the correct place."

But Curtin is also eager to get his bookkeeper on "an accounting software package as soon as possible." The reason? Much of the raw data Curtin uses for projecting his firm's sales, production, and cash flow comes from the accounting system. Timely and accurate accounting data—as uninteresting as the routine entry and posting of transactions may be—is essential to Dennis Curtin's financial planning and control.

Why isn't publisher Curtin, with his expertise in financial spreadsheeting, already using a microcomputer accounting system? "I'm not a computer hobbyist," he says. "I'm not interested in testing software for small manufacturers. I want a software package that has reached critical mass in the marketplace. So far there's nobody talking in consensus about any particular accounting software package."

What about hiring a consultant to find and install a suitable package? "The curves on buying a computer and hiring a consultant to make it run have crossed," says Curtin. "You can spend $4,000 on an IBM-PC and $5,000 on hiring someone to set up the software."

Like Curtin, few small-business executives are enthusiastic about the prospect of $50 to $100 an hour in consulting fees. In the very small firm with an unadorned double-entry bookkeeping system, the need for extensive consultation is questionable. In the larger firm with special accounting requirements, some professional assistance is advisable, if not inevitable.

Implementing any accounting system is more complex and costly than word processing, spreadsheeting, or even data-base management. The software package that works famously for the professional service with 400 clients and no inventory can be a disaster for the wholesaler with 4,000 customers and 15,000 items in the warehouse. But when computerized bookkeeping works, the benefits are profound.

Pays for Itself

Micro-power accounting can pay for itself within a year by reducing the time that business managers, professionals, and office personnel spend on the books. And a micro-power accounting system does more than merely keep the books. Invoices, purchase orders, monthly customer statements, and dozens of internal financial reports can be *automatically* prepared and *typed* on standard forms, often complete with bar graphs and pie charts to highlight essential data. Most manual typing and proofreading is eliminated. Key indicators of the firm's financial health—cash flow, inventory, aged receivables, aged payables, sales, and production levels—are monitored on a day-to-day basis if necessary. Potential problems can be identified before they get out of control.

Also, as one New Jersey bookkeeper points out, "If you make a mistake and your entries don't balance, you *have* to correct it. The program won't let you continue until you do."

How much can computerized accounting save the small business? "In terms of dollars and cents," says Tom Collins, "to get what we're getting now, I would have to hire a full-time bookkeeper at fifteen to twenty thousand dollars a year. Even so, a bookkeeper can't offer the kind of management information the computer is providing. I don't know how you put a dollar-and-cents value on meaningful information that lets you orchestrate and fine-tune the small business."

Automating a Seventy-five-Year-Old Accounting System

David Danson also uses computerized accounting software to generate management information his manual accounting system couldn't provide.

The Dave White Company had been distributing meat to New York City–area restaurants for nearly three-quarters of a century when Danson joined as the firm's comptroller. Danson recognized that the seventy-five-year-old bookkeeping system needed automation, but the cost of mainframes, minis, and even timesharing services was out of the question. A Radio Shack TRS-80 personal computer was not. "One of our office employees quit," recalls Danson, "and instead of replacing her, we found that her work could be done by the computer." Like Tom Collins, Danson concentrated on computerizing the big five accounting functions—general ledger, accounts receivable, accounts payable, payroll, and inventory.

How did the administrative staff respond to the new computer? "Everyone accepted the system," says Danson. "The start-up time was extremely quick. The greatest factor involved in getting the system running was entering the information. By the time the data had been entered our people were ready to 'live with it.' In fact, the staff actually looks forward to working with it now."

With the basics under control, Danson turned to finding new ways to put his accounting software to work. Most of the restaurants served by the Dave White Company operate on a "rotating menu basis." Says Danson: "The computer allows us to anticipate the cyclical needs of our customers so that we can supply them with their orders while keeping our inventory low." Before the TRS-80 such inventory planning "was just too cumbersome."

And that's not all. "The computer offers the potential to do a lot more things with the business—both internally and externally," says Danson. "It's opened up other areas of business for the company." For instance, the TRS-80 can generate detailed product-use reports that help Danson's customers with *their* inventory planning. "We wouldn't think of doing that manually," says Danson.

The bottom line of comptroller Danson's experience with automated accounting is better service, lower prices, and a leaner, more competitive firm. "The computer enables us to keep our overhead down," says Danson. "We remain profitable even with a lower markup. As a result we're growing faster than ever before."

Eyes Closed

What do office workers and bookkeepers have to say about automated accounting systems? Does the personal computer reduce their responsibilities and make work less interesting? Not if the experience of Sharon Divincent, office manager for Artistocrat International, an institutional hors d'oeuvres manufacturer, is any indication. "I love working on the computer," she says, "I really do. Within a week I was able to use the system efficiently. Now I can practically do it with my eyes closed."

At the height of the season, Aristocrat carries a payroll of sixty to eighty production workers. But only one employee keeps the books in Aristocrat's front office. "With the computer," says Sharon Divincent, "I run the entire office by myself, without any help. My daily job involves making invoices, entering incoming payments, purchase orders, and bills; writing out the checks for accounts payable and payroll; tracking inventory and maintaining aging reports." She also closes the books and produces Artistocrat's monthly sales and inventory reports ("it gives great reports") and financial statements. "And when I walk out the door at five or five-thirty," she adds, "my work is completed. I'm not the type of person who has work lying around the desk."

Confidence

The personal computer is building Ms. Divincent's confidence, not reducing it. She is proud of the workload she carries and of her own productivity. "I laugh sometimes because my friends work in offices where there are three or four girls and no computer," she explains. "One girl will be doing accounts receivable, someone else will be doing accounts payable, and another person will be typing up invoices. I do all that myself. And in one day too.

"The other day I did our end-of-month statements. I have a friend who says it takes her a week to get the customer statements out. Ours were in the mail in half an hour. In other companies it takes four people to do what I do in one day. And believe it or not, I have fun with it."

One reason Ms. Divincent enjoys her work: The computer takes over the mechanical drudgery of repeatedly posting entries, looking up accounts, figuring payroll, and even typing out the checks, invoices and reports. "If I want to know what customer ordered what in November," she points out, "I can ask the computer for a 'customer analysis,' and it will print out exactly what that customer bought. You don't have to plow through files and endless paperwork to get your information. And the results are printed out. You can get a 'receivables aging,' a 'payables aging,' a 'sales analysis by part number,' an 'accounts receivable distribution report,' inventory reports, payroll reports. It writes out the checks, it does the payroll register summary, payroll posting registers, employee master listing, check register . . . it's just really outrageous."

Instead of "dehumanizing" her office, Sharon Divincent says automated bookkeeping makes it a "friendlier" and less pressured place to work. "With the system, you have more time since everything gets done so quickly. There's more time to call up customers and talk to them. More time to be friendly on the phone without feeling pressured that there's a lot of work to be done. With the computer there is no pressure of that sort. Just more time to show people your product."

BUT IS THE AUTOMATED ACCOUNTING SYSTEM NECESSARY?

Collins, Danson, and Divincent are fortunate. They are pleased with automated accounting because their software does what it supposed to do. But just as good accounting software can help the small firm, bad software—or even good software that is badly matched to the firm's accounting needs—can undermine years of goodwill and honest effort. "You probably don't need an automated system that reduces cash flow by getting out late and inaccurate billing, loses track of inventory and receivables, promotes tardy and inappropriate buying and scheduling decisions, alienates customers and employees, and takes up all of your time, desperately trying to patch up the damage," computer consultant Donald Shaw writes in *Your Small Business Computer*. "Yet such a situation is an uncomfortably frequent outcome in the business-oriented small computer field."

There are over 600 microcomputer accounting programs in the marketplace. Perhaps sixty are worth considering. How do you find the right one? Begin by asking whether automated accounting is necessary at all.

"I'm gonna catch hell for this," Don French told an editor of *Personal Computing* magazine, "but I've tried everybody's software, and it's simply not worth it for me to keep my books on a computer." Such a statement might be unexceptional, were Don French not president of a well-known accounting software house. "We're a low-volume, high-price company," French explains. "I might have only fifty transactions a month. In addition to that, I have a payroll of only ten or twelve." In other words, his accounting requirements don't justify a full-blown, computerized double-entry accounting program. Even with good software available at trade prices, Don French is better served by a sharp pencil, a couple of sheets of ledger paper, and his check register.

Many low-volume, high-margin manufacturers, distributors, retailers, and small offices fall into this same category. If the payroll includes a dozen or less workers, monthly receivables number under 100, and the mechanics of bookkeeping are not siphoning time from more productive work, then the business is probably better off with manual books. The exception is the small firm that is in trouble with its accounting.

"There is a widespread belief among small-businesspeople," says a St. Louis CPA, "that if you are disorganized, the computer will only make things worse. With personal-computer accounting software, I find the reverse is actually true. The computer imposes order on what is often a chaotic manual accounting system."

ALTERNATIVES TO THE ACCOUNTING SOFTWARE PACKAGES

Home-Grown Bookkeeping

What of the very small business operating on a cash accounting basis that isn't ready for a full-blown, computerized accounting system, but still wants to use micro-power to cut the drudgery of keeping the books in order? For starters, if the price of a computer is justified for some other office application such as word processing or spreadsheeting, a home-grown cash accounting system can be cobbled together from existing software.

The most widely used of all micro-computer programs—word processing—can be adapted into a simple cash accounting system. The key is finding a word-processing package that performs arithmetic *within* a word-processing document. Not many do. Perfect Writer by Perfect Software in Berkeley, California, is among the few that offer such features as column totaling and crossfooting as part of the standard package.

Third-party math enhancement upgrades, however, are available for many widely sold word-processing packages. WordStar users, for instance, can purchase an add-on program called Math★ that allows addition, subtraction, division, and multiplication during word processing.

When Math★ and WordStar are combined, rudimentary sales, cash disbursement, expense journals, and even a general ledger can be created as word-processing documents. The computer will automatically total columns and rows. With practice it is even possible to post totals between accounts using the WordStar "block move" function. Invoices and monthly statements can even be generated by "merge-printing" data, say, from an accounts receivable file with a mailing list. But beware that the "word processor as bookkeeper" is adequate only for the simplest accounting needs. As with the other home-grown options, the time saved by automated accounting may be offset by the hours devoted to tinkering with your program. "The difference," says a Wisconsin dairy products distributor, "is in the quality of the experience. The computer is fun. It's intellectually stimulating. Every time I work with it I think of some new way to improve the business."

For Programmers Only

The executive with a penchant for BASIC programming can try his hand at writing a simple sales journal or charge account program. BASIC programs can be created from scratch, as it were, or by adapting a public-domain version from periodicals such as *Compute!* or the book *How to Profit from Your Personal Computer* by T. G. Lewis. Copying a computer program out of a book or magazine and entering it through the keyboard is a simple process—*if* the program is written in the same dialect of BASIC used by your computer. Also, beware that it takes but one inadvertent slip on the keyboard to enter a bug into the program.

Ninety-nine times out of one hundred, programming errors result in an inoperable system and a conspicuous "ERROR MESSAGE" directing you where to find the problem. But not always. A nasty bug, for instance, might print $44.00 on customer statements, instead of $440.00. Yet otherwise the program seems to work perfectly. To catch hidden bugs before they become fatal, run the program side by side with your manual system for three to six months to check for hidden flaws.

Using Your Spreadsheet

In reality, writing or even adapting a BASIC accounting program demands greater intimacy with the workings of the personal computer than is necessary or even advisable for most executives. A far easier and more practical technique is to design your books using a spreadsheet such as VisiCalc or SuperCalc. Since the spreadsheet is essentially an "accountant's ledger pad" to begin with, "programming" VisiCalc or Super Calc to keep running totals, perform crossfoots, and balance debits and credits is something even computer neophytes can accomplish.

With the publication of the books *Doing Business with VisiCalc* and *Doing Business with SuperCalc* by Stanley R. Trost, setting up your own basic accounting system with a spreadsheet program has been even further simplified. After a few hours of training in the fundamentals of VisiCalc or SuperCalc, any beginner can follow Trost's step-by-step recipes for setting up a sales register, check register, expense register, invoice generator, income statement, and even a comparative balance sheet and job log. Once your accounting is under control, you can also use Trost's recipes for a personal income-tax package. Using Trost's SuperCalc instructions, I computerized Form 1040 as well as Schedules A,B,E, and Y on a rainy April afternoon. Should you take itemized or standard deductions? Change a figure anywhere on Trost's templates and your taxable income automatically appears on Line 34. If you are eligible to use Schedule Y, the program even calculates your taxes as well.

By using predesigned templates like those in Mr. Trost's books, not only can you avoid many difficult hours spent reinventing the wheel, but you also learn how to use built-in spreadsheet functions that automatically calculate averages, choose values, count results, use "look-up" tables, and even compute the net present value of a series of cash flows. These functions streamline any spreadsheet program, but the typical novice lacks the know-how to take advantage of them.

Using a Data-Base Program

Another alternative for the small business or professional office is to program the books within a powerful data-base management program such as DB Master or dBase II. Both spreadsheet and data-base management programs can be structured to handle a double-entry ledger and to produce various key reports, financial ratios, and statements. For the typical small-business accounting applications, however, data-base management programs have two potential advantages over the spreadsheet.

First, the usual 64-column-by-254-row spreadsheet configuration limits the number of accounts, and particularly inventory items, that the spreadsheet can handle. When active accounts number in the hundreds and inventory items are in the thousands, spreadsheets become awkward and unwieldy. DB Master and dBase II, on the other hand, have powerful appetites: In its gold-plated IBM-Personal-Computer version, DB Master can maintain over one million records.

Second, the ability of the data-base program to sort records is a powerful advantage when converting accounting data into useful management information. Ashton Tate's dBase II, and to a lesser extent, DB Master, have the ability to combine, sort, and present data in new ways. These simplify the production of reports such as aggregate sales and commissions, inventory control, receivables agings, quarterly sales, and payroll tax reports, and even client mailing lists from the accounting records.

Both spreadsheet and data-base programs come bundled (included virtually for free) with many personal computers. By comparison, a set of accounting packages for the big five applications can cost between $450 and $4,500. And since the spreadsheet or data-base accounting program can be specifically designed for your business, this approach has the potential to solve unique accounting and reporting needs.

Inherent Problems with Do-It-Yourself Approach

Even so, there are some inherent problems with any do-it-yourself accounting solution. "Before the small businessman can create a successful bookkeeping program," explains one CPA, "he must understand both the principles of accounting and personal computers. Few really do. As a result, he soon becomes bogged down in problems that really have nothing to do with his business or his career."

Also, when you have special bookkeeping requirements, home-brewed books are no match for first-class accounting software. "If you need interrelationships between your general ledger and other accounting 'modules' such as accounts receivable, accounts payable, and inventory," says Boston microcomputer consultant Phil Paul, "then the accounting package is clearly a better way to go."

Publisher Dennis Curtin agrees, for a different reason. "In my opinion, it's just too complicated to set up accounting books on spreadsheets or a data-base program," he says. "That would put me in the position of being a bookkeeper for months trying to figure out how each little transaction is entered and accounted for. Those aren't the kind of problems I want to spend my time solving."

If you do opt for the accounting package, how do you begin evaluating the avalanche of off-the-shelf software? For most small firms, the logical place to start is with the general ledger.

GENERAL LEDGER

The heart of the accounting system—automated or manual—is the general ledger. In low-volume, high-margin firms, the general ledger may be the only software package needed to computerize the accounting system. For larger companies or the small firm with numerous transactions, the general ledger will be the centerpiece of a constellation of accounting software.

The general ledger records and balances the financial transactions of a business. It proves accurate and timely statements—including the balance sheet and income statement—that describe the company's financial situation. And it generates comparative data on the firm's financial position.

The typical computerized general ledger has two operating components: a "chart of accounts" and a "transaction file." The chart of accounts is the master listing containing the current balance of each account and often such additional information as the year-to-date activity, budget information, and previous-year totals. The transaction file contains a record of all financial transactions occurring within a specified accounting period—usually a calendar month. At month's end the chart of accounts and transaction files are merged by a "trial balance program" that matches each transaction to the appropriate account, performs totals, lists individual accounts and their transactions, and updates the chart of accounts to produce a current-month master file. From this master file the program then generates reports on business activity for the accounting period: the balance sheet, income statement, and often an income statement for each department. When all accounts are in balance, the reports have been produced, and a new accounting period is ready to begin, an end-of-period or month-end program clears the previous balances and prepares the system for the next accounting period.

Select It in Consultation with a CPA

The general ledger is the most critical piece of computer software the typical small business will ever buy, and it should be selected in consultation with the company's CPA. In Salt Lake City, Utah, CPA Marvin Poulsen helps his clients set up their books with a personal computer. "It does all the nitty-gritty detail work," he explains, "leaving me free to concentrate on taxes, business management consulting, and other areas I enjoy."

Among the criteria you and your accountant should consider in selecting a general ledger are provisions for multiple departments, trial balances, audit trails, quarterly income statements, financial comparisons, cash-flow analysis, reporting flexibility, expansion, and software integration with the other accounting programs.

All of these can be important. But none more so than the software integration, a term that refers to the ability of payables, receivables, inventory, payroll, and other accounting functions to link together and automatically update the general ledger. Software integration is easily overlooked in the first blush of excitement—and confusion—that accompanies any encounter with the computer. But if you ignore integration, you run the risk of saddling your business with software that operates at a fraction of your computer's potential.

The development of a full series of integrated accounting packages can take several years and cost over a million dollars in programming fees. To shortcut development expenses, many software entrepreneurs go to market with an accounting "series" that consists only of a general ledger or accounts receivable package. Perhaps more programs will follow the first two. Perhaps not. Even if the promised software is developed, there is no guarantee it will suit your business and accounting requirements. If compatible software is not forthcoming, your accounting system may soon reach a dead end.

A Terrible Mistake

San Diego businessman Maurice Maio made the mistake of purchasing a "stand-alone" accounts receivable package. "We outgrew that system in about two months," he recalls. "It was just terrible."

Without other integrated programs for payables, receivables, and general ledger, Maio soon faced a difficult decision: Scrap his stand-alone program and all that went into setting it up, or keep the program and piece together various incompatible software packages for receivables, payroll, and the other functions, and then manually post totals to the general ledger through the keyboard. Such a jerry-built bookkeeping system could certainly be made to work, but it would be inconvenient, slow, costly, and error-prone.

In the end, Maio opted to scrap the incompatible package, and even the computer it ran on, and start over with a set of integrated accounting programs. You can avoid similar difficulties in the beginning by purchasing modular software that is part of a *proven* accounting system. Even if you're positive you'll never need receivables, payables, inventory, or payroll software, buy a high-quality integratable general ledger anyway.

WHERE TO BUY

Who sells proven integrated accounting software? Peachtree software in Atlanta, Georgia (Peachpak 8 Accounting Series), is a leader in the field. So are BPI Systems in Austin, Texas; Continental Software in Los Angeles; and Software Dimensions (Accounting Plus) of Citrus Heights, California. All four software houses offer a range of integrated accounting modules including a general ledger and most of the other big-five applications. All are firmly entrenched in the marketplace, with solid reputations for product service and user support.

Peachtree Software, for instance, is a subsidiary of the world's largest independent producer of financial accounting software for mainframes. Many of Peachtree's customers are family-run businesses like Flamingo Home Sales. "We've found it's an excellent system for the small business," says mobile home dealer Tom Collins. Excellence, however, has its price: Collins's five programs retail for $3,750.

Seidman & Seidman is a thirty-eight-office international accounting firm that recommends the Peachpak 8 series to small and medium-sized companies, and uses Peachtree Software internally as well. "Peachtree offered a good, solid history in microcomputer software and is obviously going to continue as a strong product line," says Bob Redd, Seidman & Seidman's director of microcomputer services. The use of the microcomputer and its software, continues Redd, "has given us greater control over what we can do with our information and what we can get out of it. It has shortened our turnaround time. And it has given us monetary savings that are significant and will increase over time."

THE TRANSITION PERIOD

No Complaints

The transition from manual accounting to a computerized system can be brief and painless. Seven Associates is a small Northern California manufacturer of industrial electronics with thirty-five employees and annual sales of about $1 million. After twenty-three years of manual bookkeeping, president Harry B. Smith elected to computerize. "We had grown to the point where we had over two hundred customers, and keeping that many accounts straight was getting pretty hard to do by hand," he says.

Smith selected the Accounting Plus general ledger, receivables, and payables. "We had a little problem at first because our business has so many tax accounts at different percentages and rates." Smith returned his program to Software Dimensions where it was modified to accommodate his tax-account structure. "They were genuinely interested in improving their product," he says. "When we had a question, we just called them up. That made a big difference."

Although Seven Associates possessed no computer experience, installing the Accounting Plus was no big deal. "Our main problem was getting the information into the computer. It took us two or three months to get everything loaded. But as soon as we had the information entered, the system started saving one heck of a lot of time."

Tough Work Even with Computer Savvy

Computerizing the books, however, is not always so easy, even when the company happens to be a high-tech microcomputer firm. MicroRIM is a Seattle start-up with thirteen employees and a wealth of personal-computer saavy. But like many new and fast-growing firms, MicroRIM's books were not exactly a model of efficiency. "They really didn't keep any books," says office manager Carol Cissell, "until I started putting the company on an accounting system."

Ms. Cissell picked the Accounting Plus software. Yet getting the programs running at MicroRIM was anything but simple. At the root of her problem—faulty software documentation.

"When I first brought the Accounting Plus package up on the screen it was labeled as version 3.02. The manual I received with the program mentioned version 2.0, 2.2, 3.0, and others. But nowhere did it say anything about a version 3.02. The manual would tell me 'this is what you will see on the screen.' But that wasn't what I saw on the screen at all."

After many futile hours and much confusion, Cissell obtained the proper documentation. "When they finally sent me a manual that was up-to-date I didn't seem to have as many problems." Even so, getting the system to run smoothly took "many hours on the phone with Software Dimensions."

"I had the program up and running five times," she recalls, "and each time I'd go look at my chart of accounts the next day to find all the numbers reassigned to different accounts. If I hadn't had a computer background along with the accounting background there is no way I could have put this system up." Having the proper manual, she concedes, made a big difference: "Once I got the right documentation I think I could have done it as a layman." And even though she experienced "more start-up problems than should have been necessary," she remains a steadfast advocate of automated accounting. "All you have to do is push a few buttons."

Use a Consultant to Avoid a Stormy Passage

Even with top software and a knowledgeable user, the transition from manual to computerized accounting may be a stormy passage. The struggle to master an automated system can be benign, perhaps even enlightening. Or it can alienate office staff and distract attention from more pressing concerns.

A skilled microcomputer consultant increases the odds of a smooth transition. The installation of accounting software can be such a complex and potentially disruptive process that the money spent on a few days of outside consulting may head off far more costly mistakes. "The point when it makes sense to acquire technology," says Frederick Frost, owner of a Rhode Island manufacturing firm, "is when you are fortunate enough to find a consultant who is both a visionary in the microcomputer field and a practitioner with a business background. Not a moment before."

MORE CONTRIBUTIONS OF AUTOMATED ACCOUNTING

Instant Control

The contributions of computerized accounting can include the survival of the business itself. Just ask Pat McLoughlin of The Haworth Press. When a cash-flow crisis darkened the firm's prospects in 1979 it was the personal computer that turned the company around. "Our only reason for staying in business was to meet the payroll," recalls McLoughlin.

Haworth's owners used the personal computer to slash administrative overhead and boost office productivity. Word processing played a central role, as did VisiCalc and the database management program PFS. But without a computerized accounting system to provide a day-to-day portrait of Haworth's financial progress, Pat McLoughlin admits, "we'd have no way to keep track of our costs by division and section. We'd still be in trouble." Instead, two years after their brush with bankruptcy, McLoughlin and his partner Bill Cohen witnessed the doubling of their revenues. "The key thing," says McLoughlin, "was the instant control."

Inventory Control

For San Diego's Maurice Maio, the "instant control" of computerized accounting may not have been needed to save the business, but it certainly hasn't hurt. "Without the computer," says Maio, "we would be half the size we are today, and we would be in trouble."

Maio inherited the family plumbing business when he was twenty. There was a van, a set of tools, and a few parts. Eight years later, Maio Plumbing, Heating and Solar operates twenty-five trucks and is projecting nearly $2 million in annual revenues, up from $150,000 just three years ago. Why has business been so good? "Once you get hold of your accounting," says Maio, "it's all downhill. Once you can pay your bills and control the inventory and payroll and get people to pay you on time there is nothing left to do except advertise." It was not long ago, however, that Maurice Maio's accounting wasn't under control at all.

"As soon as we started growing," he recalls, "I got hit with the paperwork. In this industry there are thousands of little parts. Logging in all the invoices, purchase orders, and part numbers was just terrible. We couldn't collect our bills on time. We couldn't pay our bills on time. We didn't know what inventory we had or where to find it."

Maio hired a bookkeeper. "But it just took too long to record every part, pay every supplier, turn out every statement and meet every payroll. We didn't know who owed us what or what we owed them." Then came the stand-alone accounts-receivable software and a personal computer. Neither the software nor hardware were adequate. "I learned two lessons," he says. "First, there is no way you can run a service business like this without a computer. Second, when it comes to accounting software, you're a fool not to buy an integrated system."

Maio's second microcomputer was a powerful Altos small-business model. For software he selected the Accounting Plus system. "We're running general ledger, accounts receivable, accounts payable, payroll, sales orders, purchase orders, point of sale, and inventory. We put them all into effect at once. It took about two months to adapt to the system."

Inventory Shrinkage

In one area alone—inventory shrinkage—Maio saved enough money within the first year to more than pay for the computer and its software. "Inventory shrinkage prior to the computer was 15 percent, or about $30,000. With the computer, shrinkage is down to 6 percent. That's a $15,000- to $20,000-a-year savings."

How does the computer reduce shrinkage? "It watches every part that comes in and goes out," says Maio. "The guys know the inventory is being watched. That alone helps. Second, it tells us which parts are getting ripped off over and over again. Now that we know what's being stolen, we keep a closer eye on it."

But inventory control, not shrinkage, was actually Maio's most crucial problem. "Our warehouse and our vehicles were always running out of parts because we didn't know where things were and how many were available." With the computer, Maio now knows exactly where his inventory is located. So do his servicemen and dispatcher. "We are able to serve our customers better because when a truck pulls up in front of a house, that man knows what parts he has. Also, our office can see with the push of a button which trucks have the parts needed for a certain kind of job. We're now using a custom program that considers inventory, the servicemen's qualifications and experience, and driving mileage for scheduling jobs. We're usually able to get to a person's home with a truck equipped to handle their problem within thirty minutes." The computer recommends which truck to dispatch based on its current location, the serviceman's specialty, and parts inventory. "If it's a garbage disposal problem," says Maio, "then the computer sends the closest truck with garbage disposal parts and a serviceman who knows how to install them."

Another benefit: Maio's inventory contains what he needs, and only what he needs. "We used to buy and buy and buy. But we never could control what we bought. We now have reports that tell us when we have fallen below our 'safety stock' levels. There are no more mistakes. No more running out of parts. And when we do order stock we take advantage of quantity discounts."

Dollars on the Shelf

Maio has succeeded in financing his firm's spectacular growth entirely out of earnings. Most companies are not so fortunate. Firms that borrow to buy stock must be especially precise in their inventory control. "When there are dollars sitting on the shelf," says Boston car dealer A. Harlow Ellis, "you automatically have cash-flow problems."

Not long ago, inventory at Ellis's $2.5-million-a-year Saab and Alfa-Romeo dealership was managed by a service bureau that issued bi-monthly reports. The result? Frequent shortages of some parts, and a costly oversupply of others. Like Maurice Maio, Ellis turned to an Altos computer to track the roughly one thousand parts that move through his service department every week. A daily report shows Ellis his exact inventory level on some 4,500 year-round and seasonal items. When stock falls below a predetermined level, the computer automatically alerts the parts clerk and even prints the purchase order. Has this computerized inventory control saved money? In the first year of micropower operation, Ellis estimates reduced inventory and increased turnover "resulted in a net gain of about fifty thousand dollars."

Accounts Receivable

Another potentially serious source of cash-flow difficulty is aged receivables. Maurice Maio uses the Accounting Plus package to watch the receivables. "Nobody gets late anymore. And if they do the computer automatically adds the proper finance charge."

Virtually all the major accounting packages, including the Peachpak 8 and Accounting Plus series, include a receivables aging report as part of their accounts-receivable module. One surprising aspect of these systems, however, is that while they post to the general ledger and automatically produce month-end customer statements, they *do not* produce invoices. The Peachpak 8, Accounting Plus, and BPI systems all require an additional invoice program. One exception is Continental Software's accounts receivable module which generates both customer statements and itemized invoices.

Accounts Payable

Most businesspeople attach little importance to the accounts payable side of the ledger, but Maurice Maio is not among them. "Knowing how much you owe and who you owe it to is almost as important to your cash flow as your accounts receivable," he says. Especially when there are "cash net 10" or other discounts involved. "We're making money just by paying our bills on time. We pay our bills almost faster than we get the invoices. As a result we've got every vendor in town beating at the door trying to do business with us. The word's gotten out how fast we pay and now everyone wants to sell to us. That means faster service, bigger discounts and better deals."

Payroll

Payroll is one task most small firms prefer to turn over to their bank or a service bureau such as Automatic Data Processing (ADP). "There's no way I'd ever put a payroll on here," says MicroRIM's Carol Cissell. "There no reason to do it when ADP charges us only thirty dollars a month to run the payroll for our thirteen employees. They even do the W-2s, file the forms, and pay the taxes. There's no way you can beat that as far as I'm concerned."

Maurice Maio, however, does his computerized payroll in-house; and he has a very good reason for it. "The computer has allowed us to put the men on commission based on a percentage of parts and labor. That's been a big factor in our growth. It provides our servicemen with an enormous incentive to sell remodeling jobs and new fixtures. During the heating season, for instance, our guys were busy selling energy-efficient thermostats and heating systems."

Time for a Raise

The serviceman's commission is the principal reason Maio does his own computerized payroll, but it is not the only reason. "We used to award raises based on need or how long a man had been with us. We don't do it that way anymore." When a serviceman requests a wage review Maio pulls out a detailed payroll summary. "I'm able to monitor exactly how many dollars each man has brought into the company in labor and materials. I know if he's worthy of a raise. All our raises are based on performance now. That's something else we could never measure until we got the computer."

Chapter Ten

The Final Step: Executive Hardware

Information is the manager's main tool, indeed the manager's "capital," and it is he who must decide what information he needs and how to use it.

—Peter Drucker

Now, about that computer. At Comemco, Inc., in Mountain View, California, Dr. Roger Melen has advanced a formula that lets you assign a "figure of merit" to personal computers. According to Melen's Law, $M = R \times C \times D$.

Melen explains the variables this way: M is the "merit factor," a relative indicator of computer performance. R is the capacity of the computer's Random Access Memory (RAM) divided by 64K. C is the number of characters the computer can display divided by 2,000. D is the total floppy disk capacity divided by 100K. Under Melen's Law a computer with 64K of RAM, an 80-column-by-25-line display (2,000 characters), and 100K of disk storage is normalized with an M-factor of one ($M = 1 \times 1 \times 1$). More powerful machines will rate above one, less powerful models rate below one.

CAVEATS TO MELEN'S LAW

By plotting Dr. Melen's M-factor against price you can develop a *general* cost-versus-performance comparison for the different models of personal computers you are considering. In a moment I'll embellish Melen's Law, and show you how to use it. But first, the caveats.

For starters, Dr. Melen *is* a founder of Cromemco, a personal-computer manufacturer, and, yes, his own machine, the Cromemco C-10, rates nicely under the formula. But Melen denies that the law is skewed to make the C-10 look good. Instead, he says, he developed the formula to define which hardware values were the most important, and then designed the Cromemco computer accordingly.

Next, with many brands and models of personal computers, the three factors that Melen's Law uses as a measure of performance—random access memory, display characters, and disk drive capacity—can be upgraded at additional cost. Indeed, many personal computers today can be purchased in much the same way you would buy stereo components. Thus, although your computer itself is assembled by IBM, Apple, or whomever, the RAM expansion cards, as well as the disk drives, video monitor, and other peripherals, may be bought from third-party suppliers offering a range of options and prices. With the IBM-PC, for instance, it is possible to expand the RAM to 128K, or even 256K. Under Melen's Law this will double, or even triple, the machine's *M*-factor. Hence, when using the *M*-factor, you must be careful to calculate the personal computer as you intend to purchase it, not in the "stripped-down" or "starter" versions that are the most widely advertised.

Also, although the three factors Melen's Law uses to evaluate computer performance—RAM, character display, and disk capacity—are crucial, there is much the formula does not, or cannot, quantify. Melen's Law, for instance, has no provision for software considerations, including whether or not the computer supports CP/M, and what programs, if any, are included with the computer.

Then, there is the question of *how* you intend to use your personal computer. Word processing in the small firm, for instance, can have significantly different RAM, disk capacity, and other hardware requirements than accounting or spreadsheeting. (We'll explore these fine points momentarily.)

Other factors worth considering—and not computed in Melen's formula—include dealer support or other forms of expertise that may be available to you. The personal attention of a local vendor can be immensely valuable, but obviously your hardware choices will be limited to the machines in his or her inventory. If you have friends or employees who already own a personal computer, their experience with certain models can also save you many agonizing hours.

Finally, there is the superior speed and flexibility of the 16- and 32-bit computers to be reckoned with. Remember, these bit designations refer to how memory is transferred and stored, not the amount of memory available. An 8-bit microprocessor is limited to words that are only eight bits in length, while 16- and 32-bit machines can handle binary words that are 16- and 32-bits long. The larger the bit mode, the faster and more powerful the computer.

Crayon Comparison

At the Indianapolis Speedway it is said some racers draw the fine line of control with a razor-sharp pencil, while others use a crayon. Once you've used a 16-bit computer, you'll find 8-bit performance comparable to the crayon. Sixteen-bit computers are faster, more convenient, and more versatile. Given that the software you need is available for them, 16-bit computers are the best choice for small-business or professional computing.

For one thing, 16-bit machines have the memory capacity and processing speed to support so-called third-generation integrated programs such as VisiOn and Lotus Software's 1,2,3. What manager doesn't yearn for the ability to analyze dozens, even hundreds of pages of financial, marketing, production, or sales data with a few strokes of the keyboard and then print out the results in a detailed and graphically illustrated report? Integrated software makes such dreams reality. Moreover, with 16-bit computers it is possible to use devices such as the electronic mouse and even a "graphics tablet" that allows some data to be entered by handwriting instead of typing.

And there is more. Sixteen-bit computers can multitask—perform several applications simultaneously. This is no mean advantage once you have come to rely on your personal computer to execute your routine, and not so routine, office chores. Generating form letters or monthly customer statements, for instance, with a letter-quality printer can tie up the typical 8-bit machine for hours. Even with a speedy dot-matrix printer it takes about 20 minutes to produce a hard-copy draft of this chapter. That's 20 minutes that the 8-bit computer can't be used for writing, editing, or any other memory-intensive activity. But because 16-bit computers have greater memory and faster operating speeds, one program can be printing out while a second program is engaged in word processing, spreadsheet forecasting, or other tasks. This uses your computer, and your time, more efficiently.

Finally, for accounting, inventory control, data-base management, or even spreadsheeting operations where large files are involved, 16-bit machines can save seconds, and sometimes minutes, each time the computer performs a complex search, sort, or calculation.

MELEN'S LAW MODIFIED

With these factors in mind, let's return to Melen's Law. I've tampered with Dr. Melen's version slightly by adding a fourth variable, called *B*, to take the speed and flexibility of 16-bit circuitry into account. In the McNitt version of Melen's Law, *B* equals the bit mode of the microprocessor (typically 8, 16, or 32) divided by eight. As a result, a 64K computer with a 2,000-character display, 100K of disk capacity, *and* an 8-bit microprocessor is normalized at one. The new formula for Melen's Law as revised by McNitt is:

$$M = \frac{\text{RAM}}{64\text{K}} \times \frac{\begin{array}{c}\text{\# of columns of}\\ \text{video display}\end{array} \times \begin{array}{c}\text{\# of lines of}\\ \text{video display}\end{array}}{2000} \times \frac{\text{disk capacity}}{100\text{K}} \times \frac{\text{bit mode}}{8}$$

How to use Melen's Law? Start by plugging in the appropriate numbers for the computer you are considering. Say the apple of your eye is not an Apple, but an IBM-PC. Assuming that you'll be using the computer mostly for word processing, you'll want 64K of RAM, two disk drives (your dealer has a good deal on a pair of single-density drives with 160K each), and an 80-column-by-24-line video display. In addition, you know from the dealer's spec sheet that IBM-PC uses a 16-bit microprocessor. Thus, your equation looks like this:

$$M = \frac{64K}{64K} \times \frac{(80 \times 24)}{2000} \times \frac{320K}{100K} \times \frac{16}{8}$$

Thus $M = 1 \times .96 \times 3.2 \times 2$ for a merit factor of 6.14. The list price of this IBM-PC configuration is $3,500 (excluding a printer). To find out how this particular IBM-PC setup compares to other personal computers, refer to Figure 10-1. Here, I've calculated the *M*-factor for a number of popular personal computers and plotted it against their approximate list prices.

The beauty of Melen's Law (McNitt's version) is that it provides a systematic tool for the otherwise chaotic task of evaluating computer performance. Again, the danger with Melen's Law, however, is that there are many critical variables it doesn't take into account. Use it as a general guide to performance, and it can point you in the right direction. Use it as a hard-and-fast rule, and it just as likely will lead you astray.

With Melen's Law as a performance evaluator, then, you are in a good position to begin choosing among personal computers. But how do you decide on the fundamental requirements? Specifically, how much random access memory is necessary, how much disk drive capacity do you need, what kind of printer is best suited to your purposes, and what impact do peripheral amenities such as keyboards and video monitors have on computer selection?

The best way to tackle these questions is to look at the basic computer applications one at a time.

Figure 10-1

MELEN'S LAW, REVISED
HOW THIRTY-SIX PERSONAL COMPUTERS COMPARE

Model	M-Factor	System Price*
ACCESS MATRIX	3.5	2,190
APPLE IIe	2.7	2,390
APPLE III	5.4	3,815
BMC if800	5.8	4,995
BYTEC HYPERION	49.2	3,690
CANON CX-1	6.1	5,000
COLUMBIA MPC	32.3	3,620
COMPAQ	24.6	3,540
CROMEMCO C-10	7.5	2,380
DEC RAINBOW 100	25.3	3,495
EAGLE PC	24.6	3,495
EPSON QX-10	29.6	2,995
FORTUNE 32:16	30.7	4,995
FRANKLIN ACE 2000	2.5	2,295
FUJITSU MICRO 16	25.6	3,995
GAVILAN	6.9	3,995
HEATH/ZENITH MODEL 100	12.3	2,199
HP-150	39.3	3,995
IBM-PC	13.8	3,557
KAYPRO IV	7.7	1,995
MORROW DECISION I	7.7	3,495
NEC APC	76.8	3,598
NORTH STAR ADVANTAGE	6.9	2,999
OTRONA ATTACHE	57.6	3,795
SANYO MBC-1000+	3.2	1,995
SEEQUA CHAMELEON	12.3	1,995
SHARP PC-5000	1.6	1,995
SONY SMC-70	5.6	3,375
TRS-80 MODEL 4	3.5	1,999
TRS-80 MODEL 16	48	4,999
TELEVIDEO 1602	56.6	3,405
TOSHIBA T300	73.7	3,090
VECTOR GRAPHIC 2600	11.52	3,995
VICTOR 9000	152.0	3,495
WANG PC	27.6	3,790
XEROX 16/8	19	3,395

*SUGGESTED RETAIL PRICES AS OF OCTOBER, 1983

Note: The *M*-factor offers a *gross* comparison among personal computers based on the amount of random access memory, disc drive capacity, the number of display characters, and the bit-mode of the central processing unit. In general, the higher the *M*-factor, the greater the information-handling capacity of the system.

The *M*-factors in this list were calculated on the basis of a "typical system" including at least 64K of random access memory and two disc drives. The *M*-factor *does not* take software compatibility into account. Moreover, upgrading or downgrading the amount of random access memory or disc drive capacity can dramatically change a system's *M*-factor.

WORD-PROCESSING HARDWARE

Word processing has several idiosyncratic requirements that set it apart from other micro-power applications of personal-computer hardware. The foremost is printer quality.

There are two kinds of personal computer printers. One is the **dot-matrix** model. Dot-matrix printers are fast, cheap, and dependable. The trade-off, however, is print quality. The dot-matrix process produces characters by moving a tiny machine-gun–like head armed with blunt needles along an inked ribbon. Depending on the combination of needles, the dot-matrix printer produces a legible approximation of all twenty-six vowels and consonants, plus numbers and graphics characters. But no one has ever accused the dot-matrix typeface of elegance. Most dot-matrix characters are ungainly, fuzzy, and unsuitable for either reproduction or business correspondence.

The alternative to dot matrix is a **letter-quality** printer. Traditionally, letter-quality printers are slower, more expensive, and less dependable. Their sole advantage is the neat, crisp characters they produce, comparable in quality to an IBM Selectric typewriter. (For $500, Mediamix in Los Angeles markets a black box device that converts IBM Electronic Typewriter Models 50, 60, or 75, among others, into letter-quality printers. Such conversions are ideal for limited printing such as occasional business correspondence, but routine use can result in routine breakdowns.)

Among the most highly regarded letter-quality printers for office word processing is the NEC Spinwriter. Other frequently recommended letter-quality printers are manufactured by Diablo and Qume. The Spinwriter's imprint is comparable to the IBM typewriter, but in place of the familiar IBM golf ball–shaped print head, the Spinwriter uses a daisy wheel impact mechanism consisting of a central hub with characters arranged on spokes (reminiscent of daisy petals). It is simpler, faster, and more reliable than the Selectric-type systems. Unfortunately, at $2,500, the Spinwriter can double the price of a microcomputer word processor.

Honors for the world's first under-$1,000 letter-quality printers go to Smith Corona and a firm called Williams Laboratories in Ithaca, New York. Both companies build their machines on a typewriter chassis, sacrificing many features, including speed and durability, for low price. These printers have a top speed of about 120 words per minute, compared with over 600 words per minute for the fastest Spinwriter model. Both, however, do produce letter-quality type.

The Williams "Bytewriter" is actually an Olivetti Praxis 30 typewriter with an interchangeable daisy wheel and a circuit board that allows it to be driven by, among others, the TRS-80, Apple II, Osborne I, and IBM-PC computers. The Bytewriter does not have a **tractor feed,** a spindlelike device with pins to grip the perforations in continuous-form paper. Without tractor feed, paper must be inserted one sheet at a time, as with any ordinary typewriter. This is a profound annoyance with lengthy documents or standard payroll, tax, or insurance forms.

Unlike the Bytewriter, Smith Corona's TP-1 is a dedicated daisy-wheel printer. It has no keys and cannot serve as an office typewriter. The TP-1 can be used as a friction feed printer, like the Bytewriter, when printing on letterhead or special stationery. Also, a tractor-feed option allows continuous printing, either on blank pages or prepared forms such as W-2s and medical insurance reports. In addition to the Bytewriter and Smith Corona TP-1 there are now many other letter-quality printers on the market, some even priced competitively with good dot-matrix printers.

Taking both dot-matrix and letter-quality printers into consideration there are over 175 printer models available, but not every computer can use every printer. Software is a factor, as the typical disk operating system will drive only specific printer "families" without modification. Then there is the hardware **interface.** The computer communicates with its printer through a device known as an "I/O port." Oddly, some computers do not come with I/O ports as standard equipment. Adding a printer interface, a cable, and perhaps an adapter can up the cost of equipping some computers with a printer by as much as $200.

If a personal computer is to be used extensively for word processing, and not just for occasional correspondence, the quality of the video monitor and keyboard are important. Color television screens and even high-quality color monitors are not well-suited for word processing. Green phosphorous or amber monitors are reportedly kindest to the eyes. The higher the resolution the better. All but the cheapest monitors display 80 columns and 24 lines. Displays that are deeper than 24 lines often prove counterproductive, since much time is lost trying to find your place on the screen. Whether or not your computer can take advantage of the full 80-column-by-24-line display, however, is another story. The Apple II, for instance, displays only 40 columns, and this limitation remains unchanged on the Apple IIe, although 80-column "cards" area available to expand the displays of both machines, at additional cost.

As for keyboards, avoid "membrane" keyboards made of plastic overlays. Most typists prefer a crisp, springy keyboard over a soft, mushy one. The better and faster the typist, the more crucial the mechanical quality of the keyboard.

When it comes to word-processing control keys, not all keyboards are born equal. WordStar control keys, for instance, differ drastically from one computer to the next. A few keyboards are cumbersome for word processing regardless of what program you use. The famous Apple II is one. For word processing, the Apple II keyboard, with its meager forty-eight keys, is dreadful. It lacks a tab key for indenting paragraphs or moving the cursor from one column to the next. Nor does it have keys to control cursor movement up and down, or even a separate numeric **keypad** for punching in numbers for tables and charts. Yet, such is the power of word processing that thousands still use the Apple II every day without annoyance or regret. And, happily, most of these problems were addressed with the introduction of the new Apple computers.

The internal memory of the computer is not a major concern in word processing. Any personal computer with 64K or more is sufficient. Disk drive storage capacity, however, is crucial. No matter how much memory your disk drives have, you'll want more.

The typical floppy diskette holds from 70 to 500 kilobytes of data depending on your disk drive. This translates to between about twenty and eighty double-spaced, typewritten pages per 100K of diskette memory, depending on the software program you use. Including research notes, interview transcripts, and manuscript copy, *The Art of Computer Management* consumed over twenty-five single-density 100K diskettes. Since I seldom had compelling reasons for jumping from section to section within the manuscript, the system served me well. Even so, there were nights when, with desk awash in a sea of floppies, I yearned for a more capacious memory system. You will too. As an absolute minimum you'll need at least 200K of disk capacity. But even with 200K you won't be able to take advantage of some of the most powerful spelling-check programs such as the 80,000-word Random House Dictionary. To run these programs you'll need a minimum of about 360K.

At Kyriakis & Guralnick, attorney Steve Guralnick uses a hard-disk drive on his word-processing system. "Our office stores about 750,000 characters of master text for preparing legal documents," Guralnick points out. Guralnick's five-**megabyte** (five million bytes) hard disk eliminates the need to change floppies when assembling documents from electronic files that would otherwise be stored on numerous separate floppy diskettes. Author Warren Stallings is also using a hard-disk drive for word processing. "It allows me to do global searches of over one thousand pages of manuscript without having to change disks," says Stallings.

Hard disk drives offer speed and convenience. They "boot" and execute programs more quickly, and they save fumbling through volumes of diskettes. But until you've built a data base containing a few thousand records, they are not necessary. For the faster response and convenience of hard disk drives you can expect to pay betwen $1,000 and $4,000.

My advice on disk storage is this: Purchase two floppy disk drives with your computer, whatever the model. The bare minimum is a pair of 100K drives. Just be certain that additional storage, probably a hard disk drive, *can* be added when necessary. Be sure your programs *can run* on a hard disk, even if you don't currently need one. Transferring your programs and files onto a hard disk may be a small hassle, but your retail computer stores should be of assistance here. Solving such problems is exactly why you're paying your local vendor 20 to 30 percent over the discount mail-order rates.

SPREADSHEETS AND ACCOUNTING

The rule of thumb for spreadsheeting hardware is delightfully simple: The bigger the better.

The minimum memory requirements are 64K of RAM and a pair of 100K disk drives. This is adequate for simple accounting, budgeting, and financial modeling with programs such as VisiCalc or SuperCalc.

As your files grow and your spreadsheet models become more complex, the limitations of 64K RAM and 200K of disk drive memory will become increasingly apparent. First, with limited disk drive memory, you'll be forced to keep your spreadsheet files on numerous floppy disks. This limits the effectiveness of a key feature of SuperCalc and most of the "enhanced" spreadsheets such as VisiCalc Advanced Version that can automatically search out previous files, say, last year's budget, and retrieve vital data, including both numbers and formulas. Also, the larger and more sophisticated your spreadsheet models become, the more time it takes for the computer to perform its calculations. Then there is the question of integrated programming. These software packages that typically combine a spreadsheet with a data-base management and graphics program usually require a 16-bit microprocessor with at least 128K of RAM and 400K of disk memory. If you're serious about spreadsheeting, you'll need a serious computer: at least 128K of RAM, preferably a 16-bit microprocessor, and about 600K to 800K of disk memory.

When working with spreadsheets, the more rows and columns you can see on the monitor at one time, the less time you'll spend scrolling and searching, and the fewer mistakes you're likely to make. As a result, the comfortable minimum for a video display is 80 columns by 24 lines. A few computers offer larger displays as an option. The DEC Rainbow, for instance, can be equipped to display up to 132 columns and 24 lines. The IBM-PC will permit an 80-column-by-40-line display format.

What goes for the video display also holds for the printer. As a rule, dot-matrix printers are preferable for spreadsheeting applications because of their speed. Wide printers such as the popular Epson MX100, which can print up to 233 characters per line at the rate of 100 characters per second, are ideally suited for spreadsheeting. At its maximum setting the Epson MX100 (list price: $995) accepts 18-by-18-inch sheets of fan-fold, tractor-feed paper. A tractor-feed mechanism on the printer is also a virtual necessity for extensive spreadsheeting.

Keyboard quality is somewhat less important for spreadsheeting than word processing. One convenient feature, however, is a detachable keyboard. Another is a keypad for entering large amounts of numeric data.

Accounting hardware requirements are nearly identical to spreadsheeting with one exception—disk capacity. Where there is a high volume of financial transactions, the sheer bulk of numbers can overwhelm any floppy disk drive, especially if the accounting system also includes inventory or order entry. It is very complicated and inconvenient to update and keep track of files spread across many, many floppies. The alternative is a powerful hard-disk drive that not only can hold millions of characters of data, but also can help speed the execution of your programs. Even if you don't need a hard disk now, be certain both your computer and your accounting software are capable of supporting a hard-disk drive, should it be necessary in the future. As a rule of thumb, 600K to 800K of floppy disk memory will suffice for several hundred accounts of modest activity. When transactions are numerous, accounts number into the thousands, or significant inventory or order entry functions are involved, a hard disk drive is advisable, if not absolutely essential.

You can roughly estimate the amount of disk capacity you'll need by multiplying the number of characters in an average account by your total number of accounts. If, for instance, your typical account contains 800 characters by year's end, and you have 500 active accounts on your books, you'll need a minimum 400K of disk memory for your accounting files. But before purchasing a pair of 200K disk drives, don't forget that you will need additional disk capacity for your accounting software, perhaps as much as 100K per module, as well as room to grow.

DATA-BASE MANAGEMENT

Memory and peripheral requirements for data-base management depend on the length and number of your records, as well as how you plan to use the information they contain.

In general, the keyboard and monitor requirements for data-base management are the same as for word processing, at least if your recordkeeping is more than casual. A quality keyboard, a high resolution video monitor, and a computer capable of an 80-column-by-24-line display are advisable.

As long as your records and the reports generated from them are used within your firm, a dot-matrix printer is preferable for its speed and reliability. If, however, the data-base program is producing information for patients, clients, or customers, a letter-quality printer may be more suitable, although less efficient.

Also, as with word processing, the typical minimum memory capacity for data-base management is 64K RAM and a pair of 100K disks. If your records are brief, say 400 characters (80 words), you'll be able to fit about 250 of them on a single 100K floppy. But when your records become lengthy, and especially if you aim to take advantage of the inquiry function available through a powerful relational data-base program such as dBase II, you'll find that additional RAM, disk capacity, and 16-bit performance will be advantageous. Should you want to perform spreadsheet analysis on data from your files, with an integrated spreadsheet–data-base management program–graphics software package you can conveniently transfer large amounts of information between the different applications programs. And, as mentioned before, you'll need at least 128K of RAM and a 16-bit computer to support integrated software.

MULTIPLE APPLICATIONS

In the workplace, few personal computers perform a single task, at least not for long. But how do you select hardware for a system that will, as is often the case, be used by the boss for financial planning, the bookkeeper for accounting, and a secretary for word processing?

Budget permitting, you will still do well to follow the guidelines above. A quality keyboard, a good monochrome monitor, and a letter-quality printer are the basics for the typical office's word-processing system. One suggestion on the printer: For the price of a bargain-basement daisy-wheel printer you can equip your IBM Memory Typewriter to do double duty as an office typewriter and a computer printer for business correspondence.

Accounting, spreadsheeting, and data-base management requirements will oblige you to invest in more RAM and disk drive—or possibly hard-disk drive—capacity than you might otherwise need for word processing alone. Also, if hard-copy records are necessary, you'll find a high-speed dot-matrix printer indispensable.

Finally, regardless of how you begin using your personal computer, sooner or later you will want to tie into the international telecommunications grid. The device that allows computers to communicate across town, or across the country, is called a **modem.**

Modems

At the Stamford Hospital in Stamford, Connecticut, research librarian Joanna Faraday helps doctors locate medical literature. Two years ago, Ms. Faraday did her research manually. Back then, she recalls, "a literature search might take half a day."

Today, she has a computer connected, by way of a modem, to Medline, an on-line data base operated by the National Library of Medicine. "Now," she says, "the same search, using Medline, will take about fifteen minutes." And not only is Medline faster; with it she can perform a more thorough job, pinpointing exactly what the doctor needs. "With manual searching methods," she says, "I can only look for one subject at a time. Using the computer I can combine any number of different subjects. The result is a list of articles that are cross-referenced for two, three, or more subjects." Since Medline has been installed, she reports that requests for medical literature searches have quadrupled, in part, "because people are pleased with the results they get and in part because they seem to trust the computer more, even if it's still the librarian who performs the search."

Across town at the Stamford office of Cummings and Lockwood, a major U.S. law firm, attorney Paul Knag uses the Lexis data base for locating legal sources, case rulings, precedents, and judgments. "Originally," he says, "people thought it was very futuristic to be using a computer to do research. But today it's like library books or letterhead: We just couldn't think of operating without it. It's a much more efficient way of researching the law."

One advantage of Lexis is its flexibility. "It enables you," says Knag, "to search according to your own program, rather than some indexer's valuation of what's pertinent and what's not." An attorney, for instance, can ask Lexis to supply a list of all cases that pertain to Rule 23.C.1 and involve companies of a certain industry that were decided in Second Circuit courts. To find this manually requires reviewing the entire list of cases involving Rule 23.C.1. But Lexis performs all the cross-referencing, providing the lawyer with only the cases that fit his requirements.

Says Knag: "Lexis is a tremendous advantage to a lawyer who has it, and a tremendous disadvantage to any lawyer who doesn't. It's like trying to run a hospital without an X-ray machine. Once the X-ray was invented, you really couldn't have a hospital without one. So it is with Lexis and the computer that accesses it."

Whatever your profession, whatever your business, there are services similar to Medline and Lexis available to you—if you have a modem.

There are over fifty models of modems to select from, not counting units sold under the brand names of computer manufacturers such as Apple, DEC, and IBM. Since setting up a modem to operate with a particular model of computer is a somewhat ticklish and technically complex undertaking, there is much to be said for purchasing a modem that has your computer-maker's endorsement. If you have a choice between a "direct-connect" and an "acoustically coupled" modem, go with the direct connect. It is more reliable.

If there is no authorized modem for your machine, you might consider the Hayes-Stack Smartmodem (List: $566), which is a highly regarded direct-connect unit. In addition, you will need a software communications program such as VisiTerm, Micro-Courier, Hayes Terminal Program, or DataLink to provide your computer with the proper instructions for transmitting and receiving files from another computer. But where do you turn for advice and assistance in selecting and installing a modem and communications software, or any personal computer-equipment for that matter?

WHAT ABOUT VENDORS?

Kenneth Bosomworth is president of International Data Resources, a market research firm that not only studies the personal-computer market, but actually uses computers for word processing (producing "personalized junk mail"), payroll processing, and econometric modeling. Bosomworth is not sanguine on the quality of service and expertise that the small-businessperson is likely to find when acquiring a personal computer.

"In buying a personal computer," he says, "you're faced with the decision of trying to select the lesser of many evils. All of the microcomputers are sold by salesmen who are unable to satisfactorily demonstrate or explain anything about them. By the standards of the office-products industry the whole microcomputer business is still a joke."

Today's computer salesman is often yesterday's hi-fi salesman. He or she understands little about computers, and nothing about your business. This isn't a universal truth, but it's a valid generalization. The problem lies in the explosive growth of an industry that didn't exist ten years ago.

"The situation is improving," says Bosomworth. "But the lack of a coherent chain of distribution for most products until recently meant that companies like Apple had no control over what the service policies were going to be for the end user. A company like Radio Shack didn't have those problems, but they were faced with a huge chain of stores and service centers without any notions or policies appropriate to office users. In terms of quality control, in terms of maintenance, in terms of professionalism, in terms of the sales force, the microcomputer industry is lacking."

But while the sales and service end of the personal-computer business has yet to mature, Bosomworth sees one very bright spot—the equipment itself. "The engineering and design of the products we see in the microcomputer market today are far ahead of what's available at this time in the office automation field."

AND IN THE FUTURE?

The wild profusion of hardware, software, and computer jargon are powerful disincentives to personal computing. Moreover, by all indications the personal computer and its software are merely in an embryonic phase. As personal computers grow more powerful, programmers are finding ways to use that power to make computing easier for the user. One protype of what you can expect is the Apple Lisa computer, with its integrated software, electronic mouse, and pictograms. Most executives master the basic controls and concepts of the Lisa in twenty minutes or less. Some studies suggest that by 1990 executive workstations comparable to the Apple Lisa will cost under $2,000.

As more and more small businesses and professional offices computerize, the competitive advantages diminish. Not long from now, the personal computer will have become another standard office appliance, along with the filing cabinet, typewriter, and photocopier. But there is still time for small-business managers to gain an advantage over the competition by computerizing now.

Glossary

A

addresses A computer memory is divided into unique **address** locations at which individual pieces of data are stored. Each address is identified by its own code number.

Algorithm A set of finite, procedural steps for solving a specific problem.

Alphanumeric A convenient way of describing symbolic characters, such as those found on a computer keyboard.

Alphanumeric characters can be letters of the alphabet, numbers, or special symbols such as [, >, %, or $.

Applications software Computer programs designed to accomplish tasks such as word processing or accounting. **Systems software** or **operating systems,** by contrast, perform various housekeeping functions within the computer and its **peripheral** devices.

ASCII Stands for American Standard Code for Information Interchange. The ASCII code assigns a specific **binary** number to each **alphanumeric** character on the computer keyboard, thus providing a basic standard that allows communication between different computers.

Ascender The part of a letter (such as *b, d,* or *h*) that ascends above the top of the letter *x*. Compare **descender.**

Assembly language A "low-level" computer language used by programmers to communicate with the computer. **Assembly language** translates instructions written in "high-level" languages such as BASIC and Pascal into binary code, or "machine language," which the computer can understand.

B

Backup To err is human, but sometimes even computers make mistakes. Always make a **backup** copy of vital data on a second disk. Some programs such as Wordstar also make a second **backup** file every time you "save."

BASIC **B**eginner's **A**ll-purpose **S**ymbolic **I**nstruction **C**ode. **BASIC** is the most popular programming language for personal computers. Should businesspeople learn **BASIC**? Not usually. Chances are the program you need has already been written. Your time is better spent running your firm.

Baud rate The number of **bits** per second a computer transmits to its peripherals or another computer. Part of the "setup" procedure for most personal-computer programs involves telling the program the **baud rate** of the printer you will be using.

Binary The term for the Base-2 number system that uses 1s and 0s to store, exchange, and process information. All digital computers use the **binary** number system.

Bit Stands for **BI**nary digi**T,** the smallest piece of information (1 or 0) that a computer can recognize. Traditionally, eight **bits** are grouped into one message unit, called a **byte.**

Bit mode Personal computers these days come in 8-, 16-, and 32-bit models. The larger the **bit mode** the more powerful the computer. Small firms looking for a computer today should be paying close attention to the 16-bit machines.

Bug An error either in the computer hardware or its software program. Usually solved by "debugging."

Buffer A temporary storage area, such as that typically found in a computer printer. The **buffer** is a "holding tank" that compensates for variations in data-handling speeds among the different parts of a computer system.

Byte The fundamental unit of computer memory. One **byte** represents a single **alphanumeric** character. The **byte** itself is composed of eight **bits.** Personal computer memory is usually expressed in **kilobytes** or 1,000-**byte** increments. Disk storage is referred to in **kilobytes,** or sometimes **megabytes.** A **megabyte** equals 1,000 **kilobytes.**

C

C BASIC A popular high-level language for microcomputers. The advantage of **C BASIC** over regular **BASIC** is that it runs faster and occupies less memory.

Central processing unit (CPU) The "brains" of the personal computer, composed of a microprocessor chip and its associated circuitry. The **CPU** collects the data, decodes it, and executes the programmed instructions.

Character One letter, number, or symbol. In most personal computers each character consumes one byte of memory.

Chip Colloquialism for the silicon or germanium wafer and its integrated circuitry forming the personal computer's **central processing unit.**

Code Computer code takes the form of binary numbers, as in "machine language," or any of the various programming languages that are easier for people to read and write.

Command An instruction—usually keyed in as a word or character—that causes the computer to perform a designated operation.

Computer language Any of the numeric and alphabetic **languages** or **codes** used to communicate with and operate the personal computer.

Computer program A series of **commands** instructing the computer to perform a specific task.

Configuration The arrangement of the various units within a system.

CP/M Control **P**rogram for **M**icrocomputers, the most widely used **operating system** for business applications software.

Crash To lose data due to a software or hardware error.

CRT The televisionlike cathode ray tube used in personal computer monitors as a part of the VDT (video display terminal).

Cursor A symbol appearing on the video monitor that indicates where the next character of text or data will appear.

Custom software A computer program tailored to meet your specific requirements. **Custom software** can take months to write and cost tens of thousands of dollars. For most standard applications—word processing, financial modeling, accounting, data-base management—excellent off-the-shelf programs already exist, at a fraction of the cost of custom programming. It is also frequently possible to modify these packaged programs to meet your needs, again at a fraction of the cost of starting from scratch.

D

Data Any facts, letters, symbols, or numbers that can be acted on by a personal computer.

Data base A collection of facts, letters, symbols, or numbers that can be stored and retrieved in different combinations.

Data-base management The process of using the personal computer to store and retrieve information pertinent to the operation of a small business or professional practice in a timely and efficient manner.

Dedicated Used only for one specific task or purpose, e.g., a **dedicated** word processor is a computer that can only be used for word processing. Generally not a good idea for your business.

Default The value that a program assumes in lieu of instructions to the contrary. WordStar, for instance, assumes you want your margins to be 65 characters wide, unless you tell it otherwise.

Descender The part of a letter that descends below the baseline, e.g., *q,y,p,g* all have descenders.

Digital Refers to the off/on condition of the computer circuits represented by the **binary** digits 1 and 0.

Directory An index or catalog of the files located on a specific disk.

Disk A magnetic device used to store computer data (See **floppy disk** and **hard disk**).

Disk drive The machinery used to **read** and **write** information from a disk.

Disk operating system (DOS) A program that manages the transfer of data between the **disk drives** and the **central processor. Applications programs,** such as word processing, must be compatible with specific **disk operating systems** such as MS DOS, Apple DOS, and **CP/M.**

Documentation The instructional materials that accompany a computer and its software when you buy them. Typically, computer **documentation** is both voluminous and incomprehensible, except perhaps to computer experts.

DOS See **Disk operating system.**

Dot-matrix printer A fast, reliable type of computer printer that forms characters or graphic symbols from dot patterns. Dot-matrix characters, however, are not renowned for their legibility. (See **letter-quality printer.**)

Double-density A technique that doubles the amount of data a magnetic medium such as a **floppy disk** can hold.

Dual intensity The ability of a video screen or printer to produce regular as well as highlighted or boldfaced characters.

E

Edit The process of changing or correcting data or, in the case of word processing, text.

Error message A usually cryptic expression such as "BDOS ERROR: DRIVE B" that appears on the video screen indicating something's amuck. Many errors result from trivial mistakes such as improper syntax, e.g., putting a comma in the wrong place. Other errors can be more sinister, resulting in lost data.

F

Field In most data-base programs a **record** is composed of various **fields** containing related data groups, such as names, titles, addresses, or part numbers.

File Any collection of data on a disk that has been given a specific name or number.

Fixed disk A type of mass-storage hard disk that cannot be removed from its disk drive.

Floppy disk A flexible plastic disk contained in a cardboard jacket that is used to store data. Most personal computers use "floppies" that are 5¼-inch "minidisks."

Format As a noun, the layout or arrangement of data or text on a screen, disk, or file. As a verb, "formatting a disk" refers to the process of preparing a blank disk to accept data from your particular computer.

Also called "initializing." "Reformatting" in word processing is a technique for rearranging text, e.g., from single spacing to double spacing.

G

Graphics Computer-generated pictures. **Graphics** programs are used to translate data into charts and graphs.

H

Hard copy Printed data, usually generated by the computer printer.

Hard disk A magnetically treated metal disk capable of storing mass quantities of information—often 30 to 150 times more than a floppy disk.

Hardware The physical stuff—**disk drives,** printer, **CPU,** video monitor, keyboard, cables—as opposed to the **software** or **programs.**

High resolution (High-res) The ability of a monitor to display highly detailed graphics.

I

Iconograph A pictorial symbol, such as a wastebasket or file cabinet, used in some integrated programs to indicate various command options.

Initialize To prepare a disk for data storage.

Input Information entered into the computer.

Instructions A set of symbols representing an action that can be performed by the computer's microprocessor.

Integrated software Originally the term **integrated software** referred to various individual programs, such as accounts receivables, inventory, and general ledger, that could be used "interactively," i.e., they would "post" to one another. More recently, **integrated software** such as VisiOn and Lotus 1,2,3 have attained even greater sophistication. They combine several applications programs—usually including spreadsheeting, data-base management, and business graphics—into a single package that uses one set of standardized **commands.** Such **integrated** programs vastly simplify the process of transferring data from one program, such as a spreadsheet, to another type of application, like word processing.

Interactive A computer system in which a dialogue occurs between the user and the machine or between different programs run on the machine.

Interface Hardware or **software** used to connect computer devices.

K

Keypad Usually a separate set of calculator-type keys found on many personal computer keyboards. **Keypads** simplify the entry of numerical data.

Kilobyte Approximately one thousand bytes. Abbreviated as "K." **Kilobytes** are the data-processing world's most fundamental measure of computer power. In general, the more **kilobytes,** the more useful the device.

L

Language A set of unambiguous **commands** understood by a computer's **CPU.**

Letter-quality printer A computer printer that forms characters of quality comparable to that of an office typewriter.

Load To transfer a program from a **disk drive** or other storage device to the processor.

M

Machine Code The computer's "native tongue," usually composed of 1s and 0s. High-level languages are translated into it to make **commands** directly executable by the machine.

Mainframe computer A large-scale computer used for scientific, corporate, and government data processing.

Mass-storage peripheral A device for storing large quantities of data. **Floppy disk** drives are adequate for many small-business applications including most word processing and financial forecasting, but where extensive files, large inventories, or numerous accounts are involved, a **hard-disk** drive is often required.

Megabyte Roughly one million bytes (one thousand kilobytes). **Floppy disk** capacity is ususally limited to between one hundred and twelve hundred **kilobytes.** Hard-disk drives typically store between one and fifty **megabytes.**

Memory The data storage area within a computer. Personal computer **memory** is classified as either **read-only memory (ROM)** or **random access memory (RAM). ROM** is built in to the microprocessor chip and it never changes. Most **RAM** memory, by contrast, is "volatile," i.e., it lasts only as long as the power is on.

Memory capacity The amount of storage space in memory as measured in **kilobytes.** The minimum memory capacity for most business applications is 64K.

Menu A list of options that appear on screen when running a computer program. Menus purport to help users who are unfamiliar with a program. Some do. Others merely clutter the screen with information that is either too basic or too advanced to be of assistance. If a program uses a **menu** it's helpful to be able to turn it off.

Micro Short for **microcomputer.**

Microcomputer A low-cost computer system using a **microprocessor** as the **central processing unit.**

Micro-floppy A **floppy disk** measuring approximately three inches in diameter. The micro-floppy disk can fit more data in less space, but has been slow to make significant inroads against the well-established 5¼-inch mini-floppy disk.

Microprocessor The "brains" of the microcomputer, composed of integrated circuits etched into a silicon or germanium **chip** and capable of performing thousands of arithmetic operations each second.

Minicomputer A computer classified in terms of power as somewhere between a **mainframe** and a **micro.** Historically, the **minicomputer** handled divisional-level data processing while the more powerful **mainframes** were reserved for corporate-level tasks.

Mini-floppy or **mini-disk** A 5¼-inch **floppy disk.**

Modem Acronym for **mod**ulator/**dem**odulator. A device that allows personal computers to communicate over telephone lines.

Mouse A device somewhat resembling the rodent, used to control a computer **cursor** and enter **commands** without a keyboard.

O

Operating system A group of **programs,** usually including the **disk operating system (DOS),** that manage the housekeeping functions of the computer and its **peripherals.** Also called **systems software.**

P

Packaged software Ready-to-run computer programs available through retail stores and mail-order houses. Thanks to the mass market for PC programs, you can usually buy **packaged software** that has cost hundreds of thousands of dollars to develop, for only a few hundred dollars. Herein lies one of the great economic advantages of the personal computer.

Pascal A high-level programming **language** comparable—some say superior—to BASIC. Usually not necessary to know for most business computer functions.

PC A generic abbreviation for personal computer. In some circles, however, **PC** will be taken to mean the IBM-PC.

Peripherals Devices such as printers, **modems,** and **disk drives** that are attached to the computer.

Pixel Picture cell, many thousands of which make up the image on a video screen.

Program A series of instructions that a computer can "understand" and perform.

Q

Quad density A double-sided, double-density disk capable of storing four times the data of a single-sided single-density disk.

R

RAM (Random Access Memory) Electronic internal **memory** that can be read from or written to (i.e., accessed) at any point.

Read To retrieve data from a storage location or medium.

ROM (Read Only Memory) Internal **memory** from which information can be **read,** but onto which data cannot be written.

Real time Performing computing during the time an event is taking place, usually in order to influence the outcome of the event. Flight-navigation computers, for instance, use **real time** computing.

Record A group of related data **fields** treated as a unit, such as an employee personnel file.

Retrieval The act of finding stored data.

RF Modulator A device that allows the personal computer to use an ordinary TV as a display. OK for games, terrible for business computing. Get a real monitor; you've got enough headaches already.

Routine A self-contained collection of "program statements" that performs a specific function within a **software program.**

S

Save To store data on a **disk** or other external memory device.

Scroll A procedure that moves text across the video screen.

Sector A section of a disk's track.

Serial Computer operations that occur in a sequence, as opposed to parallel operations, which happen simultaneously.

Single-sided A **floppy disk** that uses only one side for data storage.

Software A set of instructions for operating computer **hardware.**

System An integrated collection of components serving a common purpose.

Systems software See **Operating system.**

Syntax Rules for writing statements in a computer **language.**

T

Terminal Equipment used to communicate with the personal computer, including the keyboard, video monitor, and printer.

Throughput A measure of the gross productivity of a device, such as the number of characters per second that a printer can produce.

Timesharing A process in which a single large computer is shared by many users.

Tractor feed A device equipped with sprockets to continuously feed paper through a computer printer. A necessity if you are printing multiple copies of a document or long reports.

W

Winchester A mass storage peripheral capable of storing many times more information than a floppy disk.

Window The portion of the video display that actually appears on your screen.

Write To record data on a storage **disk** or in **memory.**

Write protection A system for protecting a **disk** from being "written on" or erased.

Index